MORAL PHILOSOPHY

Historical and Contemporary Essays

Edited with Introduction

by

William C. Starr and Richard C. Taylor

With contributions by

**Bruce Aune, Fred R. Berger, Vernon J. Bourke,
Richard Brandt, John M. Cooper, Germain Grisez,
Ralph McInerny, Marcus Singer, James D. Wallace,
Nicholas P. White.**

Marquette University Press   Milwaukee, WI U.S.A.

CONTENTS

Introduction

The papers in this volume were originally presented at a conference on "Contemporary Ethical Thought and the History of Moral Philosophy" held at Marquette University in October of 1985. Of the papers here six are historical in character while four deal with contemporary thought directly. The historical essays include contributions by Nicholas White (Plato), John Cooper (Aristotle), Vernon Bourke (Augustine), Ralph McInerny (Aquinas), Bruce Aune (Kant), and Fred Berger (Classical Utilitarianism). The four contemporary papers, while clearly not historical in nature, owe much to a one or another particular tradition in moral philosophy and bear strong witness to this volume's thesis that contemporary moral philosophy is integrally connected to its historical background. These final four essays are by Richard Brandt (inspired by Classical Utilitarianism), Germain Grisez (natural law morality inspired, in part, by the thought of Aquinas), Marcus Singer (inspired by the thought of Kant), and James Wallace (virtue ethics inspired by Platonic and Aristotelian thought in part).

The editors of this collection believe that this volume contributes in a singularly valuable way to present-day discussions of moral philosophy through its effort to show the continuity that is at the base of the relationship of contemporary moral thought and its historical traditions. The expertise of the contributors whose work here constitutes the argument for this belief needs no explanation in light of the many contributions all have made to modern philosophical thought.

The most complete treatment of moral philosophy found in the dialogues of Plato lies in his *Republic*. It is with this work and Plato's efforts in it to present a comprehensive account of the preferability of the life of the just man over that of the unjust man that Nicholas White deals in the opening essay of this volume, "Happiness and External Contingencies in Plato's *Republic*." Two key difficulties stand out as particularly problematic both for the moral argument of the work and for the comprehensive unity of the work as a whole. The first problem is that of the missing response to the charge of inadequacy. No careful and critical philosophical reader can study this dialogue without considering the charge that the argument of the *Republic* is inadequate to its stated goal of proving the life of the just man is preferable and happier than that of the unjust man. Clearly, well-being or happiness, which for Plato in the *Republic* is a harmony of the parts of the soul, is far from being enough to guarantee that the just life is the better since it cannot exclude the important role of external contingencies in the attainment of human happiness. How can Plato find in favor of the just man without dealing with this? Where is the missing response to the charge of inadequacy? The second problem is that of the extra book. What function does Book 10 have? Are its contents anything but additions superfluous to the argument of the work brought to a conclusion in Book 9?

According to White, the solution to these difficulties lies in the consideration of the two problems as intrinsically connected: the missing response is to be found in the extra book. As common sense teaches, nothing can guarantee the human soul or even the reasoning part of it freedom from external contingencies. And as careful examination of his teachings reveals, Plato eshewed the extreme position on present repercussions and understood this commonsensically when he stressed the need to protect reason from the distracting hindrances of desires and sensations. Similarly, Plato does not take the position that justice is effortlessly maintained over a lifetime. The maintenance of well-being or happiness over a complete life requires strategy and planning for its accomplishment in the physical world where all that comes into being also perishes.

For White, Plato does not argue that the life of the just person is better in each moment than that of the unjust person, but rather that the former is overall better than the latter since the just person employs the rational planning that can reasonably assure lasting well-being. The just man with an orderly soul and a rational plan is not passive but rather active in making the best of a bad situation, while the unjust person with a disharmonious soul can control neither himself nor his tragic fate. And in a similar vein the final section of Book 10 with its argument for the immortality of soul and the Myth of Er illustrates the control the just person can have over the future. In the afterlife we meet with judgments and punishments and rewards but the ultimate outcome of all that is reincarnation and a choice of a new life to be led here, choice made on the basis of the character formed here in this world prior to the journey into the afterlife. The real reward for the just man is that he is able to retain his just character through incarnations. Thus, Book 10 of the *Republic*, far from being superfluous, serves to forestall exaggerated interpretations of portions of earlier books and to respond to critics who might raise questions about the role of external contingencies and present and future repercussions. It completes with further argument the reasonable understanding of Plato's assertion that the life of the just man is one of greater fulfillment in well-being and happiness than that of the unjust man in the face of present and future contingencies.

In "Contemplation and Happiness: A Reconsideration" by John M. Cooper, Aristotle's contribution to moral philosophy is addressed through systematic consideration of the distinctive Aristotelian position that theoretical activity is of higher value than practical activity and that while a kind of happiness can be had through virtuous living in the sphere of practical life, complete happiness is only had through the contemplative activity of the philosopher. Limiting his consideration to the *Nicomachean Ethics* Cooper poses the problem of the apparently two distinct and perhaps incompatible conceptions of human happiness found in that work. The first, that happiness comes through fulfillment of people in moral virtue, civic activity and practical action, is found in the general initial account of Book 1 with details of moral theory spelled out further in Books 2-9. The second is that of Book 10, chapters 6-8, which present a more refined conception, one of the contemplative life as the most complete fulfillment of human beings in happiness apparently unhindered by the entrapments of moral life's engagements in the practical life of other people. That moral life is there considered as second best to the preferred life of intellectual contemplation through what is best in us, reason.

The solution to the problem lies in the careful consideration of the accounts found in Books 1 and 10. In the first Aristotle offers only a vague and preliminary account in his search to grasp the nature of happiness, *eudaimonia*, in practical philosophy. This account implicitly includes intellectual virtue manifested in theoretical activity without explicitly endorsing it as the greatest of happiness. This does become explicit, however, in Book 10, where he uses the term, "complete happiness." Here Aristotle does not abandon his earlier analysis but rather finds happiness in two kinds of virtuous activity, excellence in theoretical study (contemplation) and excellence in the realm of the practical. The former more completely fulfills the primary criteria of happiness (it is the best activity, one immediately pleasant, self-sufficient, desired for itself and freely undertaken in leisure rather than compelled) than the latter and consequently merits being characterized as, "so to speak, the more perfect version of the general unified category of activity, virtuous activity, which constitutes happiness." The sense of "complete" in "complete happiness," then, is that of what is perfectly or completely realized; and the sense of "complete happiness" is of what is one of the constituents of happiness, not happiness as a whole. The achievement of complete happiness in a complete life does not involve single-minded cultivation of the intellect but rather encompasses all human virtues including those of character and practical thought. Intellectual virtue of the theoretical intellect is the perfective culmination of all the virtues and thereby is completive of human nature in its full perfection.

On this understanding, Aristotle seems to assert that the *eudaimonia* attained in morally virtuous activities counts as *eudaimonia* only in virtue of their relationship to contemplative activities which can yield complete happiness because of their kinship with the divine activity of contemplation. The best and happiest human life then is one divine-like but happiness is also to be found in activities of moral virtue. The best life, however, is one involving the understanding of the lasting value of the use of complete or perfected human rational abilities in all their aspects. Aristotle's *Nicomachean Ethics* thus contains one complete account of human excellence and fulfullment in happiness which asserts one life, the contemplative, to be the primary and most complete. Like his teacher, Plato, here Aristotle ultimately asserts the primacy of the role of reason in the attainment of human happiness.

The first of two essays dealing with the contributions of medieval philosophy to the development of moral thought is a discussion of three prominent issues in the thought of St. Augustine of Hippo by Vernon J. Bourke in "Some Enduring Values in Augustinian Ethics." These issues, the practice of lying, the argument to show there is one supreme good for all men, and the justification of war, all have background in classical philosophy of the Greeks and Romans but receive from Augustine a treatment characteristically Christian which endures in the medieval disputes of later centuries.

Consideration of Augustine's treatment of mendacity in his early (395) *On Lying* and some 25 years later in his *Against Lying* serves to underscore contributions that can be derived to provide assistance in an area of moral philosophy still inadequately developed. Though today we still lack what Elizabeth Anscombe called "an adequate philosophy of psychology," Augustine clearly saw the need for this. Without a generally accepted theory of mental functions, the meanings of key terms such as cognition, volition, understanding, deliberation, intention, choice and others remain uncertain and obscure even though such notions and activities are discussed frequently because they are at the center of the study of ethical concepts such as responsibility, merit of praise and blame, etc. Lying is found to be morally wrong in intention in two ways: it is a difformity or incongruity of the consciousness of the speaker, a *locutio contra mentem*, and it is a willing to harm others by deception. Lying is a kind of self-contradiction which is wrong both with respect to prior attitude (an internal willing expression of untruth) and what is consequential (possible harmful results). From the thought of Augustine in these two works there emerges an appreciation of the importance of a theory of internal willing for ethics and of the need for a comprehensive understanding of the psychology of internal mental activities and attitudes.

For persons or human actions the morally good must in the long run have a univocal meaning and a standard for moral judgment, Bourke argues. Augustine shows in the nineteenth book of his *City of God* that the ultimate end of all things, including human beings, is God who is the highest good. And it is through moral actions that we are brought closer to this good. Since the time of the Renaissance, commitment to an absolute goodness has often been left aside for utilitarian, deontological and other approaches asserting proximate goods which, Bourke believes, can be made a part of human morality only if they are made into ethical goods though an ordering to an objective *summmum bonum*.

Augustine's approach to the question of the ethical bases for the thinking behind the notion of a just war is founded on common sense and prudential judgment, sound intention, and objective moral right and was of central importance to the formation of the thought of Aquinas. First, peace is defined as the "tranquility of order," order from a divine source which permeates all things, and war must be viewed as a means to bring about peace. Secondly, war requires a just cause, the opposition of some serious evil determined to be wrong by a moral philosophy that takes its start from critical examination of societal mores. And, third, war requires a right intention or spirit which condemns viciousness, revenge, ferocity, lust and other base motives.

For Bourke, the most valuable contribution that the thought of Augustine can make today lies in the notion that contemporary ethical thought cannot be wholly deontological nor utilitarian in nature but rather must involve both the subjective and the objective aspects of moral action in such a way that the agent is further understood as being drawn by an external good which reasonable action can attain.

The specific problem of the nature of the discrepancies between the thought of Thomas Aquinas and Aristotle on the attainment of happiness affords Ralph McInerny the occasion to give critical consideration to the contention of René Antoine Gauthier (editor of the Leonine critical edition of Aquinas' *Sententiae super libros Ethicorum* and editor with Jean Yves Jolif of *L'Ethique à Nicomaque*) that Aquinas did considerable violence to the thought of Aristotle to make it consonant with Christian theology. In "The Moral Thought of St. Thomas Aquinas" McInerny argues that this would mean that Aquinas' Aristotelianism should be of interest only to theologians and that there would be no benefit to readers of his *Commentary on the Nicomachean Ethics* or of the moral part of his *Summa theologiae* unless they shared his religious beliefs. For McInerny, this is no mere esoteric point of contention, for it brings forth the whole matter of the character of Aquinas' use of the thought of Aristotle and the question of his understanding and perhaps honesty in dealing with Aristotle's text. McInerny undertakes the critical examination of Gauthier's assertion of a difference which is profound and unbridgeable between the views of Aristotle and Aquinas on the ultimate end of man. Here he examines Gauthier's position in order to show something of Aquinas' understanding of Aristotle, of the way he subsumes Aristotle into his moral theology, and of how this is of interest to contemporary philosophers.

The ultimate end of man for Aquinas is God who is both necessary and timeless, but for Aristotle this end is something contingent and temporal, a good achievable by action. Of this difference Aquinas was well aware, for he holds that the natural end of man is not destroyed but rather presupposed in the notion that man has a supernatural end which is eternal happiness in union with God. For Aristotle man's ultimate end lies in a variety of activities and ends which are an ordered set pursued under the notion of good (*ratio boni*). Aquinas distinguishes "between the notion of ultimate end and that in which the notion of the ultimate end is located" and finds in God the object in which there is perfect realization of the *ratio boni* through knowledge and love. The imperfect happiness which can be obtained in this life consists first in contemplation and secondarily in the ordering of activities by the practical intellect, just as Aristotle said in Book 10 of the *Nicomachean Ethics*. Perfect happiness, however, when the human will is quieted by the attainment of the universal good, is found in God alone who provides that human action informed by grace can merit eternal happiness. This viewpoint, of course, is one of religious belief and faith and maintained from a Christian perspective. But it does not set aside or invalidate Aristotle's contentions regarding what Aquinas calls imperfect happiness, for this sort of happiness resembles but does not equal that of the gods even for Aristotle.

Thus the moral thought of Aquinas in his theological works is not in opposition to the pagan ethics of Aristotle, as Gauthier contends. Instead the historical Aristotle is subsumed in a commodious synthesis by Aquinas on this issue as well as others. And so Gauthier's tendentious generalization that Aquinas distorted the thought of Aristotle to bring it into harmony with Christian theology is shown to be undermined by the very texts of Aquinas. Hence, rather than requiring that the *Commentary on the Nicomachean Ethics* by Aquinas be set aside a priori as distortive of Aristotle, this indicates that the *Commentary* merits careful reading before judgment is passed.

Bruce Aune in "Kant's Theory of Morals" shows that Kant held that there is a supreme moral principle. He calls this principle the categorical imperative. Aune believes that there are in Kant "four pure versions of the moral law and four corresponding topics or rules of judgment." Of course, it is controversial whether Kant actually did have different versions of the categorical imperative. Aune holds that they are different. As he sees it, Kant attempts to develop a comprehensive theory of morality which is associated with the Judeo-Christian tradition while dissociating itself from the purely theological aspects of that tradition. Kant did hold the strong thesis that the categorical is not merely acceptable, but binding upon all rational beings. This work has been continued by the well known contemporary moral philosopher Alan Donagan.

Aune, however, holds that Kant's categorical imperative is unsatisfactory in its quest to be the supreme principle of morality. He respects Kant's attempt to establish the categorical imperative. However, he argues that in the final analysis Kant fails to do this. Aune maintains that Kant does not show that different human viewpoints will not affect what one "wills" when one wills a maxim. This leaves the categorical imperative with a philosophical status similar to the golden rule, "which is perhaps a useful formula to inculcate in children who must be taught to treat others 'with consideration,' but which is virtually useless for theoretical purposes."

Aune is unconvinced by Kant's claim that human beings have natural purposes and that only those activities which are "natural" are morally acceptable. Aune holds that from a secular perspective such claims are simply philosophically indefensible. Aune has philosophical difficulties with Kant's use of "end-in-oneself," "rational kingdoms," and "autonomy" as well. He shows that it is not the case that Kant can intelligibly maintain that if a maxim cannot be made a universal law, it is not morally acceptable. Aune uses the example of one who wills to marry and have a child with his wife. Yet this maxim is not universalizable since it does not apply to women. So, Aune concludes that Kant's ethical theory, while perceptive and insightful in numerous places, is untenable as a comprehensive systematic moral philosophy. He concludes his essay with a strikingly negative assessment of Kant's moral philosophy which the reader will have to judge for oneself.

Fred Berger's paper, "Classical Utilitarianism," holds that the classical utilitarians (Bentham, James and John Stuart Mill) have been subject in the literature to the following two criticisms. First, it is claimed that the classical utilitarians desire to maximize the total amount of pleasure for a given group, e.g., a society. It is further alleged that the classical utilitarian is not concerned about how pleasure is distributed within the members of that society, hence the Rawlsian critique that "utilitarianism does not take the distinction between persons seriously" (Rawls, *A Theory of Justice*, p. 26). Secondly, it has been alleged that the classical utilitarians hold that all pleasures possess the same value, even malevolent pleasures. Berger argues that both of these criticisms are false.

Berger notes that the second claim is only plausible in the case of Bentham, not Mill. Even with this restriction in scope, the claim is badly distorted. Berger explicitly points out that Bentham held that human nature is far more inclined towards a feeling of sympathy for one's fellow humans than malevolence. Not only that, Bentham also holds that malevolence is generally contrary to utility. That is, while malevolence may be of utility to a given individual, its existence is likely to be disuseful to society as a whole. Of course, the utilitarian is concerned with the overall welfare of society, not any one individual *per se*. Finally, although Bentham does recognize the existence of malevolence as a pleasure it is relegated to "secondary status." It has neither the same status or importance of benevolence.

With respect to the first claim that classical utilitarianism is not interested in distributive justice, merely aggregative justice, Berger shows that John Stuart Mill held no such view. Mill's emphasis is on rules and individual rights. Whether one interprets Mill to be an act utilitarian or a rule utilitarian, it is clear that rules play a crucial role in the development of his brand of utilitarianism. It is also the case that the rules of justice are constitutive of what rights people actually have. This view is defended in *Utilitarianism*, Chapter V. So, individual rights which only make sense if persons as distinct individuals are taken extremely seriously are not only crucial to classical utilitarianism, but also demonstrate its clear interest in distributive justice. Utility provides a philosophical grounding for individual rights which is a notoriously difficult issue for contemporary rights-based theories.

Richard Brandt in "Fairness to Indirect Utilitarianism" argues that indirect or rule utilitarianism is a philosophically defensible moral theory. He explains the concept of rule utilitarianism, makes some perceptive remarks about a personal moral code, and then shows key differences between act and rule utilitarianism. It is worth noting that in this essay Brandt continues to emphasize, as he has elsewhere, the central importance of the role of a moral code if one wishes to defend rule utilitarianism as well as show that rule utilitarianism does not collapse into act utilitarianism. That is, the code itself possesses considerable utility which would not exist in any version of act utilitarianism in which rules are not binding.

Brandt devotes a considerable amount of energy to discussing various objections to rule utilitarianism which have been offered in the literature. He offers an analysis of the "rule worship" objection, the objection concerning "how can one identify utility maximizing moral code," the argument from integrity, the argument from justice and equality, and the argument from the problem of partial compliance. Brandt finds all of these objections unconvincing. He argues that each objection can be answered in either of two ways. Some of the objections can be successfully refuted by the rule utilitarian. Other objections simply miss the mark. That is, they object to claims which the rule utilitarian never made in the first place.

Brandt shows that rule utilitarianism can be applied to a political system such as South Africa. His point is that no societal moral code with a set of complex moral rules will promote utility by legally endorsing an invidious form of racism, such that as that authorized and practiced in South Africa. Since such rules and acts derived from them are inconsistent with a utility-maximizing system, a rule utilitarian would be opposed to social practices like those permitted in South Africa. Thus, it is unfair to criticize the rule utilitarian as one who would endorse apartheid if it promoted utility. Brandt's point is that that is simply not possible. The moral code would not be useful to society *as a whole*. Utilitarianism, as a consequentialist theory, must consider the facts before making a specific moral judgment consistent with the principle of utility. The factual evidence for this claim is overwhelming.

Germain Grisez in his article, "A Contemporary Natural-Law Ethics," offers a sketch of a contemporary version of a moral theory based on natural law. Grisez's theory is not Thomistic in its approach, although there are important points of agreement between the two theories of natural law. Grisez makes use of both deontological and teleological approaches in developing his own theory. In this paper he is not offering the reader a new moral theory; he is summarizing and developing key positions which have been developed in a series of essays and texts which appear in the bibliography he provides at the end of his essay. This particular paper provides an excellent introduction to the work of Germain Grisez that allows one to assess his attempt to develop a contemporary version of natural law ethics.

Grisez holds that a first principle of morality can be articulated and defended. It holds that one ought to choose and "will those and only those possibilities whose willing is compatible with integral human fulfillment." Grisez emphasizes that by the term "integral human fulfillment," he is referring to the good of all persons and communities, not simply individual self-fulfillment. Grisez's moral philosophy is universal in orientation, not particularized to specific individuals. He carefully explicates and defends a particular interpretation of this first principle of human conduct. From the first principle, intermediate principles are derived, e.g., the Golden Rule, which leads to specific moral judgments.

Grisez concludes with a theological epilogue which shows the relationship between natural law ethics and Christian faith. For Grisez, it is faith in Christian gospel which helps one to make choices consistent with the first principle of morality noted above. It is also worth mentioning that Grisez lets the reader know that there are others besides himself who are working to develop a contemporary natural law theory. Included among these individuals are Joseph Boyle and John Finnis. Others are mentioned in his lengthy bibliography at the conclusion of his article.

Marcus Singer in "Imperfect Duty Situations, Moral Freedom, and Universalizability" holds that the "Generalization Principle" he developed in his extremely influential book *Generalization in Ethics* can successfully withstand the most severe objections raised by hard cases. Singer notes that if he is correct, then the logic of the Generalization Principle has a great deal to be said for it in moral philosophy. It is worth noting Singer feels that the term "universalizability" has been used in so many different ways, e.g., Kant and Hare both use it, that he prefers to stick with the clarity of the term "Generalization Principle."

Singer uses the cases of Billy Budd and Sartre's well known case of a young Frenchman in 1940 who is forced to make a choice whether to take care of his aged mother or to join the Free French forces. The Billy Budd case is taken from Melville's short novel *Billy Budd*. Billy Budd is accused falsely of inciting the crew of the ship *H.M.S. Indominable* to mutiny. He is accused by the evil master-at-arms Claggart. When the charge is made, Budd cannot speak. So, in an instant of extreme frustration he strikes and kills Claggart. Even though Billy Budd is not a wicked person and Claggart is just that sort of individual, according to maritime law Captain Vere is forced to find Billy Budd guilty. This is a capital offense. He argues that neither of these two cases successfully shows an inadequacy of the Generalization Principle.

Singer shows that the Sartre case is an imperfect duty situation. An imperfect duty allows for exceptions in favor of inclination. A perfect duty never allows for exceptions in favor of inclination. So, for example, truth telling is a perfect duty. Even though one may be inclined to lie on occasion, morality does not permit this. An example of an imperfect duty is self-improvement. Although I have an overall duty to improve myself over the course of my life, I am not obligated to act this way on every occasion. So, if I wish to sit on my couch, have a beer, and watch a football game on a particular instance, this is permitted since a perfect duty is not involved. The Sartre case is one of imperfect duty, not perfect duty. Thus, there is no "one right answer" to be discovered in the Sartre case. The case is always expressed in the form "What Should I Do?" In the Billy Budd case, there may be a right answer since Captain Vere's duty is a perfect duty even though it is unclear what the right answer is. Captain Vere knows all too well what he must do. He has no choice. Yet, it surely is an open question whether Captain Vere is doing the "right" thing. So, for different reasons both are very hard cases. Yet Singer forcefully argues that neither refutes the Generalization Principle. Rather, the cases force the Generalization Principle to be interpreted very carefully.

James Wallace in "Ethics and the Craft Analogy" notes that in recent years a number of philosophers (Foot, Hampshire, MacIntyre, and himself) have revived a tradition in moral philosophy known as "virtue ethics," a tradition historically associated with Aristotle. Virtue ethics holds that one acts morally by learning and practicing the moral virtues of one's tradition and culture. The emphasis in virtue ethics is on ethical action and moral training. The emphasis is not on merely learning abstract moral principles independent of one's culture and tradition. This is the mistake, virtue ethicists believe, that both the deontological and consequentialist traditions have made. MacIntyre in *After Virtue* seems to make the exceedingly strong thesis that mere fidelity to abstract principles and a corresponding loss of "virtue" has caused a severe decline in the contemporary moral fiber of Western civilization. These philosophers have been dissatisfied with various forms of non-cognitivism in moral philosophy as well as intuitionism, utilitarianism, and deontological ethical theory. Wallace holds that much can be learned in moral theory through an understanding of the "craft analogy."

The idea here is that those individuals who possess knowledge of a craft have a given function, e.g., the function of a pianist is to play the piano well. By analogy there is also a function for man himself. This function is to live well. One who lives well is a virtuous person, that is, one who possesses the virtues. One who possesses the virtues is a truly moral person. The craft analogy helps us understand this.

How far can the craft analogy be used? Is it the case that human beings are the sorts of creatures who have a fixed-goal view of the world? Wallace points out both the strengths and limitations of such a view. He then concludes that virtue ethics should be modified so that character traits will be representative of the craft analogy and will exceed the number of virtues as explicated by Aristotle and others in the classical tradition. Wallace believes that Aristotle has the right methodology in developing moral theory. However, he does not go far enough. It is too simplistic to suppose that if we know and even practice the moral virtues, we will be doing all there is to do from a moral perspective. Wallace makes this clear when he writes, "No one supposes that by studying courage, justice, and honesty we will learn a great deal about the standards by which the practice of a craft is properly evaluated.... Philosophical accounts of the virtues lack the necessary specificity to enable us to draw out of them useful accounts of how difficult concrete practical problems are properly resolved." Thus, there is much work to be done in properly developing a systematic theory of virtue ethics.

This volume is dedicated to the memory of Fred Berger of the University of California at Davis, one of its contributors, and to the memory of Joan Kung of Marquette University, one of the participants in the conference from which this collection arose.

We would like to express our thanks to the Franklin B. Matchette Foundation for valuable funding, to Marquette University for an Andrew W. Mellon Grant and a grant from the Religious Commitment Fund, and to the Department of Philosophy of Marquette University for additional funding assistance. These funds made possible the important conference at which these papers were first presented. We would also like to thank Anthony Beavers whose expertise in computer typesetting and laser printing made this collection of papers into an attractive volume. The invaluable technical assistance of Lee C. Rice is gratefully acknowledged. The helpful suggestions of Rev. Roland J. Teske, S.J., on the introduction and other parts of this work are also gratefully acknowledged.

William C. Starr
Richard C. Taylor
Department of Philosophy
Marquette University

Happiness and External Contingencies
in Plato's *Republic*

Nicholas P. White
University of Michigan

Usually, in philosophy as elsewhere, the more problems we have on our hands, the worse off we are, and we would generally not be willing to trade one problem for two. But in Plato's *Republic* we have a case in which we are better off having two problems than we would be with one, if we look at them together. Let me explain.

The First Problem Introduced:
The Missing Response

How can Plato seriously believe, people often ask, that a just person is always happier or better off than an unjust one? Even after we take into account all of the attempts to interpret his views charitably, there remains an intractable problem: his conclusion seems, as a general contention, staggeringly implausible. Moreover it seems implausible for reasons that he is fully aware of. I shall amplify this claim shortly, but very briefly the point is this. How happy or well off a person is seems, to the viewpoint of present-day common sense, to be affected to some substantial degree by many sorts of external contingencies. For example, one can be tortured on the rack or hit by a truck, or caused both excruciating pain and anxiety about the well-being of loved ones, or one can be caused anguish when such a misfortune befalls a friend or relative. Seemingly, common sense says, these things can happen even to a person who is just. And on the other side, someone who is unjust can entirely escape such misfortunes. Can Plato seriously hold that, whatever other advantages the just may gain as compared with the unjust, the reverse weight of misfortunes can *never, ever* fall in such a way that on balance the just person is worse off than the unjust? Could he really think, for example, that the just person is inevitably happier on the rack, or under the truck, than the unjust person is away from such things?

Or consider the matter, still briefly, in more Platonic terms. For Plato in the *Republic,* happiness or well-being is a kind of harmony of the parts of the soul or personality.[1] Surely external luck, good and bad, can affect parts of the soul in ways incompatible with the existence of that harmony, as again cases of excruciating pain or grief would seem to show. Once again, could Plato seriously think that the just person on the rack always has a more harmonious soul than the unjust person off of it? Commentators on Plato tend to avoid this question, usually suggesting, openly or by silence, that Plato has no reply to make to it. But that suggestion merely adds to one implausibility another, far greater one. For surely it is simply not credible that Plato should have regarded it as anything but an absolute necessity, if he was going to make his position at all believable, to respond to this problem in some substantial way, rather than trying to sweep it under the rug. We know for a certainty that his philosophical opponents had put it to him. We can see that fact from the *Gorgias*, from Book I of the *Republic*, and from the challenge put to Socrates in Book II by Glaucon and Adeimantus, to mention only a few pertinent passages. Can Plato have thought that he could silence such opponents simply by trotting out an account of well-being that excluded external contingencies from any role in it, unless that exclusion were supported by some weighty argument? How could he have thought so for a moment?

The Second Problem Introduced:
The Extra Book

How can Plato seriously believe that Book X of the *Republic* serves any philosophical purpose in the work, or that its main line of argument is worth attending to? Thus Julia Annas:

> ... Book X appears gratuitous and clumsy, and full ...
> of oddities. [And t]he level of philosophical argument is

---

1. See, e.g., Gregory Vlastos, "Justice and Happiness in the *Republic*," in Vlastos, *Platonic Studies* (Princeton, 1973), pp. 111-139.

much below the rest [of the *Republic*].[2]

Thus, too, myself once:

[Book X] can be seen ... as an appendix to the whole work, ... [and] not a fully cohesive one.[3]

In his book on Plato's moral theory, Terence Irwin ignores Book X about as completely as he is able: of a massive total of 381 references to passages of the *Republic* listed in his *index locorum*, the references to that book number exactly six.[4] And in Martha Nussbaum's recent work, devoted to "luck and ethics in Greek tragedy and philosophy," which we shall see is the main subject of Book X, that book receives practically no attention at all.[5] One can easily understand this attitude, especially on the part of those commentators (among whom I count myself) who are mainly concerned to disentangle the strands of the argument of the work. Niceties aside, the defects of Book X appear to be three: (*a*) it seems imperfectly connected with the thoughts and arguments of the previous books; (*b*) the ideas within it seem not to hang together with each other; and (*c*) a number of its arguments seem shockingly weak. Most notably under (*a*), the most important thesis of the work seems to have been fully established at the end of Book IX.[6] Why, then, did Plato add on Book X? If it contains ideas and literary figures that he could not resist using, then why did he not write some other dialogue to contain them -- he was not reluctant to write more dialogues -- instead of disfiguring the *Republic* with them?

Those, then, are the two problems. It can of course be guessed right away what I am going to end up saying about them: that Plato does in fact attempt in Book X to provide us with the Missing Response, and that providing it is precisely the aim of Book X. Let me proceed to show that this is so.

---

2. Julia Annas, *Introduction to Plato's Republic* (Oxford, 1981), p. 335.
3. Nicholas P. White, *A Companion to Plato's Republic* (Indianapolis, 1979), p. 246.
4. Terence Irwin, *Plato's Moral Theory* (Oxford, 1977).
5. Martha C. Nussbaum, *The Fragility of Goodness: Luck and Ethics in Greek Tragedy and Philosophy* (Cambridge, England, 1986). The discussions of Book X, which are cursory, are confined to pp. 133, 203, 223, 224, and 385 (see p. 542).
6. See, e.g., my *Companion*, pp. 243, 246-247, and Annas, *loc. cit.* As I indicate on p. 247, however, I do not think that the whole of what Plato promised in Book II to show has in fact been shown by the end of Book IX. For a full treatment of this matter, see my article, "The Classification of Goods in Plato's *Republic*," *Journal of the History of Philosophy*, 22 (1984), 393-421.

The Problem of the Missing
Response Considered

Efforts by commentators to solve this problem have not been lacking. George Grote noticed that if we take the word "just" in the ordinary sense, then Plato's thesis that the just are always happier than the unjust appears implausible; and he pointed out, as did David Sachs more recently, that in that thesis Plato's word for "just," *dikaion*, does not take the ordinary sense but rather one constructed from Plato's theory of the soul. It may then turn out that his thesis is no longer pertinent to rebutting his opponents, who deny that the just are better off in the ordinary sense of "just." But his thesis will at least seem less implausible. Or will it? Not much, I think, for the reason already given. In the ordinary sense of "happy" (or "well off," "well-being," and so forth), misfortune can very substantially affect how well off one is, and the same seems to be the case even under Plato's sense of "happy," involving harmony of the soul. So what makes Plato's thesis seem implausible is not merely something about our conception of justice, but something also about our conception of happiness or well-being. The same difficulty arises in Irwin's effort to rescue Plato's thesis from unbelievability. Irwin realizes how important it is to Plato's argument *not* to take "well-being" in some supposedly ordinary sense, as if Plato might have thought that he could presuppose a common understanding of what that term meant. Irwin realizes, too, that Plato's procedure opens him up to yet a second charge of switching the sense of a word on his opponents.[7] But even if Irwin's Plato could show that his sense of "well-being" really is germane to denying what his opponents wish to assert, we still have the same problem as before. For Irwin recognizes that Plato takes "well-being" to refer to his newly-constructed notion of harmony of soul, and we have not seen any way -- nor does Irwin give us one -- of showing how harmony of soul can be compatible with such grave misfortunes as being in extreme pain or grief or the like. Irwin is aware that there is a difficulty here, and so he notes, for example, that "Plato does not claim that justice is sufficient for happiness."[8] He says, however, that Plato does claim "only that the just man is always happier than the unjust." But this too is called into doubt by the occurrence of accidental misfortunes. Plato still seems to need some response to our very obvious objection that an unjust person might meet sufficiently less misfortune than a just person to make the former better off than the latter. Plato could reply, of course, that he is comparing the just person to an unjust person *in similar external circumstances,*

---

7. This is one of the main themes of Irwin, *op. cit.*
8. Irwin, p. 326.

say, the just person under the truck with the unjust person under the same truck, and is only saying that the former is better off than the latter. But of course he often seems clearly to be saying something more than that, and is so taken.

A third way with the Problem of the Missing Response is tried by Julia Annas. On her account, Plato intends to argue that, properly understood, well-being is not a condition that is affected by external circumstances or misfortunes, but a state "that is more in ourselves than we tend to think it is," and can be shown "to depend on the agent's state rather than the way the world happens to be."[9] As stated, however, the interpretation involves a false dichotomy. Even if well-being does indeed "depend on the agent's state," it will also depend on "the way the world happens to be" if the agent's state itself does. And the problem is that on Plato's view, as we shall see more fully soon, the harmony of a person's soul can indeed depend on the way the world happens to be. At present, though, my point is that if Plato believes that it does not, he had obviously better give us a very good reason for that belief. Moreover we can see that he realizes that fact. Annas says the following:

> Plato does not defend his redefinition of happiness . . . .
> *He takes it as obvious* that once one accepts that justice
> is really psychic harmony, then the happiness that results
> from it will likewise be seen to depend on the agent's
> state rather than the way the world happens to be . . . .
> *Plato produces no real argument* . . . .[10]

I suggest that Plato knew perfectly well that he could not possibly take such a redefinition as obvious, and that if we say that he did, we are picturing him as simply turning his back on the very opponents that he undertook in the *Republic* to face. That still leaves us facing the Problem of the Missing Response.

But the problem for which the Missing Response is needed is more complex than it may at first appear, and so I am going to take some time to lay it out. It can be conveniently divided into two problems, both concerning the effects on a person's well-being of external bad or good fortune. One is what I shall call the Problem of Present Repercussions, and the other is what I shall call the Problem of Future Repercussions. Let me first briefly describe them.

The Problem of Present Repercussions Introduced. This is the sort of problem one usually has in mind when one asks whether the just person is happy on the rack. One is asking whether, if the just person is

---

9. Annas, pp. 316-317.
10. Annas, *ibid.*, with my emphasis.

on the rack during a particular period of time, he or she is happy during
that very same period of time. More generally, one can ask whether and to
what degree undergoing extreme pain or the like during an interval of
time lessens one's well-being during that same interval. Common sense
says that it does, and to a very considerable degree. Plato must somehow
deal with that view.

    The Problem of Future Repercussions Introduced. The question
here is whether and to what degree extreme pain or the like can, in
Plato's opinion, disrupt the harmony of the soul so as to make a person
cease to be happy or at least diminish his happiness later on. Even if
Plato's notion of happiness is such that being happy over a certain period
is compatible with extreme pain over that same period (so long, say, as
the pain is borne in a certain way or with a certain attitude), then he
might still hold that under some circumstances, such extreme hardship
can disrupt the soul so as to cause his well-being to deteriorate over time.
That would be to hold that the factors determining the degree of one's
well-being at a certain time include external circumstances that cause
such things as pain, and are not confined simply to one's degree of justice
at an earlier time. Thus, even if being just could not be argued to entail
being happy *now*, it would not therefore necessarily entail being happy
later, if external misfortunes interfered. Now, just as common sense holds
that external factors can have present repercussions on one's well-being, it
equally plainly holds that they can also have future repercussions. Plato
must somehow deal with this view too. Let us now take each of these
problems and look at them carefully, to see exactly how Plato comes to be
subject to them.

    The Problem of Present Repercussions Considered. It seems to
me quite impossible to deny that in Plato's opinion, common sense is
right in granting some role to external factors in determining how well off
one is during a given period. (Plato does not seem to think that one
should ask how happy a person is at an instant of time, or even over a
short period, as we shall see -- if indeed he thinks the question makes
sense -- but that fact does not affect the argument.) On Plato's theory of
the tripartite soul, such factors evidently would act mainly or exclusively
through the "lower" two parts of the soul, spirit and appetite, because of
their desires for certain external states of affairs, like being honored or
having enough to eat, which are subject to contingencies, and also because
of their susceptibilities to various influences of one's surroundings, such
as things that affect sensation and things that cause pain, which are also

contingent.[11] Since it is evident that he thinks that these parts of the soul are influenced by external contingencies, the only question remaining is whether he thinks that one's well-being can be influenced by such states of these parts of the soul. Here again the answer is clearly affirmative.

It is affirmative, in the first place, even if one thinks (as I myself do not) that in Plato's opinion the pleasures, pains, satisfactions, and dissatisfactions of the lower parts of the soul are without any intrinsic value whatsoever, either positive or negative, and that the only states of the soul to which genuine intrinsic value attaches are states of the reason, especially such things as philosophical contemplation. The strongest support for such an interpretation is to be found in the *Phaedo*, but probably the majority of scholars have thought that the view is present in the *Republic* too.[12] In any event, these dialogues certainly do show that Plato ascribed far less intrinsic positive and negative value to such pleasures and pains than common sense does. But the fact that is crucial, though almost always overlooked, is that *even if* Plato indeed ascribes absolutely *no* intrinsic value to pleasures other than pleasures of reason, he plainly thinks that the capacity of the reason to engage in its own activities is heavily dependent on not being disturbed or hindered by the appetites, particularly what he thinks of as the "bodily" appetites, and there can be no question that he urges all sorts of arrangements to prevent just such disturbances or hindrances. Indeed, the effort to protect the reason and its activity from the hindrances arising from the body -- both its desires and also the sensations that affect the reason through it -- is a repeated theme in Plato, both in the *Republic* and elsewhere, and it shows how large a role the treatment of external contingencies must play in Plato's thinking about well-being. The *Phaedo* emphasizes how assiduously the philosopher must cultivate an independence of sensory and appetitive distractions (esp. 65a-66a), and the *Republic*, in addition to warning against the same sorts of distractions (571d-572a), says that even a good man may be corrupted by dramatic performances (605a with 605b-608c), and of course establishes a strict regimen for the rulers to prevent their

---

11. There are of course many problems in making clear just what the connection is in Plato's view between appetites and sensation, but what is plain is that neither of them has its seat in the reason, and that both are closely associated, in some sense, with the body.

12. There is relevant material on this issue in treatments of the *Republic* too numerous to mention, including those cited above. Although Plato certainly accords far less value to pleasures that he associates with the lower two parts of the soul than would common sense, I think it is a mistake to think that he accords no intrinsic value to them at all. Without attempting to deal with this issue here, I would note a particular difficulty with such an interpretation that is usually neglected completely. It is that if one says that Plato accords no positive intrinsic value to "lower" pleasures, then one would seem forced to say that he accords no *negative* intrinsic value to "lower" *pains* -- an interpretation that seems to me extremely difficult to sustain.

corruption by other factors. Nothing in Plato ever suggests that (at least for the living) a desirable condition of soul can ever be guaranteed against all shocks from the outside.[13]

The Problem of Future Repercussions Considered. Consider first why this problem presents a difficulty for Plato's thesis that the just are better off than the unjust, at least if the thesis is not stated carefully. Most crudely, it can be simply misleading to say that you will be better off by being just, since that could be taken to mean that once you become just your well-being thenceforward is assured. But that will not be true if justice is a condition not automatically maintained. Being told that you will be happy if you become just may turn out to be as misleading an advertisement as being told that you will be beautiful if you have facelift, if you are not also told that the effects of facelifts wear off so that the procedure has to be repeated periodically. There is also another issue. If one now wants the greatest well-being possible over one's whole life, one needs to know what the best plan or strategy is to gain that end, starting from the present. For suppose that justice now does entail happiness now, and vice versa. Even so, it is one thing for it to be the case that being just at a given time substantially increases one's chances of being just, and happy, at a later time; but it is quite another thing for it to be the case that being just at a given time, even if it guarantees being happy *right then*, gives one no better odds than an unjust person has of being just and happy *later*. And of course it would be especially cruel if justice now made justice and happiness later *less* likely than present injustice did, though of course precisely this view is adopted by those (perhaps Cephalus in *Republic* I is among them) who think that they must first make their fortune, by hook or by crook, so that they may live virtuously later. For both of these reasons, it is evidently a pressing question for Plato whether his thesis has to be limited to saying that one is happy during a period if and only if one is just during *that same* period, or whether his thesis can be strengthened to say that subsequent well-being can always be gained, and can best be gained, by becoming just forthwith.

---

13. Nothing in Nussbaum's treatment of the *Republic* affects this claim. In her account of Plato's views two quite different issues are conflated without evident awareness of their distinctness or the relationship between them (see pp. 8-9 and Chs. 4-5). One is the question whether a thing's *being good* is dependent on events or states of affairs that are contingent. This issue dominates her treatment of the *Republic* in Ch. 5. The other issue concerns whether a thing's *being obtainable (and retainable or maintainable)* depends on events or states of affairs that are contingent, particularly ones that are outside of human control. On the former issue, she correctly takes Plato as holding that a thing's being good is independent of, in particular, human desires for it and even enjoyments of it (this point is emphasized in my *Companion*, pp. 35-37, 53-54, and in Annas, pp. 269-271). The latter issue, which is taken up in her discussion of the *Protagoras* in Ch. 4 (see esp. pp. 89-91) but does not figure in her discussion of the *Republic*, is what is being discussed here.

Although many suppose that throughout Plato's main argument in Books II-IX he must simply *assume* that justice is a condition that tends strongly to maintain itself, i.e., to guarantee its own future continuation, it is clear that this is not at all the case. For when one gives the matter a little thought, one realizes that a tremendous emphasis is placed throughout those books precisely on the precariousness of the just person's justice. However strong a child's native propensity toward justice may be, Plato insists constantly that fostering justice requires enormous efforts (376-414, *passim*, esp. 376e-379b, 412e-414a). Although Plato says that the young guardians-to-be will not willingly lose the belief that the good of the city coincides with theirs, they still might lose it by the bewitchment of pain, pleasure, or fear (413b-e). He emphasizes strongly that people with philosophical temperaments, and even those who have gone a long way in philosophy, can be corrupted by pernicious influences around them, especially censure and approval (491-494, esp. 492b-c), though those in the process of being corrupted can sometimes be saved (492a). And of course Plato's ideal city itself can deteriorate because of dissension among the rulers (545-547), which results from mistakes that the rulers themselves make in the eugenic arrangements that Plato prescribes (546b, c-d). Indeed, Plato introduces his account of this deterioration with the general statement that everything that comes to be on earth must perish (546a). From all of these indications, it becomes completely implausible to think that in his view, justice is a fully automatically self-sustaining condition. On the contrary, he is insisting that other factors beside one's present justice help to determine whether one's soul will be as harmonious in the future as it is now. Therefore we also clearly cannot say that the Problem of Future Repercussions is something of which Plato would be able to be unaware.

I think it is also clear that in mounting his argument in Books II-IX for the superiority of the just life over the unjust life, Plato has carefully taken account of the Problem of Future Repercussions, and has tailored his thesis so that that Problem will not affect it. That is because the thesis deals, as I have just indicated, with a comparison of a just *life* and an unjust *life* (581e, 583a, 587e-588a; cf. 358c). That is, he makes the *supposition* that one person is just *throughout* his life and that another person is unjust *throughout* his life, and then argues that *given* that supposition, the former is better off than the latter. Only the degree of well-being contemporaneous with a person's justice or injusice matters to the comparison, merely because no subsequent times are brought in that could be relevant to the accounting. His conclusion thus falls under the thesis that one's happiness during a period of time is proportional to one's justice during that same period, as that special case in which the period in question is a whole life, or more generally a period for which nothing later needs to be accounted for. The conclusion thus does run afoul of the

Problem of Present Repercussions, and we shall have to see what Plato does about that. But at least the Problem of Future Repercussions is neatly circumvented, for the time being. That means only, however, that Plato does not need to deal with it in order to make the particular comparison that he makes in *Book IX* in the particular way that he makes it. It does *not* mean that he can ignore future repercussions forever. On the contrary, it means that he cannot.

The Problem of the Extra Book Considered. As I have indicated, the Problem of the Extra Book is multifarious, because of the several seeming defects of Book X, involving (*a*) its connection to the earlier books, (*b*) the connections among its parts, and (*c*) the quality of some of its arguments. Let me list a series of questions that arise about it under these headings.

(*a*) The chief question about the relation of Book X to the earlier books obviously is simply one of what it can add to what they have already tried to show. The question is made more urgent by the feeling, which one can easily get at the end of Book IX, as Annas says, that both philosophically and rhetorically everything seems to have been settled. One might hope to find an answer by returning to the beginning of Book II and noting that Plato has there promised to show that justice is good both "for itself" and "for its consequences" (357a-358d, 367a-e), and then suggesting that the purpose of Books II-IX is to show that justice is good "for itself" while Book X aims to show that justice is good "for its consequences." But this cannot be right, since only past the middle of Book X, at 612a-b, does Plato recur to his promise in Book II and say that having argued that justice is good for itself, he will now consider its rewards (*misthoi*, 612b1; cf. 357d1, 367d4). So the suggestion would leave unexplained the role of the first two thirds of the book.[14]

Under the same heading, however, there is an additional difficulty about the last third of Book X that is both more serious and philosophically more interesting than the other, though it is hardly ever noticed. As I have just said, that passage maintains that justice is good "for its consequences." He has already argued that it is good "for itself," by which he means that it is good for the well-being that justice itself, without the help of any auxiliary factors, brings about in the soul.[15] Plato takes well-being, as we have seen, to be a certain harmonious or orderly

---

14. Annas claims (p. 294) that in Book IV Plato argues that justice is worth having for itself, and that in Books VIII-IX he argues that it is worth having for its results. See "The Classification of Goods" for reasons against this claim, which seems to me to clash irremediably with the clear evidence of 612a-b, among other passages.

15. See George Grote, *Plato and the Other Companions of Socrates*, new ed. (London, 1888), vol. IV, p. 102; David Sachs, "A Fallacy in Plato's *Republic*," *Philosophical Review*, 72 (1963), 141-158, esp. pp. 145-147; my *Companion*, pp. 78-79; and my "Classification of Goods."

arrangement of satisfactions and pleasures of all parts of the soul. (What distinguishes well-being from justice, as I have argued elsewhere, is that justice is a harmony of motivations and activities of the different parts of the soul, whereas happiness is a harmony of satisfactions and pleasures.)[16] But if this is so there is a problem about specifying the relationship between the well-being that justice itself brings and any additional rewards that Plato can say the just person might gain (614a). The rewards that Plato mentions are things like public offices, marrying whomever one wishes, and the like (613b-e), which are things aimed at by the two lower parts of the soul (principally the second part, which desires honor). But insofar as Plato has promised just people the orderly satisfactions of the desires of all parts of the soul, he would seem to have promised them such things as these, insofar as they are compatible with that orderliness. Certainly he cannot be promising them these things in measures beyond what would be compatible with overall orderly satisfaction, because by hypothesis their happiness would then be disrupted. And the same thing seems to hold for any particular item that might serve as a reward of justice in the sense of Book X. Thus, our question is, what can the rewards of justice be, if they are not to be reckoned as already included in well-being?

(b) Next we must ask about the connections among the parts of Book X. Actually, we should not pose the question in a way that assumes that Book X itself must possess some kind of thematic unity, since the book divisions of the *Republic* are in all probability not Plato's divisions. Instead we should ask why Plato proceeds as he does from the conclusion of the argument at the end of Book IX to the end of the whole work, and what the transition of thought might be from one section to the next. In particular, then, we must ask why Plato ends the *Republic* with the two principal sections of Book X, the discussion of tragedy and imitation, and the myth about the afterlife, with its preface, the argument for the immortality of the soul. The presence of the discussion of tragedy seems especially puzzling. As we saw, the rest of the book does treat the consequences of justice, and although we have now seen reason to wonder what that treatment involves, it at least is part of the plan announced at the beginning of Book II, whereas the discussion of tragedy is not. The usual reply to this problem seems to me hopelessly lame, though I once accepted it.[17] It is that Plato needs to disarm the poets, his main rivals to the position of moral, cultural, and political educators of the *polis*. But this explanation is quite unconvincing. Although there may be said to be some point in his having placed his attack on the poets after his exposition of his whole position in Books II-IX, that seems a very weak considera-

---

16. See "The Classification of Goods," pp. 414-416.
17. In my *Companion*, p. 247.

tion, and it appears to me that the attack would have been far more appropriately placed elsewhere, either in Book III, where he denies most poetry a role in the guardians' education, or else somewhere in Books VI-VII, to contrast the viewpoint of poetry with his own ideas about the Good and its role in the rulers' activities. After all, he includes an attack on his other rivals, the Sophists, in Book VI, long before he has fully expounded his own views. So we need to ask whether the discussion of tragedy has features that make it appropriate to place it with the other things that come after Book IX.

There is also a question to be raised about the Myth of Er at the end of Book X, and the relation of its parts to each other. For the odd thing is that the rewards and punishments in the afterlife seem to fall into two distinct classes, those that come to souls when they are disembodied, as a direct result of the judgment passed on each of them by the underwordly judges (614c). This judgment divides the souls into two main groups, those who go up and those who go down. The former see beautiful sights (615a) while the latter are punished by having various pains inflicted on them, depending on what crimes they have committed in life (615a-b). The other sort of rewards and punishments, on which Plato places much more emphasis, arise from the kinds of lives the souls lead subsequently, as a result of reincarnation. These rewards and punishments are chosen by the souls themselves (617e), and each of them seems to consist in nothing more than living a certain kind of life with a certain kind of character. (In addition, there is a third aspect of the afterlife: *all* of the souls rest in the meadow after the first punishments and rewards are over (614d-e), except for Ardiaius and the other incurables, who are dropped into Tartarus, and they *all* are then given a tour of the wheelhouse of the universe (616b-617d), which Plato describes in a rather confusing *Guide Michelin* (but, lamentably, without a map). It seems reasonable to ask whether any ethical significance is supposed to attach to all of this complexity, and if so, what it is.)

(c) Last we must ask why Plato gives some arguments in Book X that seem to be of such poor quality, so weak as to seem incapable of persuading anyone who needs persuading. For one thing, why does he use a myth to claim that the just are rewarded and the unjust are punished? It is often held that Plato uses myths to talk about matters that he regards as conjectural, and that is doubtless right. But what exactly does he take to be conjectural in the Myth of Er? That there is an afterlife? That the just are rewarded in it? Sometimes, of course, people say that he is here directing his remarks to a philosophically less sophisticated audience than he is addressing in the rest of the work. But although I have thought this too, it now seems obvious to me that it is quite an absurd explanation. For even if he is here addressing the unsophisticated, that still does not explain the thing that all of us sophisticated readers insist on having explained, namely, how the uncertainty of the claims in the myth affects his thesis that the just are better off than the unjust. After all, he *has* said, in Book II, that he will show that justice is valuable for its consequences. Is he now telling us that that was all a joke, and that all he has to say on the matter is a story for the *polloi*?

This story is made all the more urgent by the fact that Plato's other arguments about the consequences of justice, that is, the ones in 612e-614a for saying that the just are rewarded and the unjust are punished in *this* life, seem weak or nonexistent. The argument that the gods will reward justice actually is made to depend on claims about the *afterlife*, since Plato commits himself to saying only that if someone who is just "falls into poverty or illness or some other seemingly bad thing, we must suppose that this will end up well for him either while he is alive *or* after his death" (613a). The argument that men reward justice, however, must stand or fall on its own, and certainly it seems to fall. Plato has little or no argument or evidence to present, and indeed explicitly admits that he is merely contradicting what his opponents say (613c-d). We shall see that the fact that Plato *says* that he is merely contradicting his opponents is a good reason for not taking him to be claiming to have an *argument* against them. But until later, when we see how his behavior here fits with the rest of Book X, we must regard the weakness of his argumentation here as a problem.

The Missing Response in the Extra Book

Both the problems that Plato confronts and the ideas that he expounds in Book X have a clear and important theme in common: the influence of external contingencies on the well-being of the just. Understanding what he thinks about that influence is the key to understanding both his response to the Problem of Present Contingencies and also the Problem of Future Contingencies and the role of the things that he says in Book X.

The crucial thing to understand is the extent to which what Plato says in Book X, in response to the problems that we have seen, qualifies the claims of the earlier books rather than making yet stronger ones, and cancels the exaggerated interpretation to which those claims would otherwise seem to be open. So far from being a naive and uncritical declaration of faith in some eternal but inexplicable luck of the just person, Book X shows us the precariousness of any reliance on mere good fortune, and certain particular limitations on the guarantees of happiness that the just person enjoys. At the same time, however, the book gives Plato's defense

-- entirely lacking theretofore in the *Republic* -- of the advantage of being
just in the face of that precariousness, which consists in maintaining that
justice (in Plato's sense of the word, of course) is always one's best bet
over the long run.

    Plato's Response to the Problem of Present Repercussions. Does
Plato tell us that the just person is happy on the rack? Does he tell us,
that is, that the just person is happier than the unjust person over any
period, no matter how short, no matter what their external circumstances
may be -- for example, if the just person is on the rack and the unjust
person is enjoying some good fortune in the satisfaction of his appetites? I
do not know of any place where Plato makes so naive a claim. We have
seen that he does not make it in Book IX. There the comparison is
between two whole lives or substantial portions thereof. Plato does not
say that each minute of a just life is happier than each minute of an unjust
life, or, for that matter, than each minute of a slightly less just life. Of
course Plato's claim does depend on the idea that the unjust life is full of
minutes far less satisfying than many of the minutes of a just life; but that,
as we shall shortly see, is quite a different matter. Plato does think that
the unjust person who actually rules a city is extremely unlucky, and such
a person, he thinks, may well be in a state of constant anxiety, because of
the need to guard against attacks (578b-580a). But that is the extreme
case. He does not deny that over shorter periods of time an unjust person
can gain what he wants. In 613d he admits that most unjust people escape
detection when young, and then says on the other side only that *most* of
them are caught and ridiculed when older. Perhaps even this is overly
optimistic, but it is certainly not a claim that all unjust people are punished while they are alive. As for just people, he says that "for the most
part" (*to polu*, 613c4) they gain good reputations and prizes, when they
are older, but he admits that they may not do so well in this regard before
that.

    It needs explanation, however, why Plato thinks that the just life
can be guaranteed to be better overall than the unjust life, as we have
seen he argues up to and within Book IX, if he does not hold that the
former is better than the latter minute by minute. The answer is fairly
obvious, and emerges clearly in both Book IX and Book X. It is largely
that when one is dealing with longish periods of time, capacities for planning come into play sufficiently to make a substantial difference to well-
being. As Book IX takes pains to argue, the just person is the one who is
able to plan for the orderly satisfaction of a whole range of desires,
whereas the unjust person frustrates many desires in order to try to feed
the appetite or appetites that he is most attached to (571a-572b,
576b-578b, 586a-587b). Good luck may come in brief spurts, but only
rational planning, Plato believes, is capable of providing a reasonable
guarantee of lasting well-being.

What Book X adds to Book IX on this issue is an account of the role of reason and rational planning when dealing with misfortune. The problem is not dealt with seriously in the earlier books because, as we have seen, the earlier books simply assume a whole just life and a whole unjust life in order to compare them. But in the discussion of tragedy in the first part of Book X (595a-608b), Plato says that the subject of imitative poetry is "people acting voluntarily or under compulsion, believing that by acting they have fared well or badly, and suffering or rejoicing in it all" (603c). Then, as an example of what is not presented by tragedy, he reintroduces from Book III the good man who has suffered a terrible misfortune (*sumphora*), such as the death of a friend or a son or a brother or the loss of possessions (387d-e, 603e). Such a person, says Plato, will be moderate in his grief (because not grieving at all is impossible), because the good and the bad in such things is not clear, and because bearing it hard does him no good in the future, since grief is an obstacle to doing what needs to be done (604b-c). This, he says, is the way to face misfortunes (*tas tuchas*, 604d3). He then goes on to explain that tragedy does not depict this way of facing misfortunes, and discourages audiences from it (604e-606b). By focusing on the mere fact that he is attacking tragic poetry, readers tend not to notice that he is making his own substantial point here about the way in which a good man will cope with contingencies. So Plato is not ignoring such things, nor is he acting as though a just person will somehow have no reaction to them. Rather, he emphasizes that although grief and the like are unavoidable, a just person, by correctly estimating the values of things, will be able to plan rationally to make the best of a bad situation over the long run.

Although much could be said in criticism of Plato's particular recommendations about how to live one's life, it is clear what his argument is and how it bears on the problem at hand in the *Republic* as a whole. For outcomes that are to be satisfactory over a substantial period of time, one's best bet is to have the kind of character that can plan rationally to attain what is best. This is why, even though a just person can indeed be afflicted by misfortunes and can be in bad straits, being just is the best strategy for the long run. Of course, because Plato places so much more value on the satisfactions of reasoning, as compared with those of the body, he must hold that it would take a great deal of bad luck to the just person and good luck to the unjust person to bring the former down to the level of the latter. Nevertheless I do not suppose that Plato would deny that by some ghastly fluke a just person might suffer repeated pains and misfortunes for his whole life, or that this would significantly decrease his well-being. He says that we "must suppose" (*hupolepteon*) that the gods will not send consistently bad luck to a good man (612e-613b), but will make things go well eventually in this life or the afterlife. I take it that by saying that we "must suppose" this, he is acknowledging its precariousness. But even if this claim is overoptimistic, that does not subvert his contention about what the best strategy is for rational planning. For even if bad fortune strikes the just as much as it does the unjust, Plato's contention is simply that the former will be able to recognize what is of genuine value and what is not, and so maintain the psychological equilibrium necessary for rational planning to do as well as circumstances permit. This general view could obviously be endorsed even by someone who does not accept Plato's particular claims about what kinds of things a person would enjoy most or think worthwhile.

And it obviously *is* a response to the Problem of Present Repercussions. It is not the extreme and absurd response that some readers expect and think they see, namely, that the just person is always happy no matter what, or that every just person is at every moment better off than every unjust person. The response is rather that inasmuch as the comparison that is important involves the long run rather than the short run, justice is the best strategy.

Within this picture we can easily elucidate a fact that puzzles some interpreters, namely, that in his entire argument Plato is always concerned primarily with justice as a trait of character or soul, rather than justice as a characteristic of individual actions or even types of action. Plato never says, anywhere in the argument of Books II-X, that each and every just action causes some corresponding increment in one's wellbeing. He always takes as his question whether it is best for one to be just or have a just soul. The reason is obvious now. An action-by-action comparison is likely enough to meet cases in which, when there are only short-term effects, an unjust action makes one better off. In eschewing such comparisons, he is favoring the long-term comparison instead. This is also why he adopts the particular way that he does of explaining the justice of an action in terms of the justice of a soul. In Book IV, 443b-444a, he claims explanatory priority for justice of soul over justice of action, and then explains the justice of an action as the tendency to preserve that harmony of soul that he has identified with justice (443e-444a). (The same idea is echoed in Book X, when he says that we should call a life good to the extent that it makes the soul more just [618d-e; cf. 618b].) Contrary to some interpreters, he never in the *Republic* ascribes justice, or even value, to an action purely in virtue of its *proceeding from* or *expressing* a just condition of soul.[18] In that work his notion of the value to oneself of a just

---

18. PP. 210-211 of *Plato's Moral Theory*, Irwin seems to agree with this interpretation of Book IV. On pp. 240-242 he offers a more elaborate account of the view expressed in Book IX, but because it deals with the philosopher's motivations, and not the criterion or the value of just action, it does not seem to me to conflict with the point being made here. (I would not myself agree with Irwin, however, that Book IX expresses a different view from that of Book IV.)

action is only the notion of an action that *confirms or establishes* the state of character that enhances one's well-being over the long run.

Plato's Response to the Problem of Future Repercussions. In Plato's response to this problem we again see, along with the obvious insistence that justice as a strategy is enormously better than the contrary, a recognition of the relevance to well-being of external contingencies, and an awareness of the need for certain kinds of inevitable limitations on the guarantee of happiness that the just person enjoys.

As we have seen, Plato takes it to be clear, as indeed it is, that external influences can disrupt the harmony of a just soul, and he institutes stringent measures to guard against this. One of them is the stricture in Book X against tragic poetry, which is said to be "able to corrupt even good men, with a very few exceptions" (605c; 606a-c). He plainly does not believe that there is some kind of ironclad guarantee that someone who is just at one time will be just later, even though the capacity for rational planning will plainly put the just person in a better position to maintain his state of character. But Plato does think that the capacities for planning of even philosopher-rulers can fail them (546a-547a). As in the case of the Problem of Present Repercussions, his response to the problem is to admit it, and make his case around it, by stating his thesis in Book IX as a comparison of whole lives. This means that the one important thing that can be lacking to a person who is just at a given time is complete certainty -- that is, certainty beyond what a confidence in his own capacities for rational planning can gain him -- in the perfect stability of his condition. Can there be any other explanation than this of the fact that in the Myth of Er, as I pointed out, the reward of justice that Plato most emphasizes is the *continuation of the just condition of his soul* into a future incarnation? Notice again that all that the deities of the underworld provide is the *opportunity* for that continuation, by making it possible for the souls there to be reincarnated and to choose for themselves the kind of life they will lead. The Fate Lachesis emphasizes that the responsibility for the choice rests with the soul who makes it (617e), and although the souls have to pick from among a fixed supply of possible lives offered to them, Plato stipulates that the supply of possible lives is "much greater" (*polu pleio*) than the number of souls doing the choosing (617e-618a), thus making it clear that a soul's choice is not to be thought of as forced by the option available (see also 619b). Thus, when Odysseus is the last in his group to make a selection, he can search for a long time among the remaining lives and end up with the one, he says, that he would have picked if he had been first to choose (620c-d), the quiet life of a private individual. What this shows is that what the souls gain is merely the opportunity to go on having the characters that they have.[19] And indeed Plato stresses that most of them choose in accordance with their characters in their previous life (620a). Interestingly, he confirms elsewhere what this statement suggests, that the rewards and punishments that the souls receive in the underworld before they choose their future lives have little influence on that choice (619c-d). Those rewards and punishments are merely more experiences that their characters assimilate; but the choice of a future life is not determined by them, but is much more strongly influenced by their previous traits.[20]

There are two points here worthy of special notice. First of all, the primary reward of justice is the continuation of one's just state, and not any additional bonus beyond that. That fits with the fact that we observed, that it is difficult to see what further particular satisfactions one could possibly want if one was hypothesized already to have harmony of soul in Plato's sense. I am not denying that even if one's soul were harmonious and well-ordered, one might still have some desires whose further satisfaction could enhance one's well-being -- so long, of course, as it was carried out consistently with one's harmonious condition. But the important thing is to keep one's soul in a good state into the future. This is the second point that emerges from the myth. As I have said, the only really substantial reward that a just soul can in Plato's scheme hope to gain is simply the continuation of his present just condition. That is precisely what the myth offers him. It is not some extra *particular* benefit beyond the harmonious condition of soul. That would be impossible. But it *is* a *further, contingent* consequence of being just together with other factors.[21] Thus, in praising justice for its consequences, Plato is praising it in the only way that could fit his account of human goods, and in so praising it he is, precisely, responding to the Problem of Future Repercussions.

It is obviously not without philosophical significance that Plato puts his response to the Problem of Future Repercussions in the form of a myth. For it is part of his fixed view of the sensible world, as we saw him emphasizing at the beginning of Book VIII (546a), that the permanence of a characteristic like justice cannot possibly be completely assured (see also, e.g., *Symposium* 207e-208a). The point of the myth is to express his conviction -- that the just are rewarded by the continuation of their justice -- with the appropriate caution required by the fact that we are dealing with a contingent matter. For even if he believed that he could establish

19. See *Companion*, p. 265.
20. Whether Plato believes that the choice is fully determined by character, and in general whether he believes that choices are determined, are questions too involved to be tackled here.
21. See refs. in n. 16.

the immortality of the soul (608c-611a), he is generally reserved about ascribing certainty to descriptions of the contents of the afterlife. Moreover the important content of the myth, as he views it, seems to me largely independent of the actual existence of an afterlife. The important thing is to say what kind of benefit there could possibly be that would be a consequence of justice.

Secondarily, it is important for Plato to show what kind of reward could be expected of divinities that behave in accordance with what Plato takes to be an acceptable conception of divinity. He has already expounded this conception of divinity in Book II, 376e-383c, with emphasis on the idea that gods should be conceived of as good and as doing only good (379b-380c), and also on the idea that they do not fight with one another (378b-e).[22] Pause here to consider the strongest traditional Greek conception of the gods that Plato confronted: a conception of them as in constant disagreement and struggle, with each pursuing his or her own several desires with jealous capriciousness. As is well known, this is the conception that Plato is combating in the *Republic* (and that he had also had to contend with elsewhere, particularly in the *Euthyphro*, e.g., 5d-6c). His conjectures about the afterlife are a case in point. Gods like the traditional Greek ones could not be counted on to reward justice. Indeed, they could not be fully counted on for much of anything.[23] Book X holds that such a picture is incompatible with the true nature of divinities. But still the myth is less than a declaration that rewards are demonstrably assured to the just after death.

It seems to me clear that Plato is also combating traditional religious views in the first part of the Myth of Er, the part in which the souls are assessed by the underwordly judges, and before they choose their future lives. As I pointed out, Plato later says explicitly that their choices are influenced mainly by their established characters. He also says that souls who have gone upward rather than downward as a result of their judgment were as likely as the others to choose tyrants' lives (619c-d). This seems to me a declaration by Plato that an account of rewards and punishments in the underworld, such as were sometimes given in Greek religion, and such as Plato had himself indulged in elsewhere (especially the *Gorgias*), is not to the point in a discussion of the real rewards of justice.[24] The important point comes later, when the souls themselves

---

22. See *Companion*, pp. 93-94.
23. This is why, for example, the suggestion in the *Meno* that virtue might come by divine inspiration is plainly tantamount to the suggestion that it comes unpredictably and by luck.
24. Likewise, it is clear that the myth is not a chapter in a "theory of punishment," and in fact Plato does not have such a theory as a distinct part of his ethical and political philosophy, nor is it useful to view his remarks concerning punishments and rewards in that way.

choose their own rewards and punishments, in accordance with those characters that they themselves have. The only thing that a just person needs, and the only thing that is of substantial value to him, is the continuation of his justice. And since nothing in the sensible world can absolutely guarantee that, Plato must deploy his own myth, rather than a traditional one, to embody the conjecture that it will be forthcoming.

The Defects of Book X Reconsidered. I think that the foregoing remarks adequately cover the misgivings about Book X that I listed earlier. Let me briefly review them.

Under (*a*), we can see the role of the entirety of the book (that is, of the material after the end of Book IX) as a response to aspects of the problems about contingencies and their effects on one's well-being. The section on tragedy deals with the just person's ability to cope with misfortunes, and the myth presents the hope that a just person can continue to be just, which is the only reward that can be of really substantial value to anyone in that condition.

Under (*b*), the connection among the parts of Book X are clear enough, once we see how the attack on poetry plays a role in Plato's response to problems about contingencies, especially the Problem of Present Repercussions, and we no longer need to take it merely as an intrusive sideswipe at his rivals. The parts of the Myth of Er, and the myth as a whole, also appear as parts of his response to the same problems, particularly -- this time -- to the Problem of Future Repercussions.

Under (*c*), questions about the seeming feebleness of some of Plato's arguments are answered by recognizing that he is not, after all, trying to maintain the absurd theses that just lives are superior to unjust lives minute by minute or action by action, that the just are either exempt from or insensitive to disastrous external circumstances, and that a just character can maintain itself under any and all external pressures. In fact, as we have seen, Plato explicitly denies all of these things. Like his argument in Book IX, his claims about the rewards that people bestow on the just are made explicitly approximate, and, more importantly, are based on comparisons made over the long run, which rest in turn on the claim that the just are those with the capacity for rational planning for their own orderly overall satisfaction. And the rest of his claims, both in the myth and derivatively in his statement about what the gods reward (612e-613b), are made with both considerable caution and an exact awareness, contrary to traditional mythology, of what kinds of rewards are possible for a harmonious soul and genuinely valuable to a person who is already just.

So the peg of Book X has been fitted into the hole in the argument of the other books of the *Republic*, and the shape of the peg has now been explained by showing the hole that that argument contained. Let me conclude with a moral about how Plato ought to be read. The moral is: however much you may disagree with Plato (and I disagree with him a great deal), do not sell him short. His contentions may seem perverse, but he is *extremely* clever. He rarely, if ever, writes a passage that does not have some serious philosophical motivation. He also rarely, if ever, completely misses the point of his opponents' arguments. If you find a passage that seems to be pointless or superfluous, or a response to an opponent that seems completely off the mark, then think some more. There is a very good chance that, even if you must regard his position as wrong on philosophical grounds, you will see that what he says and what he needs to say will fit together more closely than you would ever have suspected.

Contemplation and Happiness: A Reconsideration[*]

John M. Cooper
Princeton University

1.

When one considers Aristotle's contributions to ethical theory one might have in mind any of several different things. One might think of his contributions to the subsequent history of moral philosophy, from Hellenistic and Greek Christian times to the Middle Ages, the Renaissance, Victorian England and nineteenth-century Germany, say. Or one might consider the ways in which his views have influenced recent and current work in moral philosophy, and ways in which they might further illuminate (or, as may be, darken) current discussions.

A distinct third possibility, which I will be following in this paper, is to discuss Aristotle's contributions to ethical theory by addressing his ideas in a systematic way and in some detail on their own, looking for what is unique or specially distinctive about them, without special reference either to contemporary theory or to the ways in which his ideas were interpreted and put to use in the subsequent history of ethics. Along these lines, one could discuss his moral psychology -- his theory of the nature and function of human reason, how reason when used fully controls nonrational desires and evokes its own kind of motivation ("rational wishes", *bouleseis* in the Greek). Or one might consider his theory of what a moral virtue is, and the ways in which, and reasons why, he thinks such fairly comprehensive states of character, involving judgment, perception and feeling, must take precedence in a philosophical account of the moral life over any appeal to principles of moral behavior (rules or laws).

[*]. This paper was first published in *Synthese* 72 (1987) 187-216. Copyright 1987 by D. Reidel Publishing Company. Reprinted by permission of Kluwer Academic Publishers.

Or one might think of Aristotle's views on the methods of ethics. Or his conception of practical knowledge, of what and how the fully virtuous person can legitimately lay claim to *know* (and so to be right, as opposed both to wrong and to neither right nor wrong) about how human beings ought to live. All these are aspects of Aristotle's moral philosophy that have recently and deservedly attracted the interest of philosophers and philosophically-minded scholars, and several of them are topics on which one might develop instructive comparisons or contrasts with Kurt Baier's work.

But if one is looking for what is unique, special, most distinctive in Aristotle's philosophy, then, as I have said, one will not limit oneself to topics that, for better or worse, are found specially attractive by contemporary philosophy. Accordingly, I want to concentrate on a single Aristotelian doctrine, one that I suppose no philosopher today is likely to find much use for but that is nonetheless a distinctive Aristotelian contribution to philosophical thought. This concerns the priority, in some sense or senses, that he claims for theoretical over practical activity. Though Aristotle's debt here to Plato in the *Republic* is plain, his momentous distinction and separation of the theoretical from the practical uses of the mind make the problems he faces and the theory he develops to respond to them distinctively his own, and not just one version of a common Platonic-Aristotelian idea. And Aristotle's immediate successors among the Greek philosophers, Epicurus and the old Stoics, were very far from sharing his outlook; this is especially noteworthy in the Stoics, who thought accurate philosophical knowledge, or devotion to study of any such recherché kind as Aristotle championed, was strictly not necessary for the fullest achievement of the natural human potential in which, as they in common with Aristotle held, human happiness consists. Human virtue, according to the Stoics, doesn't include that sort of thing, and beyond a certain fairly minimal acquaintance with physical theory, human happiness is attainable without it. Among the ancient Greek philosophers only Plotinus took over and adapted to his own uses something like the Aristotelian viewpoint, but of course the neo-Platonic metaphysics with which it gets mixed up makes for a theory of a very different shape, and one that has a different moral significance. The same is true of such medieval Aristotelians as Aquinas. So Aristotle's views on the special value of theoretical activity, and his identification of a contemplative life, in some sense of that term, as the best for a human being, are distinctively Aristotelian contributions to ethical theory. And since Aristotle's views on this topic are not easy to make out with any precision, and are currently the subject of scholarly controversy, it is perhaps especially worthwhile to offer a discussion of them, in gratitude and friendship, to Kurt Baier on his seventieth birthday.

2.

I will limit myself in what follows to discussing Aristotle's theories in the *Nicomachean Ethics*. Remarkably, only in the *Nicomachean Ethics*, and not in the *Eudemian Ethics* or the *Magna Moralia*, nor yet in the *Politics*, does Aristotle explicitly compare the value of theoretical study as against practical activity. Only in the *Nicomachean Ethics* does he, in consequence, explicitly maintain that (however this is to be interpreted) the best human life is a contemplative one. The *Eudemian Ethics*, in its only discussion (Book II, Chap. 1) of what constitutes human happiness (*eudaimonia*), says simply that happiness is "activity of complete virtue in a complete life" (1219a38-39), and there the context is explicit that "complete virtue" means all the specifically human virtues, the moral ones taken together with the intellectual (see 1219a37; 1219b26-1220a12). So Aristotle's view in the *Eudemian Ethics* is that the best life for a human being is one devoted jointly to morally good actions and excellent theoretical study: *eudaimonia* consists in a combination of these two, and does not define a form of life that he calls, or that deserves to be called, especially contemplative.[1] It is indeed an interesting question why in the *Eudemian Ethics* Aristotle rested content with this formulation, but departed from it in the *Nicomachean*. But we can only hope to give an answer after we have seen in some detail what Aristotle's view in the *Nicomachean Ethics* actually is.

In the *Nicomachean Ethics* Aristotle develops his theory of human happiness (*eudaimonia*) in two disjoint stages. There is a preliminary account at the beginning of the treatise (Book I), and the subject is taken up again at the end (Book X, chaps. 6-8), where certain details not previously entered into are worked out. In particular, it is only in Book X that Aristotle compares the values realized in excellent theoretical study with those of good practical activity and concludes that the ideally good human life will be a contemplative one. This means that the main

---

1. In the brief concluding paragraph of his discussion (Book VIII, chap. 3) of *kalokagathia*, the comprehensive virtue of "nobility" (so M. Woods: 1982, *Aristotle's Eudemian Ethics Books I, II, and VIII*, Clarendon Press, Oxford) Aristotle describes *kalokagathia* as "complete virtue" [1249a16], the virtue composed of all the particular virtues that have been discussed one by one in the course of the treatise, i.e., in Books III-V [1248a9-16]), Aristotle assigns some kind of priority to theoretical study and, by implication, to its virtue of *sophia*. I have attempted to work out in detail the sort of priority here envisaged (see 1975, *Reason and Human Good in Aristotle*, Harvard University Press, Cambridge, MA, pp. 136-43), arguing that it leaves intact the independence of the moral virtues as well as their separate and distinctive value. But whether or not this interpretation is accepted, this passage gives no basis for thinking Aristotle intended to take back his earlier identification of *eudaimonia* with the exercise of all the virtues and to identify it, in any sense, with the exercise of just one of them, *sophia*.

133,996

elements of what we think of as Aristotle's *moral* theory -- his theory of
the virtues and vices of character, of practical knowledge, deliberation,
weakness of will, pleasure, friendship, etc., all of which are set out in the
central books, II-IX -- are presented within the framework of the vaguer
preliminary account of happiness in Book I; they nowhere presuppose,
anyhow not explicitly and officially, the concluding, more refined theory
contained in Book X, chaps. 6-8. But when the later refinements are
taken into account it is, to put it mildly, not clear whether one can any
longer legitimately interpret Aristotle's *moral* theory as one would do
drawing only on material from the first nine books. Adopting the perspective of the contemplative ideal, as this is presented in Book X, threatens
to alter in significant ways one's conception of the structure and content
of the moral life as this was apparently analyzed in the earlier books.
Some people have even questioned whether there is any way to interpret
the moral theory of the *Nicomachean Ethics* so as to make it compatible
with the contemplative ideal of Book X. Perhaps, in the end, one should
simply admit that Aristotle works with two distinct, mutually incompatible
conceptions of human happiness in the *Ethics*: a preliminary, vaguer one
that supports a life of moral virtue, citizenship, and practical activity taken
seriously for its own sake, into which Aristotle fits his account of moral
virtue and related topics in the middle books of the treatise; and the
refined, contemplative conception, which makes no room for the kind of
engagement with other people (anyhow, fellow-citizens) quite generally
that provides the fabric of the moral life as previously analyzed. On that
reading, when in the end Aristotle argues that the contemplative conception gives the more correct account of human happiness, it will follow
that his attitude towards moral virtue is strictly qualified at best, if not
actually comprised altogether. For his preference for the contemplative
conception will mean that he can defend the life of moral virtue only as
the second best, not the best, life for a human being. (And, indeed, on
one plausible interpretation, he says precisely that in a prominent place in
his discussion in Book X, at the end of chapter 7 and the beginning of
chapter 8, 1178a4-10).

3.

As this brief sketch has, I hope, made clear, it is extremely difficult to decide whether Aristotle has a consistent theory of the good human life, and if he does, what place in that theory he gives to theoretical study. An unusual number of valuable discussions published in the last 15 years or so, and especially some work done in the past several years, have done a great deal to advance our understanding of the relevant texts, despite the fact that their authors continue to come to divergent conclusions on the central question.[2] I think we may now be in a position, if not to construct a definitive interpretation, at any rate to elaborate and defend one particular interpretation as the most convincing of the possibilities the texts leave open. For further progress requires the candid admission that Aristotle is himself, partly for good reasons that he states, to some extent responsible for the confusion that surrounds his views on this topic. He emphasizes that both the preliminary and the final accounts of happiness are given in sketches only (1094a25; 1098a21; 1176a31; 1179a34). And he repeatedly warns against speaking on ethical topics with "exactness" (*akribeia*), since so much here depends on particular facts about individual agents and their situations (1094b11-27; 1098a26-1098b8; 1103b26-1104a11). Any correct statement about *all* human agents must be subject to exceptions, and the more detailed one makes one's account the more subject to exceptions it will be, since it is not possible to produce a satisfactory qualified generalization, listing the exceptions and the respects in which and the reasons why they count as such. Hence, Aristotle insists, if one wishes to make one's general theories as true as possible, one must be content often not to enter into details at all. Thus Aristotle himself warns us not to expect anywhere in the *Ethics* a fully articulated account of happiness, and so (perhaps) not to expect one that would make it clear precisely what role moral virtue and what role theoretical study must occupy in the best human life: if one is to speak correctly of *the* best life, perhaps one must leave these matters in

---

2. I may mention here J. L. Ackrill, 'Aristotle on *Eudaimonia*', British Academy Lecture 1974, in A. Rorty: 1980, *Essays on Aristotle's Ethics*, University of California Press, Berkeley; W. F. R. Hardie: 1965, 'The Final Good in Aristotle's *Ethics*', *Philosophy* 40 277-95, reprinted in J. M. E. Moravcsik: 1967, *Aristotle: A Collection of Critical Essays*, Doubleday, Garden City; Hardie: 1979, 'Aristotle on the Best Life for a Man', *Philosophy* 54 pp. 35-50; David Keyt: 1983, 'Intellectualism in Aristotle', in J. P. Anton and A. Preus (eds.), *Essays in Ancient Greek Philosophy*, Vol. II, State University of New York Press, Albany; Richard Kraut: 'A Dominant-End Reading of the *Nicomachean Ethics*', (as yet unpublished); Jennifer Whiting: 1986, 'Human Nature and Intellectualism in Aristotle', *Archiv fur Geschichte der Philosophie* 68, 70-95; Timothy Roche: ' *Ergon* and *Eudaimonia* in *Nicomachean Ethics I*: Reconsidering the Intellectualist Interpretation', (unpublished).

some respects undetermined, subject to individual variation. In any event, it is essential to recognize that because he intended to write only a sketch Aristotle has left us a text that is unavoidably open to alternative interpretations, even ones which one feels sure, and can to some extent successfully argue, were not intended by Aristotle himself.

When I first thought of writing something on Aristotle's theory of human happiness, more than fifteen years ago now, I quickly became convinced that in his final account of happiness in Book X of the *Nicomachean Ethics* Aristotle so elevates the value of intellectual activity of the highest kind that he leaves no room at all in the ideal, contemplative life for morality as ordinarily understood and as analyzed by himself in earlier books.[3] I thought commentators failed to see this, or actually denied it, because they found this view so repugnant, even outrageous, that they simply did not allow themselves to consider whether Aristotle, after all a very great philosopher, could have adopted it. In any event, the palliatives they introduced in order to avoid attributing this discredited view to Aristotle seemed to me on examination altogether without merit as interpretations of Aristotle's actual words. Aristotle certainly *seems* to say plainly and repeatedly in Book X that happiness, or as he sometimes says instead, "complete happiness", is -- actually *consists* in -- contemplative activity, carried on for a complete lifetime (1177a7-8, 17-18; 1177b24-26; 1178b7-8, 32). And if one takes seriously Aristotle's treatment of happiness from the very beginning of the *Ethics* as the (one and only) end for the sake of which we rational, adult human beings should do *everything* that we do, I did not see how to combine this apparent equation of human happiness with the activity of philosophical thinking with the kind of commitment to morally good action that on Aristotle's own, as I thought, excellent analysis is essential to having a morally virtuous character.

The morally virtuous person has a permanent and deep attachment to his family, his personal friends, and his fellow-citizens, to serving their needs and furthering their short- and long-term good. He is also attached to his own normal and natural emotional and bodily satisfactions, and to the exercise of a normally wide range of intellectual capacities and interests. It is hardly credible that he should see this complex balance of attachments as just what one should induce in oneself and regularly express in one's more particular choices and actions, in order to further one's philosophical work. Aristotle does say once in the *Nicomachean Ethics* that *phronesis*, the intellectual virtue of practical wisdom or understanding that dictates the structure of evaluations making up the morally virtuous state of character, gives instructions for the sake of

---

3. See John M. Cooper: 1975, *Reason and Human Good in Aristotle*, Harvard University Press, Cambridge, MA, Chap. III.

philosophical wisdom (1145a9), i.e., in order to make theoretical understanding of the metaphysical first principles of reality, and its exercise, possible. And in other works of Aristotle and in the ancient Aristotelian tradition one finds moral virtue described as, in effect, a condition of quiescence in which nonrational desires and interests impinge on and distract the mind as little as possible from its own work, which is wholly philosophical.[4] In the passage just cited Aristotle does not, however, say that in shaping and supporting one's moral character in just the way it does one's practical understanding (*phronesis*) has *solely* in view the aim of providing conditions favorable for the acquisition and exercise of philosophical wisdom. And a careful reading of his detailed descriptions of the particular moral virtues makes it clear that he thinks the morally virtuous person values the multifarious persons, things, experiences and activities that he cares fundamentally about independently of the effects that so valuing them has on his capacity and opportunity for philosophical work.[5] No doubt the full development of our theoretical capacities does depend upon a due measure in our emotional and other nonrational attachments to other people and in the satisfactions of social, political and family life; otherwise, with excessive or even in some cases deficient likings for other things, we might well not be able to take enough interest in theoretical concerns or to enjoy them sufficiently in order to come to actually *experience* for ourselves what (as Aristotle thinks) is so uniquely and overwhelmingly valuable in them. And knowing this will be a central item in the knowledge on the basis of which the man of practical understanding strives to maintain for himself that due measure in his other attachments.

But what makes the measure in question a due one in the case of each range of nonrational desires and satisfactions is not merely that it makes possible, for those whose native endowments tend in that direction, the development and uninhibited exercise of their theoretical powers. It also answers to the independent values for a human being of all those other objects, activities and relationships on which the nonrational desires themselves are immediately directed. It is a cardinal fact about human nature if, as Aristotle in effect claims, the morally virtuous state, in answering to the objective values of this wide range of objects of ordinary human concern, also provides a condition of quiescence in which the higher intellectual interests can be awakened, developed and satisfied. But it is important to realize that it is this already fairly optimistic application of natural teleology on which Aristotle's moral theory rests,

---

4. *Eudemian Ethics*, 1249b22-23; *Magna Moralia*, 1198b12-20; Theophrastus in a scholion found in a Vienna manuscript and published by G. Heylbut; 1888, 'Zur Ethik des Theophrast von Eresos', *Archiv fur Geschichte der Philosophie I*, p. 195.

5. See Cooper, *op. cit.*, pp. 105-10.

and not the much more extreme, altogether implausible, belief that the state of desire characteristic of moral virtue is fully dictated by the pursuit of intellectual self-development alone.

So I found myself forced to the conclusion that Aristotle's final and fully considered theory of human happiness in Book X of the *Ethics* does not build upon his analysis of moral virtue in the earlier books, but is actually inconsistent with it, in the sense that anyone who successfully led the contemplative life recommended in Book X as the ideal one for a human being would not and could not be at the same time a morally virtuous person, leading a moral life as we, and Aristotle in the earlier books, understand it.

This was not a conclusion I was happy to come to. Not because I thought this substantive moral view was without merit or was unworthy of the great Aristotle: on the contrary, I thought there was something possibly salutary in the idea that the practices of morality and the moral way of life were suitable only for most human beings under most circumstances, and not necessarily for those whose capacities and fundamental interests set them apart from the communal life that is the best most of us can aspire to. What was bothersome was rather the thought that Aristotle had composed the *Nicomachean Ethics* with so little regard for consistency that in most of the work he could write as if moral virtue and the practices of morality are an essential part of the happy life, the best life for a human being (any human being), while in one fell swoop at the end of the work he takes this back -- and without properly explaining what he is doing by, for example, revisiting moral virtue briefly to draw out the consequences of his revised theory of happiness for the moral life. (The cryptic remark that the life according to moral virtue is a secondarily happy one [1178a9] can only be interpreted as, at best, a gesture in that direction). One might rather have expected the second treatment of happiness to supplement and complete the vaguer first one, without overturning any of the substantive conclusions about the best life and its contents that are arrived at by working out the implications of that first treatment. If Aristotle had been intending eventually to present two separate life ideals -- a less ideal but more widely suitable life devoted largely to moral virtue, and a more ideal contemplative life suited only for philosophers and not involving common morality at all -- surely he ought to have made this clear in a preliminary way already in the first book and to have presupposed it at many places as he proceeded through the intervening discussions.

That he does not do this certainly encourages the hope that it may be possible, despite what I argued in my book, to interpret the theory of happiness in Book X so that it does cohere with the rest of the treatise. Several attempts in this direction have recently appeared, or are about to appear, in the scholarly literature, and though in my opinion none of them

succeeds in disposing adequately of the formidable obstacles Aristotle's
text throws up, enough real progress has been made to incline me now to
think an interpretation along these general lines has rather more
favourable prospects than I used to think. In what remains I will develop
and defend one such interpretation.

4.

I said above that the strongest evidence in the text of Book X
supporting an intellectualist ideal that leaves no room for morality is
found in those passages where Aristotle says, or at least *seems* to say, that
happiness (*eudaimonia*) is, actually *consists* in, the single activity of
excellent theoretical thinking. Eventually I will want to suggest that this is
not in fact what Aristotle intends to say in these passages. We can take a
first step toward understanding what Aristotle does mean by considering
the first of these passages, the very first sentence of Book X, chapter 7,
with which Aristotle introduces his account of the contemplative life. In
the preceding chapter he has argued that happiness does not depend
essentially upon pleasant leisure-time activities (*ouk en paidia ara he
eudaimonia*, 1176b27-28), various forms of play, even although these, or
some of them, are in fact both chosen and worth choosing for their own
sakes. The happy life, he insists, requires seriousness; happiness depends
not on bodily pleasures and such like, indulged in for fun, but rather on
activities of virtue (*ou gar en tais toiautais diagogais he eudaimonia, all' en
tais kat' areten energeiais*, 1177a9-10). Aristotle begins chapter 7 by
recasting this conclusion from chapter 6 as follows: "If happiness
(*eudaimonia*) is activity of virtue, it is reasonable (that it should be) of the
most superior virtue" (*ei d'estin he eudaimonia kat' areten energeia,
eulogon kata ten kratisten*).

Now in order to appreciate accurately the significance of what
Aristotle is saying here one must notice that he is using the word
eudaimonia in a way that is very common (in fact, overall the most common) in the *Nicomachean Ethics*, but is rather unusual for the English
expressions proposed as translations for it -- "happiness", "flourishing",
"a good life", and so on. We expect "happiness", for example, to denote
a property or condition either of a person or of his life, perhaps during
some particular, relatively brief time, perhaps over major portions or even
the whole of his life. We don't ordinarily use the word "happiness", as
Aristotle uses *eudaimonia* here, to refer to a single, concrete activity or
type of activity, and when we meet such uses, as when someone says that
happiness is a full stomach and a dry diaper, our amused response is

partly due to recognizing a transferred usage -- roughly, calling a cause by the name of its effect. Aristotle does sometimes use the Greek word *eudaimonia* with this first sense, that a property or condition of persons or their lives. We have an example of this in *Nicomachean Ethics* Book X, chapter 6, as just summarized: Aristotle says that the happy life (1177a2-3) and again that happiness itself (1177a10) does not depend upon the fun one has in leisure-time pursuits. But this is not for Aristotle's theory the basic usage of the term. The basic use is only reached when he goes on to specify what happiness in the first sense *does* depend upon: virtuous activity in general, activity of the most superior among the human virtues, or whatever. It is through the presence of that in a person's life, or as engaged in by him, that it becomes appropriate to describe him and his life as being happy (*eudaimon*). In the first book of the *Ethics* d Aristotle makes the search for the nature of happiness the first business of practical philosophy, saying (1095a17-20) that "happiness" is the name usually given to the highest of goods achievable in action, i.e., to that good which is rationally wished for itself alone, every other thing that is pursued or done being done for the sake of it. Plainly, happiness here is not to be understood as a property or condition of a person or his life; it is some simple or complex specific good that human beings can attain in their lives that will, in the derivative usage of the term, make them and their lives happy. That is why he immediately goes on to mention concrete things like pleasure, wealth, honor, health, the Form of the Good, and virtue as sample candidates for what happiness really is. The question "What *is* happiness?" which Aristotle takes up in the first book and returns to in Book X is a question in the first instance about particular good things we can possess, use or do. Which one of these, or which combination of them, is of such a nature that it is appropriately regarded as the best good, in the sense of a good that is choiceworthy for itself alone while other lesser goods are all of them in one way or another choiceworthy for its sake? People who succeed in attaining this best good are the happy ones, the ones whose lives are happy, but the happiness that Aristotle's theory is supposed to clarify for us and advance us in the pursuit of is not the happiness that we ourselves and our lives come to be qualified by in virtue of the fact that we are in possession of some such good, but rather that good itself, whatever it turns out to be.

Hence if in the first sentence of Book X, chapter 7, Aristotle says, as it certainly seems that he does, that happiness *is* excellent theoretical thinking of some sort, he will be saying that excellent theoretical thinking is the *whole* of what a person should aim ultimately at in his life, the sole thing such that by having and engaging in it his life is made happy. Nothing else but this will make any independent contribution to the goodness of his life; in particular, moral virtue will not make one. Is this what Aristotle means? I think now that there is good reason to doubt it.

5.

To see this, recall that Aristotle formulates his own theory of the nature of happiness in Book I -- what I've been calling his preliminary, vaguer account -- in language that closely resembles his language here in Book X. In that well-remembered passage Aristotle states his theory as a conclusion from what he has argued is the essentially rational nature of human beings and the rational character of specifically human virtue: "if that is so, the human good turns out to be virtuous activity of soul, and if there are more than one virtue, of the best and most complete virtue" (*ei d'houto, to anthropinon agathon psuches energeia ginetai kat' areten, ei de pleious hai aretai, kata ten aristen kai teleiotaten*, 1098a16-18). It is legitimate to expect that whatever relationship is intended here between happiness conceived of as virtuous activity of the soul and activity of the best and most complete virtue, the same relationship would be intended in the Book X passage, where Aristotle says that if happiness is virtuous activity it is *reasonable* that it should be of the most superior virtue. Now the Book I passage is surrounded by a rich context which offers a multitude of aids for its interpretation. If by drawing on this context, we can gain a full understanding of the sentence from Book I, we can hope to use what we learn there to help us understand the sentence of Book X. I want to suggest that the sentence of Book I does not, despite initial appearances, identify happiness with the single activity of the best virtue; likewise the sentence of Book X does not do so.

Two principal features of the Book I context are immediately relevant to the interpretation of this sentence. First, as I have noted, this sentence formulates the conclusion of an argument; so one would expect what it says to follow from the premises, or at any rate to be related to them in such a way that one can see how on the basis of just these premises Aristotle means to recommend just this conclusion. Second, in seeking confirmation for his theory, as expressed in this sentence, in the remaining six chapters of Book I, Aristotle has no fewer than four occasions to restate, in substantially different language, the essentials of his own position. One would expect the original statement of the theory to be interpretable so that it supports all four of these paraphrases.

Let us consider first the four paraphrases. In three of the four (1100a4-5 [cf. 1099b26]; 1101a14-16; 1102a5-6) Aristotle says clearly that according to his theory happiness is activity of *complete* virtue (in two of the three he adds: under certain conditions, viz., over a complete life and equipped with sufficient external goods).[6] He does not say explicitly in any of these passages, as he does in the *Eudemian Ethics* where he actually includes a reference to complete virtue (*teleia arete*) in his official formulation of this theory of what happiness is (1219a35-39), that by "complete virtue" he means all human virtues, but there is little doubt that that, which is anyhow the most natural meaning of the phrase, is what he intends. Several times, in describing the activities that make up happiness in these chapters, Aristotle makes it clear that he thinks of virtuous activities of all types -- moral as well as intellectual -- as included within happiness, that is, as all of them constituents of it.[7]

Now just this view -- that happiness is activity of complete virtue, activity of specifically human nature perfected in all its relevant aspects -- is the conclusion that the premisses of Aristotle's own earlier argument in 1097b24-1098a15 themselves most strongly suggest.[8] He argues that happiness or the human good must be some sort of active exercise of our rational power, namely the employment of that power as it exists when perfected by its and our specific virtue, because the good of any living thing consists in the perfected exercise of its specific nature as the kind of thing it is. And since (see 1098a4-5)[9] our rational power is a complex thing, having several aspects and functions, the perfected exercise of our specific nature will require several activities, the activities of the virtues that perfect the several aspects and functions of our rational power. Thus Aristotle's own argument seems to require the conclusion that happiness is activity of complete virtue, i.e., activity of all the specifically human virtues, the ones belonging to our rational capacities.

---

6. J. L. Ackrill, *op. cit.*, p. 28 in the Rorty reprint, draws attention to these passages (anyhow two of them, the first and third) and emphasizes their bearing on the interpretation of Aristotle's theory as earlier formulated. Ackrill, conveniently for his interpretation, omits to notice the fourth passage, on which see below.

7. See especially 1099a17-20; 1100b19-20. Furthermore, as Grant and Gauthier have seen (see their notes to 1098b22-23), Aristotle's intention in the whole passage 1098b22-1099b8 is to argue that *his* theory makes *all* the features that different previous thinkers have identified one by one as essential to happiness, essential to it: *arete, phronesis, sophia, hedone, he ektos eueteria*, 1098b4-7. So his theory of happiness was intended to make the exercise of *sophia*, the virtues of character, and practical wisdom (I take it that with *phronesis* at 1098a24 Aristotle is referring to Socrates' theory, cf. 1144b17-19) all elements in the activity that, according to him, happiness is.

8. This is asserted by Ackrill, *op. cit.* p. 28, and explained in detail by David Keyt, *op. cit.*, pp. 365-67.

9. Grant, followed by Ramsauer, Burnet and Gauthier, argued that these lines were not written by Aristotle, but by an early reader, who added them in the margin of his text as a gloss, drawing on what Aristotle says in Book I, Chapter 13, about the division of the soul. This *may* be so, for all we are able to tell now; but since we have no actual record of any manuscript's ever having existed that omits these words we do not possess any evidence that Aristotle did not write them. Certainly the existence of the *hapax legomenon epipeithes* at 1098a4 is no sign of other than Aristotelian origin. So we have to assume that these lines were written by Aristotle.

But does Aristotle's conclusion, stated in the sentence at 1098a16-18, actually say this? J. L. Ackrill, with the eager acquiescence of David Keyt, has claimed that it does: when Aristotle says that happiness is "virtuous activity of soul, and if there are more than one virtue, of the best and most complete virtue", Aristotle simply means by "the best and most complete virtue" the virtue that is constituted by the sum of all the human virtues, moral and intellectual -- in short, just what he means later by the simpler and more perspicuous phrase "complete virtue".[10]

However, this construction of the phrase "best and most complete virtue" is certainly a very unnatural one (no less so in Greek than in English), and two textual considerations show that it cannot be right. First, as Ackrill himself notices, the expression "most complete virtue" cannot fail to remind the reader of Aristotle's elaborate discussion and classification a page earlier of ends as more or less complete, and his characterization of *eudaimonia* itself as the "most complete" *end*. But Ackrill is wrong to think that the explanation of completeness given in this passage supports his construction of the phrase "most complete *virtue*" as meaning the sum of all the particular virtues. Aristotle says that happiness is the most complete end, in a semi-technical sense he specifies -- it is the end that is *most* chosen for its own sake and so *least* chosen for the sake of anything other than itself (1097a25-1097b6). But Aristotle in rapid succession goes on to assign two further related characteristics to happiness. Happiness is also (1097b6-16) a self-sufficient end, as one would expect a complete end, anyhow one chosen for its own sake alone and not for the sake of anything else, to be. And (1097b16-20) happiness is best and most choiceworthy good in a special sense: the value that one has in having it cannot be increased by adding anything good to it, for the reason that it is to be conceived as a comprehensive good, somehow already containing whatever good you might think to supplement it with by adding to it. But if his mention of these further features of happiness shows that on Aristotle's view the most complete good is also a comprehensive end, including other goods somehow in it, that does not show that the most complete *virtue* must similarly be a complex construction out of particular virtues like justice, courage, practical wisdom, philosophical wisdom, and so on. Aristotle says quite plainly

10. Ackrill, *op. cit.* p. 28; Keyt, *op. cit.* p. 365. Keyt writes as if this interpretation is "available" to him simply because Ackrill has offered it in print. Beyond pointing out that the conclusion so interpreted makes it follow naturally from what precedes, he does nothing to defend this construction of the sentence against the very powerful objections to it that I had already made in *Reason and Human Good in Aristotle*, p. 100n.; he does not even repeat Ackrill's reasons for thinking the Greek *can* mean what he says it does. On the interpretation of this phrase see further W. F. R. Hardie: 1979, pp. 38-40; Hardie is right to stress the relevance of 1099a29-31 to this issue (see below).

(1097a30-34) that the predicate "most complete" *means* chosen always for itself alone and never for the sake of anything else. The most complete virtue will therefore be the virtue that is chosen always for itself alone and never for the sake of anything else. And in Book X when he returns to take up the topic of happiness again, Aristotle does precisely argue at some length (1177b1-4, 12-18) that the single virtue of philosophical wisdom *is* chosen for its own sake alone, and not, like the practical virtues, chosen also for further goods it brings us. To be sure, Aristotle does not compare philosophical wisdom and the other virtues in Book I with respect to completeness in this sense, but there seems no possibility for doubt either that it is this comparison which he is anticipating when he speaks of the activity of the best and most complete virtue, or that he expects his reader, having been told explicitly what "most complete" means, to recognize that the virtues may vary in respect of completeness in this special sense, and that if they do, then happiness requires the most complete of them.

This conclusion is confirmed by what Aristotle says in the fourth of the subsequent passages of Book I where he refers back to his own theory of happiness and paraphrases it. This time (1099a29-31) Aristotle says that on his theory as earlier stated he has identified happiness with "the best activities or with one of these, the best one". Unless by "activity of the best and most complete virtue" Aristotle meant activity of the *single* particular virtue, among all the particular human virtues, which is best and most complete, this sentence has nothing to refer back to. In particular, if by the best and most complete virtue he means the sum-total of all the virtues, as Ackrill thought, then nowhere in his account of happiness has Aristotle previously said a word about the best single activity and its role in happiness.[11]

6.

There seems, then, no way around the fact that by "activity of the best and most complete virtue" Aristotle is referring to the activity of a single virtue, whichever is most chosen for itself and least for other things -- in fact, as he will only make clear in Book X, but not until then, the activity of perfected theoretical study. But what then is he saying happiness is? Is there any way for us to interpret his statement so as to make it

---

11. One could add, with Hardie: 1979, p. 39, that "activity of the *best* and the most complete virtue" at 1098a17-18 can hardly mean anything other than what "the best activity" does at 1099a30.

(1) follow reasonably well from its premisses, (2) *amount* to saying that the human good is activity of complete virtue, of the sum total of the moral and intellectual virtues, as three of the four paraphrases require, and (3) contain in its second half a special reference to some one particular virtue (in fact philosophical wisdom, as it turns out) as required by the human good?

I think there is. In the past those who have understood the reference of Aristotle's expression "best and most complete virtue" in the way I have argued is correct have supposed the purport of the sentence is this: happiness or the human good is virtuous activity in general; or rather, if it turns out that there are several virtues of distinct types, happiness is the activity of the best virtue, the one that is worth choosing for its own sake most and least for its contribution to other wished for things -- in fact the activity of philosophically accomplished study. So construed, Aristotle will be offering two alternative, mutually incompatible conceptions, the choice between which will depend solely on whether there are differences among the human virtues with respect to completeness. The first, but not the second, of these alternatives follows acceptably enough from the premisses of the argument. And in the four subsequent passages we have examined Aristotle will be referring first to the one view, then to the alternation of the two views, as what on his stated theory happiness is: three times saying that his view is the first (happiness is activity of *complete* virtue), once saying it is either the first or the second (happiness is either the best activities, or a single activity, the very best of all). This is surely intolerable. And, I now think, it is unnecessary.

Bearing in mind that what Aristotle professes to be offering us here is a vague and preliminary sketch, one which we know he will take up and develop further in Book X, one ought not to expect him to be offering a choice between clear and discrete, incompatible alternatives at this point. Rather, the alternatives ought to be related as vaguer and less vague versions of the same view, so that consequences developed on the basis of the vaguer conception will stand firm when the refinements brought by the less vague conception, once it is fully presented, are taken into account.

If, now, we consider just the first part of the sentence, we notice two things. First, it does follow strictly from the premisses of the argument as Aristotle has formulated them. Throughout, he has spoken of *a* work and *a* virtue for human beings as such, as for eyes and hands and feet and flute-players, the other terms of the analogies he exploits in reaching his conclusion. He nowhere mentions multiple works or multiple virtues of human beings or any of these other things. So what follows and, strictly, all that follows, from the premisses is that human good is activity of human virtue. But second, if there *are* multiple works and multiple virtues that human nature encompasses, then the vague formulation ("happiness is activity of human virtue") leaves it open that someone should count as having achieved happiness by exercising only one or some of these virtues over a sufficiently extended period. Anyone who exercises even *one* human virtue will satisfy this "definition": he will have engaged in "activity of human virtue" for a "complete lifetime". In particular, and particularly outrageously, if the virtues differ in value (if there is a best one among them), someone will count as having achieved the human good just because he has acquired and exercised the *lesser* virtues, without having the highest and best. That is, he will, given this vaguer conception which *does* follow from the premises as actually stated, have achieved the human good without having *fully* perfected his nature as a human being. Plainly, however, this does not accord with the general tenor of the argument: though the premises speak only of *a* human work and *a* human virtue, Aristotle obviously means to imply that happiness should involve *all* of a human being's natural works being done in accordance with the virtue or all the virtues appropriate to each.

So Aristotle has good reason to amplify and clarify his "definition" in order to rule out this unwanted inference, and it is reasonable, in the light of what I have just said, for his reader to understand that that is what he is doing. Read, then, as following from the preceding argument, its explicit premises together with their evident general import, this concluding sentence will be understood in the following way: happiness is virtuous human activity, and if there are more than one human virtue happiness is activity of all of them, including most particularly activity of the best among the virtues. In other words, the result of considering what to say happiness is, if it turns out that there are more than one human virtue, is not to identify happiness with a single virtuous activity, that of the best virtue, but rather to emphasize the need for them all, *including* in particular the best one among them.[12]

Now this is not all that needs to be said about this sentence (I have not yet taken fully into account Aristotle's description of the best virtue as also the most complete one). But let us pause to take stock. I have suggested that there is a way of understanding the conclusion of Aristotle's argument in Book I that both makes it follow well enough from the argument's stated premises, and permits sense to be made of each of Aristotle's four paraphrases of his theory in the immediately following chapters. The three places where Aristotle says his own theory has identified happiness with activity of complete virtue correctly summarize the import of the whole "definition" as earlier presented. Aristotle's conclusion that happiness is "virtuous activity of soul, and if

---

12. In arguing for this interpretation I am in agreement with Timothy Roche, *op. cit.*

there are more than one virtue, of the best and most complete virtue" does say that happiness is the active exercise of *all* the specifically human virtues. But it says this indirectly and by implication, as following from the insistence that happiness requires activity of the best and most complete virtue. And it is this special mention and emphasis on the activity of the best and most complete virtue, neglected in these three passages, that is taken up again in the fourth reformulation (1099a29-31), where Aristotle says his theory makes happiness "the best activities or one of these, the best one". To be sure, Aristotle omits to make it explicit here that, in its earlier context, his reference to "activity of the best and most complete virtue" was intended to make happiness consist in the best activity of all, not singly, but as completion to the activity of the other virtues. Nonetheless, it is easy to see on my interpretation of 1098a16-18 how what Aristotle says here could seem to reformulate what he said earlier on about happiness, whereas on Ackrill's interpretation it manifestly could not.

But how can Aristotle say here that, on his view as earlier stated, happiness (that is, as we have seen, the good thing that by itself makes a person and his life happy) may *be* the single activity that is the best of all activities? After all, I have argued that his intention in mentioning activity of the best virtue was to say, not that happiness might *be* that single activity, but that it might be that one taken together with all the other specifically human virtuous activities. But one must remember that Aristotle's theory of happiness throughout Book I is a preliminary sketch only. It points forward to the discussion in Book X, where it is resumed and completed, albeit still only at the level of a sketch. In fact the relationship to the Book X discussion is immediately marked for the attentive reader by the double characterization of the virtue that Aristotle says is particularly needed if there turn out to be more than one virtue, as "the best *and most complete* virtue". As I have argued, it is plain in the context why happiness requires the activity of the best virtue, along with the others: happiness requires the perfection of our nature as human, i.e., rational, beings, and that in turn requires the exercise of the best virtue. But why the "most complete" virtue, in the sense of the one chosen most for its own sake and least for the sake of other good things? Nothing in the premises of the argument, which set out connections among a thing's natural work, its virtue (*arete*) and its good, offers any basis for saying that, if there are several essential human works and several human virtues, the virtue that is "most complete" will be especially needed. It is only when the topic of happiness is taken up again in Book X that the importance (as well as the identity) of the "most complete" virtue is explained; and in explaining it, as I will show in a moment, Aristotle develops his theory of happiness in such a way that he can then say (with a certain qualification) that the activity of the most complete virtue, philosophical wisdom, *is* itself happiness. In short, when at 1099a29-31 Aristotle says that on his already-stated theory happiness may *be* the single best activity, he is reformulating that theory in anticipation of the development it will undergo in Book X. Hence, in order to understand what he means by this reformulation, and to see how it might really *be* a reformulation of the theory as previously stated, we must look ahead to Book X.

7.

        As I noted above, Aristotle begins his reconsideration of happiness in Book X by remarking, in language reminiscent of his preliminary account of happiness in Book I, that "If happiness is activity of virtue, it is reasonable (that it should be) of the most superior virtue". We have now seen that in the similar language of Book I Aristotle does not mean to say that happiness consists in the activity of some single virtue, but rather to emphasize the special need for the activity of the best virtue, as completion to the others, if one's life is to express the full perfection of human nature. So we ought to interpret this opening sentence of Book X, chapter 7, in the same spirit and sense: having argued in the previous chapter that happiness does not consist in amusements and games but rather in the serious side of life, in fact in "the activities of virtue" (1177a10), he now adds that, if that is so, happiness especially requires the activity of the most superior virtue. This first sentence of Book X, chapter 7, should not be taken to identify happiness with any single virtuous activity alone, as at first sight it might seem to, and as it is often taken to do.

        But having said that happiness must be in accordance with the most superior virtue, Aristotle goes on at once to say that the activity of the most superior virtue, which will be an activity of contemplative study, *will* by itself constitute (not happiness, but) "*complete* happiness" -- *he teleia eudaimonia* (here the word for "complete" is the same word used in Book I to talk about "complete virtue" and the "most complete" of the virtues). What does this mean? The concept of "complete happiness" is introduced here for the first time in the *Nicomachean Ethics* (it is completely absent from the other ethical treatises), and it is not obvious at first sight what it amounts to. However, Aristotle explains it implicitly in what immediately follows (1177a19-1177b26), where he takes some pains to confirm that to say that the activity of contemplative study is "complete happiness" is in agreement with the various criteria of happiness that he has argued for previously. In order to understand this we must remind ourselves of what I emphasized above: that in seeking an account of *eudaimonia* or happiness Aristotle is looking for that single type of activity or experience, or whatever, or naturally unified set of activities or experiences, which is the best we are capable of, and that, by its presence in a person's life, makes him and his life a happy (*eudaimon*) one.

Now in earlier discussions, and particularly in Book I, Aristotle has appealed to several "criteria" that he thinks people are antecedently agreed any candidate for happiness, in the sense specified, ought to satisfy: if happiness is an activity, then it ought to be the best activity, an immediately pleasant one, something desired as far as possible for its own sake alone, self-sufficient, and freely engaged in at leisure rather than forced on us by circumstances and our need for mere survival. Taking these criteria up one by one, Aristotle argues here that the activity of contemplative study, of all the activities human beings are capable of, best and most fully exemplifies the antecedently agreed on criterial characteristics of happiness, and he infers from that that this activity is "complete happiness". By this expression, accordingly, he means to describe the activity of contemplative study as the one that best and most fully exemplifies the (as it were) "nominal essence" of happiness, the conception we have antecedently of engaging in philosophical theory about what constitutes happiness. The force of the "complete" in "complete happiness" is therefore, as David Keyt has argued,[13] "perfect or fully realized", but in the sense of most completely satisfying the criteria that give preliminary focus to the inquiry into the nature of happiness. Aristotle has argued in Book I, as we have seen, on independent grounds that happiness is virtuous activity carried on throughout a complete life, including morally virtuous actions as well as excellent theoretical study within the scope of this "virtuous activity". He does not take this back now, but only points out that one of the two types of virtuous activity in which happiness consists, namely excellent theoretical study, satisfies the preliminary criteria of happiness more fully than the other does, and so deserves to be singled out as, so to speak, the most perfect version of the general unified category of activity, virtuous activity, which constitutes happiness. If, after all, happiness itself (i.e., virtuous activity through a complete lifetime) satisfies the preliminary criteria, as Aristotle of course claims it does, that will be in special measure due to the presence in it of excellent contemplative study, since this activity *does* unreservedly possess the required characteristics.

---

13. Keyt, *op. cit.*, pp. 377-78.

Once one sees that by "complete happiness" Aristotle means only one of the constituents of happiness and not happiness as a whole, special significance attaches to the fact that in the whole of Book X, chapters 7-8, where Aristotle develops and explains his views on the place of contemplative study in the best life, he is concerned solely to argue that contemplative study is "complete happiness" in the sense that we have seen he gives to this phrase at its first appearance, at 1177a17. He repeats this characterization of contemplation twice later on (1177b24 and 1178b7), and when near the end of his discussion he does once say (1178b32) simply that "happiness" itself (not "complete happiness") is "some sort of contemplative study", the omission of the crucial qualification is surely not significant. It comes in a passage that draws consequences from the fact, argued just before (1178b7-23), that "complete" happiness (not happiness altogether) is contemplation. (This passage announces its theme at the outset (1178b7-8) by saying: "And that complete happiness is some activity of contemplative study can be shown also from the following considerations.") So he probably means simply to repeat his earlier statement that contemplation is complete happiness, i.e., the kind of virtuous activity that most fully exemplifies the properties that we antecedently expect happiness to have. (I return to this passage in the conclusion below.)

8.

Once (by 1177b26) Aristotle has established to his own satisfaction that excellent contemplative study is "complete happiness" in this sense, he uses this conclusion to develop his notorious contrast between two lives, a "life of the intellect" and a "life of the other kind of virtue". We are now in a position to offer a natural and satisfying interpretation of the sense of this contrast. When Aristotle first refers to the "life of the intellect" at 1177b26 (*ho toioutos bios*) and 1177b30 (*ho kata touton,* i.e., *ton noun, bios*), the immediately preceding context makes it clear that he is referring to the life that someone leads who has achieved "complete happiness" in a complete life, i.e., who has engaged in excellent contemplative study regularly in his mature lifetime, with a clear and full understanding of the place and importance of this activity in the best human life.[14] And, as we have seen, the life of such a person is one devoted not solely to the cultivation and exercise of the intellect, but

---

14. See the Appendix for the full text of this note.

rather to the exercise of *all* the human virtues, with the virtue of the theoretical intellect occupying a special place as the culminating perfection that, when added to the virtues of character and practical thought, completes the full perfection of human nature. Aristotle argues on three grounds (1177b26-1178a8) that this life really is the best and happiest one for us, despite the fact that it is beyond the powers of ordinary human beings and something that we can aspire to only insofar as there is something divine and not merely human in us, viz., our theoretical intellects. In interpreting his arguments we must bear carefully in mind that it is this mode of life, devoted jointly if differentially to theoretical study and moral action, for which he means to be arguing. So understood, his arguments are as follows.

First, the intellect is the best thing in us, so that its excellent exercise is better than the exercise of the other virtues (1177b28-29), and precisely because it is something divine we will add something of superior power and worth to our lives by doing everything we can to realize as fully as possible the presence of this immortal element in it (1177b33-1178a2). Second, it can plausibly be argued that each person is (1178a1-2) his intellect (or, at any rate, is his intellect more than he is any of the other elements in his make-up, 1178a7), because his intellect is the "controlling and better" element in him, and a thing should be identified with that in it which controls and is better than the others.[15] So one ought to choose the life that includes and places proper emphasis on excellent theoretical study, rather than one that omits this, being devoted only to the exercise of the moral virtues: to choose the latter is to choose not one's own life, but that of a different kind of person, one not having a theoretical intellect and so not properly to be identified primarily with that (1178a3-4). Finally, as has been argued previously (see 1113a25; 1113b2; 1176b24-27), what is by nature proper to each thing is best and most pleasant for it, so that if each of us is (by nature) more than anything else his theoretical intellect, the "life of the intellect", that is, a life devoted to the exercise of all the human virtues but with special emphasis on the virtues of the theoretical intellect, will be proper to us, and so best and most pleasant, and, in consequence, happiest for us (1178a4-8).

Throughout this discussion, then, the life of the intellect that Aristotle champions is one devoted to all the human virtues but in a special degree to excellent contemplative study. It is not, as I used to think, a

---

15. I accept what Keyt says about these qualified identity-statements, *op. cit.* pp. 379-80; even if, as the context shows, the intellect here in question is the theoretical intellect (this controls by being not what exercises control but what controls is exercised on behalf of - cf. 1145a6-9), a full account of the identity of each person will identify us in part, though in lesser degree, with the practical intellect, the non-rational desires and, in fact, the living body as a whole.

life led in single-minded devotion to the intellectual values realized in such contemplation.[16] Accordingly, when Aristotle contrasts with this lifea "life of the other kind of virtue", and ranks this second life below the other one in happiness (it is happy "in the second degree", 1178a9), he is referring to the life someone leads who has recognized the value of the moral virtues and the practical, citizenly life they support, and has perfected himself in respect of them, but has not carried his self-perfection further to include the development and exercise of the virtues of contemplative study. It is reasonable of Aristotle to say that this life, too, is a happy one, since it contains virtuous activities, activities of the type which constitute happiness and which by their presence in a life over a sufficient duration, according to his theory throughout the *Ethics*, confer happiness on it. But since such a life is at the same time deficient with respect to that very type of activity, it is not, morally good though it be, the best life for a human being. Happy it is, but not the happiest we are by nature capable of it.[17]

9.

At the end of his discussion of *eudaimonia* in Book X (1178b7-1179a32), Aristotle confirms these conclusions by taking up and developing the connections, only adumbrated in what precedes, between the human "life of the intellect" and the life the gods lead. I conclude my own discussion by considering the bearing of what Aristotle says here on the proper understanding of his conception of human happiness and the place of contemplative study in it.

---

16. Accordingly I no longer have the reason I had in my book (*op. cit.*, pp. 163-65) for denying that the person leading the life of the intellect would be a morally virtuous person who would not just engage regularly in actions required by the virtues but would do them in the full possession of these virtues. So I would now interpret the reference to the contemplative person's acting "according to virtue" at 1178b6, 1179a5-6, 9, straightforwardly, as meaning "acting virtuously".

17. It is perhaps worth emphasizing Aristotle's seriousness and explicitness in holding that a human life devoted to moral virtue but without special attention to philosophical and scientific inquiry and knowledge would, despite the primacy of the latter in what is in *fact* the best life for a human being, nonetheless count as a happy one. He says at 1178a9 (with *deuteros* I understand *eudaimon* from the previous line) that this life will be a happy one in the second degree, and at 1178a21-22 he speaks of "the happiness (*he eudaimonia*) that depends upon the moral virtues", thus referring to the morally virtuous actions that occur in the "life of moral virtue" as (a) *eudaimonia*. This is in accord with his general usage of the term *eudaimonia* as described above (pp. 31-32): the morally virtuous activities in the life of moral virtue are the good it contains in virtue of which it can be characterized as happy, and so they count in the primary sense of the term *eudaimonia* as the *eudaimonia* of or in this life.

Aristotle points out (1178b8-9) that we take it for granted that not only some human beings, but gods too, are happy (*eudaimonas*), and indeed that the gods are in the highest degree happy, happier than any human being ever is or can be. The gods' happiness cannot, however, consist even in part in morally virtuous actions since the gods are not affected by the conditions that make that kind of action either possible or appropriate. Their happiness must instead consist exclusively in (some kind of) excellent contemplative study: it is that that makes them and their lives not just happy but happy in the highest degree, happier than any human being. So the excellent contemplative study that human beings are capable of, being the human activity that is most akin to the activity of the gods that constitutes their *eudaimonia*, must be our "complete happiness" (1178b7-8), the element in our happiness that most fully realizes the characteristics that make an activity count as a happy one in the first place; it must be the *eudaimonikotate* (1178b23) human activity -- the one most of the nature of happiness, or (perhaps) most contributory to the happiness of the happy human life.

Earlier Aristotle argued that some contemplative study is "complete happiness" by enumerating various preliminary "criteria" of *eudaimonia* and arguing that contemplative study possesses these characteristics more completely than the other human activities do. Now he confirms this conclusion by adding that such study is the whole of the happiness of the gods, and the happiness of the gods must be the most perfect and most fully realized kind of happiness. But he immediately takes his argument one step further. He recalls the fact of ordinary (Greek) usage, one he has mentioned previously (Book I, chap. 9, 1099b32-1100a1), that we don't speak of any other animal than human beings as being happy or as possibly "sharing in" happiness (*eudaimonia*). Other animals can lead better or worse lives, and of course for each of them there is by nature a kind of living that realizes their good, but we do not call these lives happy, nor do we describe whatever in an animal's life makes it good as (a kind of) happiness. (We don't speak of canine *eudaimonia*, as it were.) Earlier Aristotle had explained this restriction by remarking that other animals do not engage in "noble actions", the actions in which, as he had explained, the virtues or excellences of reason are expressed; especially relevant in the context was, of course, the absence from animal lives of the *moral* virtues. But now (1178b24-32) he argues that this usage correctly reflects and is grounded in the narrower fact that among animals only human beings are capable of contemplative study. It is because we can, while other animals cannot, contemplate in much the way that god does, that the best human life is not just best, but *happy*, and that a certain activity, or certain activities, in that life are entitled to be called "happiness". So, he says, human life is happy to the extent that there is in it something resembling the divine activity of contemplation. "Happiness extends just so far as contemplative study does, and those who contemplate more (or in a higher degree) also have more (or a higher degree of) happiness, not incidentally but in virtue of the contemplation" (1178b28-31).[18]

Here Aristotle claims that, in the nature of things, divine and human contemplation are the only things that are entitled to be described without qualifications as *eudaimonia*. And ordinary usage, he says, which recognizes *eudaimonia* as a particularly wonderful sort of good, reflects this fact when it denies to other animals any share in happiness. Nonetheless, in the case of human beings, Aristotle's own theory throughout the *Ethics* has maintained that all the human virtuous activities of all types, both the theoretical and the moral and practical ones, are entitled, when they occur as part of a complete life, to be counted as elements in our *eudaimonia*. There is no good reason to think he withdraws, or contradicts, that theory here. If human beings are capable of *eudaimonia* only because they are capable of contemplative study, that does not mean that the *eudaimonia* they achieve, when they do achieve it, consists of nothing but the contemplation they engage in. Likewise, the assertion that one human being is happier than another the more he contemplates does not imply that the human being who contemplates not at all but lives a thoroughly "practical", but morally good life, has no *eudaimonia*.

Aristotle's claim seems rather to be that those very morally virtuous activities, which *do* partly constitute a human being's *eudaimonia*, only count as a (kind of) *eudaimonia* because of some connection in which they stand to the activities of contemplative study in which the happy person also engages. These latter, by contrast, get their title to the name *eudaimonia* directly, because of their intrinsic character, a character that makes them appropriately akin to the gods' contemplation. But what is this connection? Aristotle does not say, but perhaps his thought is this. We have known from the beginning (from Book I, chapter 7, onwards) that human reason, by contrast with divine reason, is complex: it

---

18. I have translated the second part of this sentence, admittedly somewhat awkwardly, in such a way as to bring out what I take to be its double import. In the first part of the sentence Aristotle says, in effect, that *eudaimonia* extends only to gods and human beings, because only they can engage in contemplative study. In the second part I take him to convey simultaneously two connected points: (a) gods are happy in a higher degree than any humans, because they contemplate in a higher degree (more continuously, and with a higher type of contemplation); (b) among human beings, the ones who contemplate more are happier than those who contemplate less. In both cases the difference in happiness is a direct consequence of the contemplation found in the superior lives: the happiness that consists in the gods' contemplation is superior because of the superior character of that contemplation, and the happiness in the lives of human beings who contemplate more is superior to the happiness in the lives of those who contemplate less because of the character and value of the added contemplation.

encompasses practical as well as theoretical functions, and its practical functions again are divided between those consisting simply in thinking and those consisting in ways of feeling and (in general) in non-rational desirings. The good for a human being is accordingly a combination of all the activities in which these functions, when perfected, express themselves. So morally virtuous action and excellent contemplative study are linked together as perfections of human reason and so as aspects of the overall human good. But since, of these activities, only excellent contemplative study is found in the divine life, the life which consists of nothing *but* happy activity and is the paradigm for happiness wherever else it is met with, it turns out that it is the happiness of the human contemplative activities which makes morally virtuous activities also instances of happiness. Given the common character of both these types of activity as expressions of the perfection of human reason, then, Aristotle seems to be saying: if one of them because of its kinship to the divine activity counts as happiness, so does the other. On this view, the whole perfection of human reason, in each and every one of its aspects, gives us a share in that wonderful good that common usage testifies to by recognizing gods and humans as the only living beings that can have happiness. Because we *can* contemplate, the other uses of our minds, when they express virtues proper to us as human beings, also, though in lesser degree, give us a share in happiness.

Carefully interpreted, then, Aristotle's bold derivation of human happiness from our kinship with the gods grounds, and does nothing to undermine, the theory of happiness that he has presented throughout these concluding chapters of the treatise. According to this derivation, "complete happiness" is found in excellent contemplative study, but happiness is also found in morally virtuous activity, and the best and happiest life for a human being is a life successfully and effectively led in recognition of the permanent value to a human being of the use of perfected human reason i n all its aspects and functions. The net effect, then, of Aristotle's return at the end of the Nicomachean Ethics to the topic of happiness as sketched in a vague and preliminary way in Book I, is indeed to bring out the priority in several connected respects of excellent contemplative study to the other types of excellent rational activity. But he does this in such a way as merely to refine the earlier account, while preserving intact its central claim that the human good consists in the regular and full exercise over a complete lifetime of all the human virtues. The revised theory of happiness in Book X is, after all, fully compatible with the accounts of the moral virtues, practical reasoning, friendship, and the other topics taken up in the middle books of the treatise.[19]

Appendix: Complete text of note 14

Keyt, *op. cit.* pp. 372-74, ignoring the evidence of 1177b26 (where *ho toioutos bios*, being the *bios* of the previous line, cannot be the activities themselves of study that constitute "complete happiness", when they occupy a "complete length of life", but must rather be the complete life in which they occur), interprets the "life of the intellect" here and later in Book X to be the contemplative activities themselves that occur within the best life. I had already argued in *Reason and Human Good in Aristotle,* pp. 159-60, that this cannot be right, since *bios* in Greek means not a part or aspect of a life (as when we refer to a person's sex life, or his religious or intellectual life), but a whole mode of life. Keyt misinterprets Aristotle, *Politics,* I, chapter 8, and Plato, *Laws V,* 733d7-734e2 in a bizarre attempt to show that in Greek *bios* has a use parallel to this modern one of "life".

In fact, in the *Politics* passage Aristotle discusses the various lives, i.e., modes of life, that different peoples live, depending on how they sustain themselves: some have marauders' lives, some lives of hunting, others the farmer's life, and so on. Keyt draws special attention to 1256b2-6, where Aristotle remarks that some tribes combine more than one distinct way of gaining a sustenance: some lead "a nomadic and at the same time marrauding (life), others a farming and hunting (life)". He apparently thinks that such combined lives are combinations of the one *life* (a nomad's or a farmer's) and the other *life* (a marauder's or a hunter's); the combined life has as its two constituents these distinct lives, i.e., the distinct activities of wandering in pursuit of food, or marauding, or hunting or farming. But that is neither what Aristotle says, nor any implication of it. It is just a mistake to think that because in leading a combined life a population combines two or more distinct ways of sustaining itself, which is all Aristotle says here about such lives, their life combines two or more *lives.* Significantly, he speaks of each combination as *a* life, e.g., "a nomadic and at the same time marauding *life*"; he does not say those who live this way lead a nomadic life and at the same time a marauding one, nor yet nomadic and marauding *lives* at the same time. And even if the reference of *touton* in *mignuntes ek touton* at 1256b2-3 is the five simple types of life just named, it doesn't follow that what one finds in the combined nomadic and marauder's life is the nomadic *life* and the marauding *life*, rather than the wandering and the marauding in virtue of engaging in which one group is said to live a simply nomadic and another a simply marauding life. To suppose that this does follow just begs the question at issue. An alternative understanding, which is moreover consistent with the undoubted usual sense of *bios* as "(mode of) life", is that in the "nomadic and marauding life" the tribe moves about from place to place getting its living, as nomads do, but supplements this with raids on resident populations as they pass them by. They lead one and only one *bios*, (mode of) life, which combines these two ways of sustaining themselves. Throughout this passage, then *bios* can, and I think does, mean "mode of life"; it is nowhere used to refer to an aspect or part of any person's or any group's mode of life.

The Plato passage seems superficially more amenable to Keyt's interpretation. It comes at the end of the long general preface or preamble (V, 726a1-734e2), in which the Athenian lays down and justifies the central idea that the city's laws, as he will detail them later, should aim at making the citizens be as thoroughly virtuous and act as thoroughly virtuous as possible. Granting (733a3-4) that we all individually want a predominance of pleasure over pain in our lives, the Athenian argues that the way to achieve what we want is to live a life of physical fitness and virtue -- that is, a life at once characterized by physical health, courage, temperance (or self-control), and wisdom (or prudence). Hence, by living under laws effectively designed to promote these characteristics, we will be getting the sort of life we all recognize that we want. To make this case the Athenian first considers separately the "temperate life" (*ho sophron bios*), the "wise life", the "courageous life" and the "healthy life" and argues that each of these lives is superior in the balance of pleasure over

---

19. This paper was first prepared for and presented at a conference on Contemporary Ethical Thought and the History of Moral Philosophy held at Marquette University, October 4-6, 1985, with support from the Franklin J. Matchette and Mellon Foundations.

pain it contains to its opposite -- the self-indulgent, the foolish, the cowardly and the diseased life respectively. From this he concludes (734d2-734e2) that since each of these lives is thus superior to its opposite, then, putting them all together, the life that has the virtue of the body (health) and also the virtue of the soul (courage, wisdom and temperance) is superior to *its* opposite, and so the person who has this life lives overall and as a whole more happily than his opposite.

It is in this concluding sentence, if anywhere, that Plato uses the word *bios* in the way that Keyt needs in order to support his interpretation of the *Nicomachean Ethics*, viz., to refer to separate phases or aspects of a person's life as parts of the overall life, or way of life, that results when they are added together. What suggests that he does mean to use it so is the word *sullebden* which I have translated as "putting them all together", i.e., as Keyt would have it, putting all these four lives together. But again this *need* not be the meaning (what gets put together may instead be the four virtues of body and soul that characterize and define in turn the four lives previously mentioned: it is by reference to this combined virtue, *arete kata soma e kai kata psuchen*, 734d4-5, that the Athenian goes on to characterize the "combined" life), and reflection on Plato's theory of the unity of the virtues strongly suggests that it is not. For Plato holds that no one can have any one virtue without having them all, so that the temperate (mode of) life, that led by the person who possesses the virtue of temperance, will be the same (mode of) life as that of the wise, or the just or the courageous. Accordingly, when in this passage he speaks separately of the temperate, the wise (prudent) and the courageous life, he is speaking throughout of the same life, the overall virtuous one, considering in turn the pleasures and pains that it has as a direct consequence of the temperance, wisdom and courage respectively of the person leading it. One does not produce the overall virtuous life mentioned at the end by adding the temperate life of someone who has only that single virtue to the wise and the courageous life led by other individuals, much less by adding together the temperate actions of the one person (as if those, rather than the life he leads in consequence of them, actually constituted the temperate life being referred to here!), and the courageous actions and the wise actions of yet other persons. (It is true that since the unity of virtue doctrine does not cover physical health, the healthy life can be a life led by a separate individual, so that one might in Platonic terms try to make *sense* of the idea of adding this life to the other, the virtuous one; but Plato's way of describing the overall life here in fact treats physical health in parallel to the moral virtues.) So the life of physical health and moral virtue that Plato refers to is a life which combines, not the four previously mentioned *lives*, but the four previously mentioned *characteristics* used to describe those lives. It is exactly as with the passage from Aristotle's *Politics*: *bios* means "(mode of) life" throughout, as it means elsewhere in Greek literature, and is nowhere used to refer to distinct aspects or phrases, or distinct sets of actions or activities, found in a single mode of life.

Ironically, as I argue in the text, Keyt did not need to adopt the desperate and foredoomed tactic of arguing that the "life of the intellect" just *is* the intellectual activities that are part of the best human life, in order to reach the conclusion he wanted to reach, that the best life is one devoted to the exercise of all the virtues, and not just the virtues of the theoretical intellect.

Some Enduring Values
in Augustinian Ethics

Vernon J. Bourke
St. Louis University

Since the ethical views of St. Augustine of Hippo were most characteristic of Christian philosophy written in Latin before the thirteenth century, this paper is limited to the consideration of three issues prominent in that type of moral philosophy.[1] The first of these issues centers in an analysis of moral action, starting from Augustine's reflections on the practice of lying and leading to further ramifications in St. Anselm, Hildebert of Tours and Peter Abelard. Our second issue has to do with a famous argument intended to show that there is but one supreme good for all men and that all other lesser goods get their moral value from this *summum bonum*. This reasoning starts with Augustine, continues in Boethius and culminates in the third book of Aquinas' *Summa Contra Gentiles*. The last issue focuses on the justification of war and the sorts of rational considerations that may apply to such a problem.

All three of these issues have some background in classical Graeco-Roman philosophy but they are given a characteristically Christian treatment by St. Augustine -- and this is the reason why they point to lasting values in Augustinian ethics. While he has been the butt of much recent criticism for some of his special ethical views, Augustine has much to offer in the field of moral psychology. Some of his critics have read a very small part of Augustine's writings. This paper will attempt to show that the positions taken by Augustinian thinkers on each of these three issues have some relevance to the doing of ethics in the present day.

---

1. For the history of Patristic and Medieval ethics: Dittrich, Otto, *Geschichte der Ethik*, 3 Bd (Leipzig: Meiner, 1926); Lottin, Odon, *Psychologie et morale aux XIIe sieclès,* 7 vols. (Gembloux: Duculot, 1942-1960); and Forell, G. W., *History of Christian Ethics* (Minneapolis: Augsburg Publishing House, 1979-1986; V. Bourke, *History of Ethics* (New York: Doubleday, 1968) Part Two.

The Need for an Acceptable Moral Psychology

Almost thirty years ago, in a paper criticizing recent work in ethics, Elizabeth Anscombe wrote that it is not profitable at present to work at moral philosophy, because we lack what she called "an adequate philosophy of psychology."[2] She was right, I think, because even now it is difficult to discern the psychological position of most contemporary ethicists. Much of experimental psychology seems concerned with very special problems of limited scope. That is probably why Anscombe spoke of a *philosophy* of psychology.

What is the difference between cognition and appetition? Is there some important distinction between acts of volition and feelings of affection? Is there an important difference between sense perception and intellectual understanding? These and similar questions are either not considered by contemporary ethicists, or they are answered in a variety of conflicting ways. Even among ethicists using the English language there does not seem to be any commonly accepted theory of mental functions in terms of which one might get at the meaning of actions such as deliberating, intending, consenting, choosing, ordering, and so on. There are almost as many theories of human emotional life as there are psychologists who write on it. Yet such activities would seem to require to be clearly understood before one could study ethical concepts such as responsibility, imputability, or entitlement to praise or blame.

Augustine faced some of these questions in two treatises on mendacity which are not much read today. One is entitled *On Lying (De Mendacio)* written early in the year 395, before he became a bishop. The other is called *Against Lying (Contra Mendacium)* written twenty-five years later, in 420. The early treatise is much more interesting to philosophers, for it studies the morality of telling lies very thoroughly, while the later work is confined to the problem of lying for presumed religious reasons. It is important to keep these treatises distinct, even though there is little in *Contra Mendacium* that differs from what is said in *De Mendacio*. Oddly, although Thomas Aquinas made much use of Augustine's judgments on lying, he consistently cited the early treatise under the name of the later one.[3]

_____

2. G. E. M. Anscombe, "Modern Moral Philosophy," *Philosophy*, 33 (1958) p. 1; cf. her *Intention* (Oxford: Blackwell, 1959).
3. Thomas Aquinas, *Summa Theologiae* II-II, q. 110, art. 1 to 4; in the notes to the Ottawa edition I. T. Eschmann's notes point out the confusion of the two treatises by St. Thomas.

The governing definition of lying is introduced near the beginning of *De Mendacio*: "that person lies who has one thing in his mind but expresses something different verbally or by any other signs" (*ille mentitur qui aliud habet in animo et aliud verbis vel quibuslibet significationibus enuntiat*).[4] This formula does not include any reference to the deception of others by the liar. The definition is more simply expressed in later medieval usage as *locutio contra mentem*, speaking contrary to one's mind. However, shortly after giving his key definition, Augustine asks whether willing to deceive is essential to a lie (*De Mendacio*, 3; P2, 244). He decides that such an intention is not part of the primary definition but that it adds something to the completeness of the action. If one does include willing to deceive in the meaning of lying, then there must be two different acts of intention: 1) willing to speak contrary to one's judgment; and 2) willing to deceive others (4; P2, 250). A moral wrong may be found in both intentions; the first consists in a difformity within the speaker's own consciousness, between what he thinks to be true and what he wills to express; the second evil lies in the will to harm other persons by deception. This immediately raises another question: whether a lie may sometimes be useful (*utile*) as a deception and in that sense good? (4; P2, 250 *ad finem*). Eventually Augustine offers four proofs that all lies are immoral: these include condemnations of lying from the Old and New Testaments (6, 7 and 8; P2, 254-262) and the fourth argument, from reason, refers briefly (9, vi; P2, 262) to the condemnation of lying that is supported by the facts of ordinary life. He admits that there are people who question this argument, however.

So, he proceeds to examine certain difficult cases raised by objectors. The most interesting perhaps (for it is a forerunner of Kant's famous case) is where you have a man concealed in your house and an enemy comes along and asks whether the man is there; you say he is not, in order to protect him (5, v; P 2, 252). Or there is the case of the very sick person whom you do not tell that he is in grave danger: you speak falsely in order to reassure him. Augustine admits that many people think that these and similar hard cases are morally approvable (5, v; P2, 254). He even brings up what we might call Joseph Fletcher's case, that of the person who commits adultery to achieve a good end (5, v; P 2, 266). There is also the case of the woman who lies, or expects others to lie, in order to protect her chastity (10 vii; P2, 266 bottom). Finally there are those who say that one may lie for religious reasons, for instance in order to convert someone to the true faith (11, viii; P2, 270). This is the problem that Augustine faced in the later *Contra Mendacium*, when in A. D. 420 a

---

4. Augustine, *De Mendacio* 3, 3; Latin and French text in *Oeuvres de S. Augustin*, ed. G. Combes (Paris: Desclée de Brouwer, 1948) vol. 2, p. 242; later citations abbreviate this edition as 'P'.

Spanish bishop named Consentius asked whether it would be good to have his representatives pretend to agree with some heretics, in order eventually to correct these heretics (*Contra Mendacium*, I, 1; P 2, 350).

All these cases are fully discussed by Augustine but he staunchly maintains that no apparently good end is sufficient to remove the basic intramental evil of willing to express an untruth (*De Mendacio*, 17, x; P 2, 284). And this is what he reaffirms twenty-five years later in *Contra Mendacium* (3, 4; P 2, 358): *Nullum est enim mendacium quod non sit contrarium veritati*. Even for the most important religious purposes, or good ends, lies are not ethically approvable. To Augustine lying is a sort of self-contradiction, so a misuse of one's ability to express one's judgments correctly. Clearly, he employs both a prior-attitude and a consequential approach to this problem of lying, for the first evil that he discerns lies in the internal willing to express an untruth and the second evil consists in the possibly harmful result to others.

In a second part of *De Mendacio* (18, xi ff. ; P 2, 286 ff.) eight types of lies are discussed. A lie may be willed: 1) to bring someone to the Christian faith (and this is most objectionable, because of the importance of its subject-matter); 2) to harm one's neighbor; 3) for the pleasure of deceiving someone; 4) to help someone to harm another; 5) to help someone without harm to others; 6) to preserve agreeable interpersonal relations; 7) to save someone's life; and 8) to save a female from sexual violation (all summarized at 42, xxi; P2, 336-340). It is striking that all these types are differentiated in terms of the consequences of conveying an untruth to others. Augustine numbers and grades these kinds of lying from the most seriously evil (for religious ends) to the least objectionable (to preserve chastity).

Whatever our views about the absoluteness of his condemnation of all lies (jokes are not lies, he thinks), we may observe two things about his underlying ethical convictions. First, he employs both prior-attitude considerations and objective consequential reasonings throughout his long analysis. Obviously his psychology includes a full awareness of the difference between mental acts of knowing and will acts of intending, consenting, choosing and commanding oneself to perform bodily actions that influence other people. No reader of the *Confessions* can avoid being impressed by Augustine's labored efforts to will to free himself from his early habits of sin. Much of his psychology of cognitive and volitional activity is already developed in his early treatise *De Libero Arbitrio*. There he is not discussing "free will" but free *decision* as an act of will. The term *voluntas libera* (free will) occurs but rarely in Augustine's writings. This is so for two reasons. First, he thinks that all men must will *beatitudo,* that is, one's own ultimate well-being. This universal desire for a good life is the theme of the nineteenth book of the *City of God*. As Augustine says in an earlier passage (DCD XIV, 4; Doubleday Image Books, 1958, p, 300):

"Man indeed desires happiness, even when he does so live as to make happiness impossible. What could be more of a lie than a desire like that. This is a reason why every sin can be called a lie." So this necessary desire for happiness means that the human will (*voluntas*) is not free in all its actions, for all men *must* desire to live well. The second reason for his rare use of the term "free will" is the fact that many people think that such freedom means complete indetermination. But he is aware that cognitive reasons affect willing and make it rational.

For Augustine, psychological functions are not tied to a faculty psychology. The last books *On the Trinity (De Trinitate,* IX to XV) distinguish mind, memory and will: but these are not faculties, each is identical with the whole soul. Man's will is not some part of the human mind; it is the whole soul as dynamic, as initiating every kind of human activity. He even thinks that sense perception involves willing attention to changes that take place in man's bodily organs, as the famous analysis of auditory sensations in the sixth book *De Musica* suggests.

So the first thing that emerges from our consideration of Augustine's study of lying is a realization of the ethical importance of a strong theory of willing. Greek philosophy had tended, from Socrates onward, to reduce volitional functions to cognitive judgments. Even Aristotle lacks a satisfactory account of will: his third book (*De Anima* III, 10-11, 433a9-434 a22) treats appetite and desire as sources of self-motion in man but there is an air of incompleteness in this treatment of will. Indeed Aristotle has no single word to designate what the Latins called *voluntas*: neither *boulesis* nor *thelesis* has this meaning. It is my impression that a strong view of the role of will in human life is only found after the advent of Christian writings. Augustine and John Damascene are responsible for this development in moral psychology.[5] The faculty psychology of Thomas Aquinas presents a highly organized re-thinking of Augustine's less systematic but more empirically-based analysis of will functions. For those who may regard this Thomistic psychology as too complex, perhaps Augustine's examination of the mental approaches to lying could be of assistance in the development of ethics today.

The second point that emerges from a reading of *De Mendacio* is that Augustine is quite open to both prior-attitude and consequential considerations in ethics. It is unfortunate, I think, that many present-day ethicists suppose that one must either be a deontologist or a teleologist. This bifurcation is due in great part to the continued tendency of continental European thinkers to follow the lead of Immanuel Kant and of British ethicists to adopt a utilitarian stance. Our quick survey of

5. See my *Will in Western Thought* (New York: Sheed and Ward, 1964) for this view of volitional psychology.

Augustine's procedure may suggest that it is quite possible for a present-day ethical thinker to attend to both the inner mental preludes to good moral action, and also to the consequential results of well-considered activity, results to the agent and to other persons who may be affected by his action.

In the twelfth century we find influential writers like Anselm of Canterbury and Peter Abelard concentrating on the subjective factors in moral activity. Both retain Augustine's psychology in spite of their knowledge of Aristotelian logic, but they pay little attention to consequential considerations. In the same century, however, there appeared a treatise on *Moral Philosophy* (now printed under the name of Hildebert of Tours) which moves in the opposite direction. It is a product of the cathedral schools, rather than of monastic centers of learning. Hildebert's *Tractatus Theologicus* (PL 171, 1067-1154) shows a close allegiance to St. Augustine. But the *Moralis Philosophia De Honesto et Utili* (PL 171, 1007-1056) tells a different story: Augustine is not mentioned or used in it. This moral philosophy is a collection of well selected passages from the ethical writings of classical Latin times. Cicero predominates but there are texts from Seneca, Juvenal, Sallust and Lucan. An ethics of the four cardinal virtues emerges but it is organized in terms of the contrast between the *bonum honestum* and the *bonum utile,* as described by Cicero.[6] The latter is a useful good, something desired and used for the sake of attaining some other good that is desirable for its own sake alone. It is not easy to translate *bonum honestum* into two English words: and that is a defect of our language and possibly of our thinking. It is defined by Cicero and Hildebert as "that which attracts by its own power and worth."[7] Such a means-end analysis presupposes, of course, a teleological emphasis in this study of the cardinal virtues. Question III (*De Utili,* col. 1043-1052) explains that useful goods are divided into goods of the soul, of the body, and of "fortune" (that is, of external physical and societal advantages over which no one person has complete control). As such these *bona utilia* are means subordinated to the achievement of the only *bonum honestum* that is wholly desirable for its own sake, the *summum bonum.*[8]

---

6. Anselm's ethical position is found in *De Casu Diaboli,* passim, and in *De Veritate;* English versions are in *Anselm of Canterbury,* trans. J. Hopkins and H. Richardson (Toronto and New York: Mellen Press, 1974-5) pp. 77-102 and 128-177.
7. The treatise *De Inventione Rhetorica,* from which ch. 53 is a source for the *Moralis Philosophiae,* is probably a product of Cicero's school.
8. *Honestum est quod sua vi nos trahit et sua dignitate nos allicit. Moralis Philosophiae* PL 171, 1009. (There is some dispute as to the authorship of this work: it represents one type of 12th c. ethics.)

In this type of medieval ethics the morality of human actions is not determined by reference to proximate goods, such as great knowledge, good health, or social reputation. All these and similar limited objectives are but means to the attainment of the highest good. This brings us to our second ethical issue.

The Argument for One Supreme Good for All Men

At the start of the nineteenth book of the *City of God* Augustine examines the teachings of many schools of philosophy on the goal or end of a good human life. This is in preparation for his discussion of the ends of the City of God and the Terrestrial City. He uses a treatise by the encyclopedic writer, Marcus Varro, in which two hundred and eighty-eight different philosophic opinions on this matter were described. Since Varro's treatise is no longer extant we will not need to examine all of them. But it is obvious that at the end of the period of ancient philosophy the majority of thinkers were teleologists: that is, they thought that there was some sort of ultimate good at which all men should aim. Augustine reduces the various opinions to three: goods of the body, of the soul, and of both. He notes that importance was given to objectives such as pleasure, good health or strength, mental ability, great virtue, good reputation and political power. Throughout this nineteenth book, and in many of his other writings, Augustine is at great pains to show that although subjective conditions such as virtue and knowledge are good for humans, the only ultimate end of all things (and especially of mankind) is the highest good, God. For Christians, he says, "eternal life is the supreme good." (DCD XIX, 4). There is no question that Augustine thought that morally good acts are those which bring a person to some sort of close association with God in a future life.

A century later, in the third book of *The Consolation of Philosophy,*[9] Boethius expanded on this same theme. True felicity, he argued, consists in "neither sufficiency by riches, nor power by kingdoms, nor respect by dignities, nor renown by glory, nor joy that can be gotten by pleasures." (*Consolation* III, prose ix; Hyman-Walsh, p. 117). Except for sense pleasures, these goods excluded by Boethius as ends of the moral life came to be called "goods of fortune" in later medieval writings.

---

9. This section of *De Consolatione Philosophiae* III, ix to xii, in the English version revised by H. F. Stewart (Cambridge, Mass: Harvard U. Press, 1936) is reprinted in *Philosophy in the Middle Ages,* ed. A. Hyman and J. J. Walsh (Indianapolis: Hackett, 1973) pp. 117-127.

He also criticizes the various goods of mind and body and concludes "that Goodness (*bonitas*) is the end of all things." (*ibid.* prose ix; Hyman-Walsh, p. 124).

This theme of finality in the moral order runs through medieval philosophy, up to the Renaissance.[10] It is developed into an organized series of arguments by exclusion in the third book of Aquinas' *Summa Contra Gentiles.*[11] All types of medieval ethics, that I know, were in basic agreement on this claim, that the goodness of human actions and character depends on the extent to which these acts enable a person to merit eternal happiness through an approach to the highest good.

In the Renaissance final causes were banished from many philosophies. Francis Bacon did not like this talk about finality. British utilitarianism substituted the greatest good of mankind in this life for the concept of eternal happiness. Immanuel Kant talked about a *summum bonum* but felt that, if you did the right thing for the sake of gaining some reward, you were not entitled to ethical credit. It seems to me that ethics lost something quite valuable when it abandoned the quest for absolute goodness. In particular I am concerned by the move of certain theistic ethicists in the present Catholic tradition to replace God as man's ultimate end by a set of so-called basic goods, such as life, knowledge, play, esthetic experience, friendship, practical reasonableness and natural religion.[12] These proximate goods are not yet ethical goods. To bring them into the domain of human morality, the Augustinian ethicist thinks that they must be ordered to a still higher ideal, the *summum bonum*.

It seems to me that this is still applicable today. To say that a person, or a human action, is ethically good must have a univocal, not a polyvalent, meaning. In the long run some unique standard of ethical judgment is required.

The Ethics Behind Just War Thinking

It is well known that certain Renaissance Scholastics proposed several conditions under which a war might be waged justly, at least by one side in the conflict. In brief these conditions were: 1) some sort of public authority had to be in charge; 2) a just cause was required, usually

---

10. Cf. Jean Rohmer, *La Finalité Morale de S. Augustin à Duns Scot* (Paris: Vrin, 1939).
11. Thomas Aquinas, *Summa Contra Gentiles,* Bk. III; Providence, trans. V. J. Bourke (Notre Dame U. Press, 1975) Part I, ch. 25-63, pp. 97-206.
12. This list is from John Finnis, *Natural Law and Natural Rights* (Oxford: Clarendon, 1980) ch. III and IV; it depends on an earlier list in G. Grisez and R. Shaw, *Beyond the New Morality. The Responsibilities of Freedom* (Notre Dame U. Press, 1974) ch. VII.

some great evil that had to be remedied; and 3) the intention of this public authority had to be right, that is, designed to remedy the evil and not for some other purpose.[13] Eventually some later Scholastics added a fourth consideration; whether the means used to wage war were proportionate to the evil involved and the good to be achieved by victory.

Now we are not concerned here with the validity or present appropriateness of these just war conditions. The reason for introducing this topic is to examine the ethical bases on which they depended. To do this I propose to work back from the main place in which Thomas Aquinas treated this problem, that is, *Summa Theologiae* II-II, q. 40. What we find there is that St. Augustine is his chief guide in setting up his three original just war conditions.

The problem that Aquinas faces in the first article of Question 40 is whether it is always sinful to make war. As reasons for considering this he cites three passages from the New Testament which seem to say that all participation in war is sinful. A third objection to wars is an argument in logical form: nothing is contrary to a virtuous act unless it is a sin, but to fight a war is contrary to peace, therefore war is a sin. The fourth and last objection to the view that Thomas is going to advocate in his response is that the Catholic Church condemns the warlike exercises in the tournaments used to train soldiers, for it denies Christian burial to those killed in such games.

Augustine is not mentioned in any of these four preliminary objections but in the statement opposing these difficulties (the *Sed contra*) the Bishop of Hippo is quoted for the first time. In a *letter*, which Aquinas calls a sermon, on the son of the Centurion,[14] Augustine explained that the biblical injunction (as in Luke 3:14) against war was intended for Christians dedicated to a life of perfection but not for the ordinary person who has to take an active role in society and earn a living.

In comment on this Augustinian position, may I point out the plain common-sense quality of St. Augustine's approach? His *Letter to Count Marcellinus* in which the above passage appeared was written in the year 412. The invading Goths had just sacked Rome; they were later to extend their war across North Africa, eventually to lay siege to Hippo, at the time of Augustine's final illness. He knew the evils associated with war but he was also aware that self-defense is sometimes needed. As an ethicist Augustine realized that judgments on practices, such as warfare, are not to be made on the basis of unusual circumstances or personal con-

---

13. On this topic two recent works are: E. B. F. Midgley, *The Natural Law Tradition and the Theory of International Relations* (New York: Harper and Row, 1975); and J. T. Johnson, *Can Modern War Be Just?* (New Haven: Yale U. Press, 1984).
14. Actually the reference is to Augustine's *Epist.* 138; PL 33, 531, to the Roman official, Marcellinus.

ditions. While members of the clergy or monks may be told not to fight in wars, ethical conclusions about the validity of fighting in self-defense are made on the basis of the circumstances of the ordinary person. I think this is still a useful guideline.

The main answer by Aquinas in this article says that three things are required to justify going to war. His first requirement is that the war be waged under the authority of the chief of government (*auctoritas principis*). Today we might simply call this public, rather than private, authority. After two citations from the Bible, Thomas again calls upon Augustine. In his treatise *Against Faustus the Manichee* (XXII, 75; PL 42, 448) Augustine wrote: "The natural order (*ordo naturalis*) suited to the peace of mortal men demands this, that the authority and decision to undertake a war be the prerogative of the chiefs of state (*penes principes sit*)." What Augustine is appealing to here is his principle of order (*ordo*). Peace was defined in a famous passage in the *City of God* (XIX, 13) as the "tranquility of order." In early life Augustine had written a dialogue *On Order (De Ordine)* in which he argued that the world and mankind are governed by orderly relations which make the whole universe intelligible. He finds traces of divine ordering in all things. Now this principle of universal order is applied to social life and the concept of peace, in the above chapter of the *City of God*.

> Thus, the peace of the body is the well-ordered organization of its parts; the peace of the irrational soul is the well-ordered repose of its sensual desires; the peace of the rational soul is the well-ordered agreement of thought and action; the peace of the body and soul together is the well-ordered life and health of the living being; the peace of mortal man and God is the well-ordered obedience of living in faith under the eternal law; the peace of men is well-ordered concord; the peace of the home is the well-ordered concord of its residents, in giving commands and in obeying them; the peace of the city consists in the well-ordered concord of the citizens, both commanding and obeying; the peace of the Heavenly City is the perfectly ordered, and completely concordant, association of those who enjoy God and cherish one another in God. The peace of all things is the tranquility of order.

We may learn something today from this lyrical account of the principle of order. Ethics deals with persons and human actions in the context of a universe embodying a structure of complex relations. Modern science has discovered many more instances of natural order than

Augustine knew. We also must admit that many things in nature appear to us to be disorderly and irrational. But inter-personal relations of humans in society may be made orderly and good by greater efforts on the part of all humans to set up reasonable socio-political institutions. Certainly war is not such an institution; war is but a means to obtain peace, as Augustine insisted (DCD XIX, 12). One of the duties of ethicists should be to set up and explain ideals in terms of which human living may be bettered. One such ideal is the Augustinian theme of universal good order.

The second condition for justifying war is that there be a just cause (*causa justa*). Some serious evil must demand to be opposed, before the admitted physical and social disadvantages of warfare can be ethically approved. To support this Aquinas goes to the *Questions on the Pentateuch* (VI, 10; PL 34, 781), where in comment on *Joshua* (8:2) Augustine said, "Just wars are customarily defined as those which avenge injuries, if a people or a state (*civitas*) must be punished because it has failed to correct some wrongdoing by its members, or has failed to restore what has been injuriously taken over."

Here the ethical appeal is to a customary definition. Augustine knew that moral philosophy starts with the critical examination of the *mores,* the customarily approved principles of behavior in a given society. Even though he was an African Augustine was much impressed with the *Pax Romana,* the socio-political conventions of the Roman empire. This does not mean that he considered all ethical judgments to be governed by the customs of one's current society. He thought that Rome in its early days was much more devoted to the simple virtues than it was in the fifth century. But Augustine also realized that established and generally accepted terms are useful to the philosopher who is writing for an average audience. Too frequently today, I think, we invent new terminology without need -- and thereby fail to make our best ideas understood by the public. Even a very wise person, or a prophet, has to express his wisdom in words that his audience can understand.

In the third place Thomas Aquinas argues that the intention of those making war must be right. His meaning of intention had the etymology *in-tendere,* to incline toward some objective. This ties in with his teleological outlook. The purpose of a state in going to war must be to remedy some great evil. It is not justified in doing so, if it intends something else which is unreasonable. To underscore this point about right intention Thomas first gives a quotation attributed to an unknown work of Augustine, "On the Word of the Lord," actually the passage is from Gratian's *Decretum* but there are similar statements in the *City of God* (XIX, 12 and 28). The text is: "Among the true worshipers of God those wars are not considered sinful that are waged, not for evil desires, but for the sake of peace, in order that evil men may be restrained and good people supported." Of course this does stress the importance of proper motivation on the part of those who fight a war but another passage that he cites from Augustine's *Contra Faustum* (XXII, 70; PL 42, 444) makes the point in a more striking way; "The urge to hurt, the cruel wish for revenge, the spirit that is unsatisfied and incapable of satisfaction, the ferocity of rebellion, the lust for domination, and other such motives, these are the characteristics of wars that are rightly condemned."

Similar assertions on the importance of a proper intention, of aiming at an approvable objective, may be found throughout Augustine's moral writings. It is not simply a question of having a good moral attitude before performing an extra-mental act, such as declaring a war: one must look also to the objective results calculated to follow the whole action. Thus a war that is declared because a state has been seriously injured by an enemy cannot be justified if there is no possibility of victory over the enemy, or if the obtainable results are of much less importance than the physical evils associated with war. Clearly there is a lesson here for us: a well developed ethics cannot be wholly deontological, in the narrow sense of the term, nor can it be completely restricted to consequential reasonings.

In the reply to the first objection, in this article, (where it is said that he who takes up the sword shall perish by it, Mat. 26:52) Augustine (*Contra Faustum, ibid.*) is again quoted: "He who takes up the sword and arms himself to draw blood for another person is the man who does so without being commanded or given permission by a higher or legitimate power." Likewise, in answering the second objection (that the New Testament teaches us not to resist evil) Thomas appeals to Augustine's treatise *On the Lord's Sermon on the Mount* (I, 19; PL 34, 1260) where he says that one's general attitude as a Christian should be to avoid the use of physical force in cases where it is not needed -- but that sometimes it is necessary to fight for the common good, or even for the good of one's attackers. And Aquinas follows this with another reference to Augustine's *Letter to Marcellinus (Epist.* 138, 2, 14; PL 33, 531). The passage is rather long but the gist of it is that, in spite of the Christian dislike of the use of physical force, it is sometimes necessary to fight against evildoers, "for nothing is more unhappy than the happiness of sinners, whereby their guilty impunity is nourished and their bad will, like an inner enemy, is reinforced."

The last reference to Augustine is in the reply to the third objection (that the Church disapproves of warlike games). There he quotes a *Letter to Boniface (Epist.* 189; PL 33, 856). "Peace should not be sought," Augustine says, "in order to wage war; rather, war is waged to obtain peace. So, in fighting a war be peaceful, so that you may lead your enemies through victory to the useful value of peace (*ad pacis utilitatem*)."

So we see how Augustine continues to stress the importance, in making ethical judgments, of examining the instances in which general rules should be applied to particular cases with prudent care. There may be exceptional conditions to be noted in the mind of the person performing a moral act -- and there may also be special circumstances surrounding other persons affected by the action -- all of which require prudence on the part of the agent.

Nothing better illustrates the enduring influence of Augustine in the thirteenth century than this article of Question 40 in Aquinas' *Summa Theologiae*. The nine citations from a variety of Augustine's works show something of the extent of Thomas' dependence on the Bishop of Hippo. I know of no other article in the *Summa of Theology* that makes as much use of Augustine's ethics.

Conclusions

The lack of an accepted and standardized moral psychology has made it difficult for twentieth-century ethicists to make a convincing analysis of moral activity. Vagueness in the meaning of the term "mind" has led to a failure to distinguish clearly between the cognitive and appetitive aspects of such action. Nor are the cognitive functions of sense perception and intellectual judgment always clearly distinguished. There is no standard psychology of human emotions, yet they play an important role in moral activity. Instead of each new ethical treatise, today, inventing a new and highly personal set of key terms, it would be better, in my opinion, to adopt a simple psychological terminology similar to that of Augustine.

In the second place is the problem, still very evident at the present time, of ethicists who do not think that all human beings are naturally directed toward one supreme good. Of course part of the difficulty here lies in the abandoning by philosophers of the concept of final causality. Without the acceptance of a unique meaning for human fulfillment, ethics cannot give a univocal meaning to the moral life. The resulting variety of ethical stances leads to a lack of credibility. The general public no longer sees moral philosophers as having something to offer as a guide to the good life.

Finally we have the character of Augustinian thought in the background of just war reasoning. What seems to emerge from this is a certain way of doing ethics. Of course Augustine and his followers throughout the middle ages derived many of their ethical values from the Bible. But they brought to their interpretation of Scripture a philosophy which was partly Platonic and partly the result of personal meditation on the facts of conscious decision-making. That man lives and works in an orderly universe, under a Supreme Orderer, was basic to this type of ethics. Frankly, I don't think that an ethics without such a base has much practical value today.

Augustine's discussions of a just cause for going to war point up the importance of the reason why one performs a moral act. Latin writers spoke of the *propter quod,* French uses *pourquoi,* the English loses something by saying "why" instead of "for what." We have noticed Augustine's appeal to a popular definition of a justifiable war: like Plato he made use of the analysis of ordinary language.

The emphasis on *intending* to remedy an evil, or promote an obvious good objective, is important today. It stresses how Augustine's thinking embraces both the subjective and the objective facets of the moral act. Motivation is not simply a matter of being pushed within consciousness by a feeling of agapistic love, or by a sense of moral duty; it is also a matter of being pulled by some external good that is to be attained by reasonable action.

I think this is the greatest lesson that can be learned from Augustine today. The notion that ethics can be wholly deontological is just as self-defeating for the moral philosopher as the idea that morality depends solely on a calculation of greatest goods for the greatest number of people.

The Moral Thought of St. Thomas Aquinas

Ralph McInerny
University of Notre Dame

Although it is no easy thing to attempt a brief statement of the moral doctrine of St. Thomas Aquinas I have been guilty of several such efforts in the past, each time -- I say this in extenuation -- at the invitation of someone. Once the impossibility of the exercise is accepted, there is a certain exhilaration to be had from plunging forward nonetheless. To do the thing at all, it is necessary to select an angle of approach with the hope that the very selective and partial account based on it is nonetheless faithful to all the unmentioned features of the doctrine.

For purposes of this summary, and of course with an eye to the wider purpose, I will say some things about the way in which Thomas incorporated Aristotle into his moral theology. You recognize at once that this is far from being non-controversial. No less a scholar than René Antoine Gauthier, editor and translator (with Jean Yves Jolif) of the *L'Ethique à Nicomaque*[1] and editor of the critical Leonine edition of St. Thomas's *Sententiae super libros Ethicorum*[2] insists that St. Thomas must be put in the forefront of those who did violence to Aristotle's thought in making it fit the Procrustean bed of Christian theology.[3]

If Gauthier is right, then the Aristotelianism found in Thomas can be of interest only to theologians. Aristotelians, and indeed historians of philosophy, would have to recognize it as an abuse of Aristotle for purposes unshared by the Stagyrite.

---

1. Aristote, *L'Ethique à Nicomaque*, Introduction, Traduction et Commentaire, par René Antoine Gauthier et Jean Yves Jolif, Deuxième édition avec une introduction nouvelle, 3 vols. Tome I, Introduction par René Antoine Gauthier, Louvain, Paris, 1970.
2. *Sententiae Libri Ethicorum* Tomus XLVII in *Opera Omnia Sancti Thomae de Aquino*, Rome, 1969.
3. "Les responsables en sont les théologiens, notamment un Thomas d'Aquin, précisément parce que, théologiens, ils ont dû faire violence à la sagesse grecque pour la faire tenir dans le lit de Procruste de leur système." Tome I, Introduction, pp. 274-5.

   To this it could be replied that Thomas wrote a commentary on the *Nicomachean Ethics* and that we can look there rather than in the moral parts of the *Summa theologiae* and other theological writings for a purer Thomistic Aristotle. Alas, Gauthier stands athwart this path as well. Thomas's fellow Dominican and editor is one of the most caustic critics of the commentary, warning that it is nothing like a modern one.[4] There are those who might detect oblique praise of Thomas here, but that is not Gauthier's intention. Gauthier's animadversions on the quality of Thomas's writing must be unique among critical editors. So extreme a criticism seems unlikely to be true; if it were, the tack I am taking in this paper would be worse than misguided. What I want to suggest is that those who do not share Thomas's religious beliefs, those for whom moral theology holds no charm, can nonetheless read with philosophical profit both the commentary on Aristotle and the moral part of the *Summa theologiae.*

   This claim could perhaps be made without differing from Gauthier. That is, one might agree that Thomas radically distorts Aristotle for theological purposes, but that, nevertheless, there is an extractable philosophical doctrine contained in the moral theology which, when extracted, could be described both as non-Aristotelian and as moral philosophy. This, it might be said, is the moral philosophy of St. Thomas Aquinas.

   Some, hearing this, will be reminded of disputes between Etienne Gilson and Van Steenbergen.[5] Gilson came to insist more and more on the fact that Thomas was chiefly a theologian and this led him to maintain that the only order of doctrine in Thomas is that displayed by the *Summa theologiae.* James Collins' demur[6] did not prove a rallying point for a rival school and it can be said that, by and large, students of St. Thomas came to see more animosity between Thomas and Aristotle than anything else. The "real" Aristotle, that is. The Aristotle who figures in the work of Thomas under the honorific *Philosophus* is something of an imaginary character whose speeches, taken out of literary context, mean things in Thomas they could not have meant for Aristotle.

---

4. "Saint Thomas n'a donc écrit ni une philosophie morale, ni une interprétation d'Aristote pour Aristote; mais il n'en a que davantage marqué l'exégèse aristotélicienne, car, pour pouvoir utiliser la philosophie morale d'Aristote dans une théologie animée par un esprit étranger à l'esprit d'Aristote et construite selon des exigences étrangères aux exigences de la philosophie, il lui a fallu en bouleverser le sens et l'équilibre." In short, Thomas's moral thought is "la négation de l'enseignement exprès de l'Aristote historique." *Ibid.,* p. 275.
5. See Etienne Gilson, *History of Christian Philosophy in the Middle Ages* New York, 1955, and Fernand Van Steenbergen, *La philosophie au XIIIe siècle,* Louvain, 1966.
6. James Collins, "Toward a Philosophically Ordered Thomism," *The New Scholasticism,* 32 (1958) pp. 301-326.

You will appreciate, I know, that this is not an esoteric point of disagreement. The relation between Thomas and Aristotle is one of the most pressing topics before Thomistic scholars, at least in my estimation. The innocuous cliché that Thomas baptized Aristotle has taken on a meaning, as with Gauthier, which -- let us be frank -- calls into question either the honesty or the intelligence of St. Thomas. Knowingly to distort a text is a serious matter and it will not do to say this was the literary custom of the time -- this is a question begging explanation.[7] The truth seems rather to be that Thomas meant to say what Aristotle meant when he attributes a position to Aristotle. If he is systematically wrong about this, there is a word to describe such a deficiency.

My own view is that attributed to Pico della Mirandola: *sine Thoma Aristoteles mutus esset*. I hold that Thomas's commentaries on Aristotle are precious aides in understanding the text of Aristotle. I think it is nonsense to state universally that these commentaries do not achieve what they clearly set out to achieve. Chenu's view is one difficult to hold when one has spent years with those commentaries. Mine is, I am glad to note, not an isolated position at the present time. Giovanne Reale's magnificent study of the *Metaphysics* goes a long way toward validating the accuracy of Thomas's commentary on that most vexed work of Aristotle.[8] If *that* commentary can be defended, the task of defending the others is much easier.

Difficulties of another sort await me on this side, of course. If it be granted that Thomas set out to understand and explain the text of Aristotle as such, he could still have been *honestly* mistaken in his views. No doubt. But this possibility is one amenable to the usual kind of philosophical and textual discussion -- just the sort of thing Thomas is engaged in. I need not maintain that Thomas's interpretation of Aristotle is noncontroversial in order to deny that he proceeded in the way suggested by Gauthier and others.

To put an end to this introductory matter, let me say that if I did not take the position I do, if I agreed with Gauthier, I would have advised that Thomas be left out of this conference. Not that I wish to suggest that Père Gauthier is the village idiot, of course, though his caustic style is contagious. I propose to take one of his remarks and examine it closely with a view to showing something of (a) Thomas's understanding of Aristotle, (b) the way Aristotle is subsumed into his moral theology, and (c) how this is not without interest for philosophers like ourselves.

---

7. M. D. Chenu, *Introduction à l'étude de Saint Thomas d'Aquin*, Montreal, Paris, 1950, pp. 173-198.
8. Giovanni Reale, *The Concept of First Philosophy and the Unity of the Metaphysics of Aristotle*, translated by John R. Catan, Albany, 1980.

Gauthier mentions as a profound, crucial and unbridgeable difference between Aristotle and St. Thomas their views on man's ultimate end. For Thomas, our ultimate end is God, who is a necessary timeless being. For Aristotle, on the contrary, the end is a good achievable by action, thus contingent, embedded in time.[9] Gauthier's indictment continues with such zest that this item can easily be forgotten in the blur of charges. But how better test his assessment than to closely scrutinize this charge? There is at least a prima facie plausibility in Gauthier's remark about the final end, man's good. The opposition he suggests between Aristotle and Thomas is just the one that Aristotle in NE I 6, sees between himself and Plato. Aristotle is not interested in the Idea of Goodness, a necessary being independent of the human order; he wants to discover a good achievable by action, a contingent quality of acts and thence a quality of the character of the human agent. Gauthier does not discuss at all this supposed opposition between Aristotle and St. Thomas on ultimate end. Someone unacquainted with Thomas might think that Gauthier is drawing attention to something that was not thematic in Thomas himself. It would be incredible if Thomas, in speaking of man's ultimate end, had not adverted to the distinction Gauthier is relying on. But as students of Thomas know, he discusses it quite explicitly and it is in terms of that explicit treatment that Gauthier's cavalier remark must be assessed. When this is done, it may be asked whether Thomas's claim that there is no conflict is well-founded or not. If Thomas is right, Gauthier's assertion of a conflict between Thomas and Aristotle is thereby weakened.

The opening five questions of the *Prima secundae* of the *Summa Theologiae* provide the focus for the discussion. They begin the moral part of the work with a treatment of man's ultimate end with explicit reference to Aristotle's treatment of the same matter. Indeed, throughout these five qustions, Aristotle is repeatedly cited, though he may seem to be keeping

---

9. "Sans doute, à première vue, la construction thomiste semble-t-elle calquée sur celle de l' *Ethique à Nicomaque*: ici et là, n'est-ce-pas le bonheur qui est mis au principe de la morale? Trompeuse apparence! La construction thomiste a son principe non pas chez Aristote, mans dans le *Beati* du*Sermon sur la montage*; l'analyse aristotélicienne du bonheur ne fournit que l'instrument conceptuel qui sert à mieux mettre en relief la béatitude évangélique: l'idée que le bonheur est fin et que la fin est le principe de l'ordre moral. Mais, pour pouvoir les utiliser dans sa théologie morale, saint Thomas a dû faire subir à ces idées mêmes une transmutation si profonde qu'il prend le contre-pied de ce qui était, au delà des mots, l'essentiel de la pensée d'Aristote. La fin morale, qui est pour Aristote réalité essentiellement contingente puisqu'elle est action de l'homme, est pour saint Thomas la réalité la moins contingente qui soit, car elle est Dieu même, non pas le dieu-objet des philosophes, mais le Dieu-Personne des Chrétiens: la fin de l'homme n'est pas dans une action de l'homme, pas même dans l'action quelle qu'elle soit par laquelle il s'unit à Dieu .... Saint Thomas dès lors pourra bien en garder des mots, des formules, jamais l'esprit." *loc. cit.*, pp. 275-6.

strange and anachronistic company -- St. Augustine, St. John Damascene, Holy Scripture. The concern of those questions is:

(1) *De ultimo fine hominis*
(2) *De his in quibus hominis beatitudo consistit*
(3) *Quid sit beatitudo?*
(4) *De his quae ad beatitudinem exiguntur.*
(5) *De adeptione beatitudinis.*

After discussing end and ultimate end, and having identified the latter with happiness, Thomas continues the discussion, in qq. 2-5, in terms of happiness. The tone and context are indisputably different from that of the *Nicomachean Ethics*. Thomas, after all, is doing moral theology, and theology is an inquiry which accepts as true a good many claims undecidable by appeal to what everyone knows on the basis of ordinary experience. The word for this acceptance is "faith." Among the things Thomas believes about human action is that it is the means, when informed by grace, whereby in this life we can merit an eternal happiness with God. This destiny is not something owed man on the basis of what he is, his nature, but is the gratuitous complement of the reparation of sin, which is why Augustine spoke of original sin as a *felix culpa*: the last state of the redeemed person is higher than that lost through sin. The short form of his claim is that eternal felicific union with God is man's super-natural end. This means (a) that it is not read off the exigencies of his nature and is thus undreamt of by philosophy and (b) that it presupposes and does not destroy man's natural end.

This enables us to express an initial reaction to Gauthier's claim of an opposition between Aristotle and Thomas. If he means to say that Thomas speaks of man's supernatural end whereas Aristotle does not, his observation, however true, is banal. Aristotle was not a Christian. In order to have any interest, Gauthier's claimed opposition would have to mean that the supernatural end is in every way an alternative to what Aristotle discussed as man's good. That is, it replaces or destroys or supplants it. But if Thomas's position is as I have described it, and as Gauthier must know it to be, the question becomes: what is the relation between man's natural ultimate end and his supernatural ultimate end in the doctrine of Thomas Aquinas?

Does Gauthier wish to say that what Thomas says of man's natural end is opposed to what Aristotle says of man's natural end? Clearly, it is only if he does mean this that the criticism is interesting. Then he must be taken to be saying that whereas for Thomas God is man's natural ultimate end, this is not the case for Aristotle.

Now as it happens, it can be maintained that, in one sense of the claim, Thomas holds that God is man's ultimate end *sans phrase*, that He is the human good, *no mention being made of the supernatural order.* But, to the extent this is so, a case can be made that Aristotle held the same thing. In speaking of Aristotle's view of human destiny, we cannot afford to ignore that grand panorama with which the *Metaphysics* begins, where Aristotle traces the perfection of man through a multitude of hierarchical stages culminating in Wisdom, such knowledge as man can attain of the divine. The Tenth Book of the *Nicomachean Ethics* picks up this theme. If Gauthier were making a serious point, he would have had to consider such matters.

But enough for the nonce of our adversary. Let us turn to the five questions mentioned to see what light they cast on the points at issue.

Question One, despite the strangeness already alluded to, provides much that is familiar to the student of Aristotle. If nature is teleological, and man is included in nature, man can nonetheless be said to act for an end in a way peculiar to himself. The point is made, not simply by contrasting human activity and the activities of other things (a. 2), but also by drawing a contrast among the activities ascribable to man. That is, Thomas distinguishes between human acts, those deliberately produced, and acts of a man, a category which includes everything from falling when dropped to digesting. Like Aristotle, Thomas is not content to say that anything that counts as a human act is undertaken for the sake of some end. He also wants to say that there is some end for the sake of which any human act is undertaken. That is, there is an ultimate end of human life (art. 4). "Life" here is a term which covers the sum total of properly human activities (Cf. IaIIae 3. 1. 1m). That Thomas means this end to be ultimate and comprehensive is clear when he asks (art. 5) if one man can have several ultimate ends. Holding that there is but one (art. 6), he asks (art. 7) if àll men have the same one and finally, (art. 8), if other creatures share in man's ultimate end. What light do these opening considerations throw on Gauthier's charge?

Thomas cites Augustine to make a distinction in the sense of "end." The end can mean a ceasing to be or it can mean that which fulfills or perfects (art. 5). It is the second sense Thomas has in mind here. The first important clarification concerning end in the second sense is found in the discussion of whether an agent wills everything for the sake of the ultimate end. The basis for the affirmative answer is this: whatever man desires, he desires under the note of the good, and if it is not desired as the perfect good, which is the ultimate end, it must be desired as tending to the perfect good, because the beginning of something is always ordered to its consummation.[10]

Before there can be any discussion of what among various possible candidates can be man's ultimate end, there must first be an understanding of what counts as an ultimate end, what formality has to be realized in it. Thomas suggests that in doing whatever we do we think it to be good for us to do it, that is, think it to be perfective or fulfilling of us. Doubtless no one thing we do is thought to exhaust the formality of "perfective of us," since any objective is perfective only up to a point and would presumably enter into a complete account of what perfects the human agent.

This distinction is operative in *Nicomachean Ethics* I, though not all have noticed it. Failure to notice it leads to a premature identification of some particular goal or activity with the human good. But it is obvious that Aristotle thinks of man's ultimate end as constituted by a variety of activities and ends. Only if one of these activities, or one of these ends, exhausted the meaning of "perfective of man" could it be identical with the human good. But it is notorious that Aristotle does not say that even of contemplation. The good for man remains a set, an ordered set, of activities and their ends. The *notion* of the ultimate end, the *ratio boni*, can be distinguished from any one activity and, in a certain sense, identified with a carefully developed ordered set of activities.

The distinction mentioned plays a crucial role in answering the question as to whether all men have the same ultimate end. "I answer that it must be said that we can speak of ultimate end in two ways: first, according to the notion of ultimate end; second, according to that in which the notion of ultimate end is found." (art. 7) Men may differ widely in discussing ultimate end in the second sense, but only because they are in agreement on it in the first sense. Needless to say, this is a very weak claim for agreement. Any human agent does whatever he does under the aegis of the good; implicit in any choice is the judgment that "*x* is good for me." The values of *x* may differ as you like, but the function remains the same.

Of course, no one chooses the *ratio boni*, the notion of the good; a person chooses something or other as good because he judges that it saves or embodies the notion "perfective of me." The difference is one between quality and carrier, form and supposit, idea and participant. The Aristotelian will resist the suggestion that the idea of Goodness is another item in the world, together with the things called good. As one related to many, "goodness" exists only in the mind. Good as it exists is a feature of

---

10. "Primo quidem, quia quidquid homo appetit, appetit sub ratione boni. Quod quidem si non appetitur ut bonum perfectum, quod est ultimus finis, necesse est ut appetatur ut tendens in bonum perfectum: quia semper inchoatio alicuius ordinatur ad consummationem ipsius . . ." *IaIIae*, q. 1, art. 6.

things relating them to the appetite of those other things whose perfections they are.

It remains controversial to claim that this explanation of choice entails anything like a dominant goal. One of the most frequent objections to ultimate end is that only the rare person aims at some one objective to which he subordinates all else. If ultimate end meant only the *ratio boni,* of course, the claim that all men have the same ultimate end, while not without interest, would be less than what it has usually been taken to mean. And indeed Thomas, in citing Paul to the Phillipians 3:19 (*Quorum deus venter est.*), suggests that there is, at any given time, some dominant thing with which the notion of good is identified. This is something that needs discussion, no doubt. But the appeal to Paul suggests that Thomas, for whom God is that object in whom the *ratio boni* is perfectly realized, sees defective human action as an attempt to make something other than God into God. This was the point of Chesterton's remark that the young man knocking on the brothel door is looking for God.

The distinction between the notion of ultimate end and that in which the notion of ultimate end is located does not suggest that just anything can rightly be taken to be perfective of the human agent. If there is no one activity whose end is identical with the good for man, there is nonetheless a set of such ends which variously realize the *ratio boni* and which together can be seen as perfective of the kind of agent man is. Given the plurality of constituents of the human good, there seems to be room for much legitimate and desirable diversity in ordering those constituents. In this way, the notion of ultimate end is seen as providing just what traditional objections to it argue it does not provide.

We may also note here that moral error or sin is understood by Thomas, not as pursuit of something whose nature is evil, but rather as pursuit of a good in a disorderly way. The glutton pursues a human good in a disordered way; so too the miser and the lecher and thief. Some kinds of action, some ways of pursuing constituents of the human good, are ruled out by what is meant by the *ratio boni* (IaIIae. 18. 5 and 6). When is a good not a good? The distinction Thomas makes when he asks if all creatures share in man's ultimate end is important here.

When Thomas identifies man's ultimate end with happiness (*ultimus finis hominum est beatitudo*) he does so in order to distinguish man's pursuit of the ultimate end from that of irrational creatures. The distinction is this: "the end is said in two ways, namely *cuius* and *quo*, that is, the thing in which the notion of good is found, and the use or attainment of that thing (art. 8). In the first sense, God is the ultimate end of all creatures. (This is the first statement that God is man's ultimate end and it is important to notice that it is a cosmic observation: God is the ultimate end of all creatures.) Aristotelian universal teleology is presupposed and then the question becomes: what is different about the way God is man's ultimate end? The term *beatitudo* expresses that difference: "man and other rational creatures pursue the ultimate end by knowing and loving God, which is not the case with other creatures" (art. 8). From this point on, *beatitudo* and man's ultimate end are identical in meaning, with *beatitudo* the preferred term.

Gauthier's claim was that Thomas, because he identifies man's ultimate end with God, is in a totally different conceptual universe from Aristotle, for whom the good for man is a quality of action. We are assuming that something more interesting than the distinction between the supernatural and natural end of man is meant -- more interesting philosophically, that is. If the supposed difference between Thomas and Aristotle is meant to obtain in the realm of man's natural end, then Gauthier is being willfully obtuse. Both Aristotle and Thomas will hold both of Gauthier's options as elements of their doctrine of ultimate end.

We have thus far drawn attention to three distinctions Thomas makes with reference to the end: (a) a distinction between end as terminus and end as fulfillment or perfection; (b) the distinction between the *notion* of ultimate end and the *thing* in which the notion is taken to be realized; and (c) the distinction between the thing which is the end and the mode of attaining it. The first distinction draws attention to the fact that "when something desires its own perfection, it seeks it as an ultimate end which it desires as its perfect and complete good." (art. 5) The second distinction we have discussed sufficiently. The third produces an important assertion: "*beatitudo nominat adeptionem ultimi finis:* beatitude means the attainment of the ultimate end" (art. 8). But the *adeptio* or attainment of the ultimate end is accomplished by "knowing and loving God," that is, by means of certain human acts. Gauthier's opposition begins to evaporate.

Having identified ultimate end and happiness, Thomas goes on to discuss, in Question Two, what happiness is not and, in Question Three, what it is. The failed candidates for identification with happiness fall into groups: exterior goods, bodily goods, spiritual goods. The denials in article 7 that human happiness can consist of a good of the soul and, in article 8, that it could consist of any created good, may seem to provide the opposition Gauthier had in mind. But do they? Article 7 begins by recalling the distinction between the thing we desire to attain and the attainment of it. "If then we speak of ultimate end with regard to the thing itself we seek as the ultimate end, it is impossible that man's ultimate end should be his soul or any part of it. For the soul, considered in itself, is as it were existing in potency: one becomes an actual knower from being a potential knower and actually virtuous from being potentially virtuous." Thus the very thing Gauthier has in mind as the Aristotelian alternative to God as ultimate end is explicitly rejected by Thomas -- *taking ultimate end to stand for that which we seek to possess.*

"But if we are speaking of ultimate end with regard to its attainment or possession or whatever use of the thing which is desired as the end, then something of man's soul pertains to ultimate end, since man pursues the ultimate end with his soul." (q. 2, art. 8) Thus it is clear that Thomas sees no opposition of ultimate ends here, but rather two ways of speaking of the ultimate end: *what* we wish to attain and our *attainment* of it.

Question 2, article 8, the denial that any created good can be our ultimate end, does two things. First, it provides a crisp recalling of what is meant by ultimate end. Second, it shows that only God can be our ultimate end, given the meaning of ultimate end.

St. Thomas gives this account of happiness: "For beatitude is the perfect good which totally quiets desire, since otherwise, if something still remained to desire, it would not be the ultimate end." This is the *ratio boni perfecti*, the notion of the ultimate end. The fulfillment of all our potentialites, the completion of our nature, such that nothing more could be desired, that is what Thomas takes happiness to be. It may seem that he has thereby defined happiness out of existence. There seems to be no way in the world in which anyone could be happy in that sense. The objection anticipates Thomas's next move. "The object of the will, which is human desire, is the universal good, much as the object of intellect is universal truth. From which it follows that nothing can quiet the will of man except the universal good." We have already suggested that nothing we seek as good is identical to goodness; the objects of appetite have goodness, they share in it. There are many good things. Nor is the class of all good things identical with goodness. There is only one value of the variable in "x is good" which exhausts the attribution such that that good is identical with goodness. "Which is not to be found in any created thing, but in God alone, because every creature has participated goodness."

The use of "participation" suggests that, whatever else might be said of what Thomas is doing here, it seems more Platonic than Aristotelian. That we have here an instance of Thomas's quite considered employment of a Platonic notion there can be no doubt. Of course what has been called logical participation is present in Aristotle [Fabro], as the analysis of the predication of substance in Book Zeta of the *Metaphysics* makes clear. While Aristotle denies the Platonic sense of the claim that a thing is not identical with its essence, he provides his own account of the same claim, one that does not entail subsistent essences. The upshot is that while Socrates is not identical with what-it-is-to-be-a-man, and the same is true of any other individual man, there is no Man apart from them which they are not. We find in Thomas's prologue to his commentary on the *De divinis nominibus,* a sort of treaty with Platonism, a laying down of the conditions of acceptance. If the Platonic Ideas are a misunderstanding of logical participation, then the position is not only false but contrary to faith. If, however, the Ideas are taken to be names of

God, then the doctrine is most true and in conformity with faith and casts great light on the way things are. Ontological participation is a way of regarding creatures as manifesting some *scintilla divinitatis*, as diminished versions of some aspect of the divine perfection. And just as any given creature falls infinitely short of the complete perfection God is, so does the sum total of all creatures, actual and potential. Any creature will be to the degree that it is thanks to God's causality. We have here the ontological difference between God and creatures which is the point of Thomas's claim that in any creature there is non-identity of what it is and that it is, whereas in God essence and existence are one. He makes the latter point by calling God *Ipsum esse subsistens*, stretching the language and hurting our non-Platonic ears.[11]

Question 3, article 1, begins by recalling the by now familiar distinction, but puts a new twist on it. The distinction is, again, between the thing that is the ultimate end and our possession of it. "If then man's happiness be considered with regard to its cause or object, it is something uncreated, whereas if it be considered with regard to the very essence of happiness, it is something created." Thus, for Thomas, *pace* Père Gauthier, the *essence* of happiness is a good achievable by action, contingent, embedded in time. In the third question Thomas wishes to speak of the essence of happiness and he will first establish that it is an activity, citing Aristotle in *Nicomachean Ethics* I. Then he will exclude certain possibilities and identify the activity in question as of the intellectual part (art. 4). Speculative or practical? Rather the speculative than the practical. It is here that Thomas makes another distinction of maximum importance for the difficulty raised by Gauthier. If contemplation is the perfection of the speculative use of our mind, it is in contemplation that human happiness will consist. "Therefore the ultimate and perfect happiness, which is expected in the future life, consists wholly in contemplation. Imperfect happiness, however, such as can be had here, consists first and principally in contemplation and secondarily in the operation of practical intellect ordering human actions and passions, as is said in the *Ethics* X." (art. 5)

This distinction between imperfect and perfect happiness, the happiness that can be attained in this life and that for which we hope in another, is clearly not one Aristotle could make. Indeed he is quite mystifying when the question of the alterability of the happiness or unhappiness of the departed comes up in the first book of the *Nicomachean Ethics*. Thomas says things about Aristotle's teaching, then, which could only be said from the vantage point of religious belief -- namely that the happiness he defines is a this worldly one -- although even

---

11. See David Burrell, *Knowing the Unknowable God*, Notre Dame, 1986, pp. 19-34.

on that score he points to Aristotle's insistence that he is speaking of the happiness appropriate to a man. (NE I 7, 431a16). That Thomas says things about Aristotelian doctrine from a Christian perspective should not, of course, be identified with the claim that he distorts the teaching of Aristotle. Thomas is right to point out that Aristotle himself notes the discrepancy between the concept of the good for man and the way we can hope to realize it. The notes of self-sufficiency and permanence must be modified in terms of the facts of human existence and it seems fair to say that Aristotle's idea of the ultimate end and our chances of realizing happiness, and of the happiness we realize filling the bill so far as the concept goes, are not identical. In short, Aristotle himself has a measure according to which he could say that the happiness we achieve is an imperfect one. What he does not say of course is that there is a possibility of attaining perfect happiness elsewhere.

Throughout Question 4, St. Thomas continues to contrast the happiness achievable in this life with that hoped for in the next in such a way that, far from disagreeing with Aristotle, he underscores his agreement with him. The assertion that perfect happiness is not possible in this life is taken to be a reiteration of Aristotle. "And because of this in out present state of life, perfect happiness cannot be had by man. Hence, the Philosopher, in *Ethics* I, speaking of man's happiness in this life, calls it imperfect, concluding, after much consideration, 'Happy we mean as men'." (q. 3, art. 2, ad 4).

The discussion of the concomitants of happiness in Question 4 glosses much of Aristotle. So too, asking in Question 5 about the achieving of happiness, Thomas sounds almost Pelagian in his optimism about our ability to achieve the imperfect happiness discussed by Aristotle, while stressing its imperfectness. "For happiness, being 'a perfect and sufficient good,' excludes all evil, but in this life every evil cannot be excluded. Our present life is subject to many evils which cannot be avoided." (art. 3) He lists these evils: ignorance, inordinate desire, bodily ills. "So too the desire for good cannot be satisfied in this life." We naturally desire the permanent possession of the good, but in this life goods are transitory and evanescent.

In saying that perfect happiness is impossible in this life, Thomas is underscoring the discrepancy Aristotle saw between his definition of happiness and what we can hope to achieve of it. That Thomas does and Aristotle does not speak of a perfect happiness after this life does not affect their concord on earthly happiness.

Although Thomas locates perfect happiness in the next life, there is an anticipation of it in this thanks to grace. The acts which can be constitutive of imperfect happiness in this life can also, when informed by grace, merit the perfect happiness of union with God. The sequel to these opening five questions is a remarkable theory of human action.[12]

These few remarks indicate that the complete moral thought of Thomas Aquinas as we find it in his theological works is not in opposition to the pagan ethics of Aristotle in the way suggested by Père Gauthier. It is unfortunate that a scholar who has devoted so much time and energy to the study of Thomas and Aristotle should have conceived so wrong an understanding of them. The Aristotle subsumed within the commodious synthesis of Thomas is the historical Aristotle. It is libelous to suggest that Thomas simply took words and phrases from Aristotle and turned them to purposes he knew they could not truly serve. How odd that those who claim to be friends and followers of Thomas should ascribe such a practice to him. The real test of the relation between Thomas and Aristotle is the commentary on the *Nicomachean Ethics*. That the editor of the critical edition of that work should be our old friend Père Gauthier is cause for concern. He has dismissed the commentary as useless. There is only one way to know whether that judgment, or an opposite affirmative one, is true, and that is to read the commentary carefully. It is lamentable that the editor of the text derides it as Gauthier has done. That he is not a sure guide is suggested by our analysis of one of his misunderstandings. To say that Thomas baptized Aristotle is no more helpful than to say that the *Divina Commedia* is the *Summa theologiae* in verse. It is time to consider the relation between Thomas and Aristotle independently of tendentious generalizations.

---

12. See Alan Donagan, "Thomas Aquinas on Human Action," in *Cambridge History of Later Medieval Philosophy*, edited by Norman Kretzmann, Anthony Kenny, Jan Pinborg and Eleonore Stump, Cambridge, 1983, pp. 642-654.

Kant's Theory of Morals

Bruce Aune
University of Massachusetts, Amherst

Although Kant is one of the classic writers on morality, his actual theory of morality is not well understood. His philosophical elusiveness is generally attributed to the striking difficulty of his writing, but I think it is equally owing to the complexity of his views. Faced with the task of discussing his moral philosophy in a single talk, I am particularly conscious of its complexity. Perhaps the most I can hope to accomplish today is to expose some of the complexity and to offer some critical remarks.

From a highly general point of view, Kant's theory of morals is an attempt to identify, circumscribe, or define in a purely secular manner a system of morality associated with the Judeo-Christian tradition and to prove that it is rationally justifiable in the strong sense of being not just acceptable to but actually binding on all rational beings. The system of morality is derivable and thus identifiable, Kant thought, from a supreme principle that he called "the moral law." His famous name for this law, which he formulated in a number of different ways, is "the categorical imperative." The system derivable from the law consists of general rules or precepts that Kant classifies under the headings (among others) of duties of justice and duties of virtue.

Since in Kant's opinion the system is not only justifiable by, but identifiable (or definable) by reference to, the moral law, I shall begin with the latter. As I mentioned, Kant offered several different formulations of his categorical imperative; in fact, by my count he offered seven distinct principles in his *Groundwork of the Metaphysics of Morals*. Critical questions that cry out for answers here are: Why did Kant offer such significantly different formulations of the moral law? How many different formulations did he really have in mind? Why did he think (and can one actually prove) that these different formulations are in fact equivalent? How did he think they could be justified in the strong sense I mentioned?

To understand any of Kant's formulations of the moral law, one must have some grasp of a more primitive Kantian notion -- of action on a "maxim." Although most of us would probably acknowledge that in our high-minded moments, at least, we act on principle, Kant thought that whenever we do something for a reason or purpose, we are acting on some "practical principle." If, for example, I intentionally do A to satisfy a purpose P, I am (at least tacitly) acting on a principle that can be expressed by the hypothetical statement, "If my purpose is P, I will do A." It is my acceptance of this principle, this maxim, that *accounts* for my doing A when I have the purpose P. The explanation is a rational one in the minimal sense that it gives my immediate (or low-level) reason for doing A.

According to Kant, maxims are "subjective" practical principles, that is, practical principles that are accepted (at least potentially) by some subjects or other. If a maxim is, in Kant's terms, "universally valid" -- that is, accepted or acknowledged by all rational beings -- then it is a "practical law."[1] Such laws correspond to nonpractical laws descriptive of the behavior of rational beings in the following way: If "I will do A if p" is a practical law, then all rational beings necessarily do A when p. When Kant, in his first formulation of the categorical imperative, speaks of a maxim becoming a universal law, I think we can reasonably interpret him as referring to the descriptive (or nonpractical) laws that would exist if the relevant maxim were adopted by (and thus valid for) all rational beings.

Kant's first formulation of his categorical imperative is as follows:

Act only on that maxim through which you can at the
same time will that it should become a universal law.

If we use "m" as a schematic letter for maxims and "U(m)" as a schematic symbol for corresponding universal laws, we can express his formula a little more precisely by saying:

Act on m only if in acting on m you can also will that
U(m) is a universal law.

Though a little more precise than the former, this last formula is still not satisfactory as a version of *the* fundamental principle of morals. I say this because, as Kant himself assumes in developing his system,[2] the fundamental principle of morals is supposed to be sufficient to identify what is morally permissible as well as what is morally obligatory -- and the for-

---

1. Kant, *Groundwork of the Metaphysics of Morals*, trans. H. J. Paton (New York: Harper Torchbooks, 1964), p. 69 (=p. 401 of Prussian Academy). My subsequent reference to Kant's writings will be to the Prussian Academy edition.
2. *Groundwork*, 440; *Metaphysics of Morals*, 221.

mula above does not (at least explicitly) provide the means by which the first of these tasks can be accomplished.

Fortunately, the necessary amendment is easy to identify. Since the categorical imperative is supposed to constitute *the* moral law, anything not forbidden by it is not (morally) forbidden at all. If we explicitly incorporate this assumption into a formulation of the categorical imperative that also contains the "ought" Kant says we are entitled to insert,[3] we can say that the idea Kant wants to convey by his first formulation amounts to the following:

> You ought not to act on a maxim m when and only when
> you cannot act on it and, at the same time, will that
> U(m) is a law.

This formulation yields a principle of permissibility because, if you cannot satisfy the condition it contains, you can infer that it is not the case that you ought not to act on m -- in symbols, $\sim O \sim (Am)$ -- and this implies that you may act on m -- in symbols, $P(Am)$.

Although Kant's formula, thus qualified, provides a basic law logically capable (at least in principle) of yielding moral permissions as well as moral obligations, it has a logical peculiarity that makes it an unpromising instrument for Kant's theoretical aims. The peculiarity is that the obligations derivable from it (if any) are essentially negative: they amount to prohibitions against acting on various maxims. Yet Kant believes that we have numerous "positive" obligations -- to promote the happiness of others, to seek our own perfection, and the like.[4] The difficulty is that one cannot, logically speaking, infer any obligation to act on some maxim from obligations not to act on various other maxims. A "positive" obligation is, therefore, difficult to derive on Kant's approach. Even if one could show, for example, that *every* maxim allowing one to neglect some talent is morally objectionable (such that one ought not to act on it) one could not *infer* that there is any maxim on which one ought to act. Yet if the categorical imperative provides no basis for this inference, it is hard to see how it could possibly provide a basis for inferring that one ought positively to do (or seek) anything at all.

If we ask how Kant's categorical imperative is supposed to be applied, we run into a different sort of problem. Suppose we ask if it is morally all right to act on the maxim m:

> I will attack and attempt to kill anyone I don't like.

---

3. *Groundwork*, 412.
4. *Metaphysics of Morals*, 419, 452.

Although Kant would certainly urge a negative answer, it is not immediately obvious how such an answer is to be defended. Note that if it is really wrong to act on this maxim, no person should be able to "will" (as Kant puts it) that the maxim m should become a law. Yet this creates something of a mystery about the meaning Kant attached to the words "being able to will," or about the conception of being able to will that he had in mind. I say this because, in a normal or ordinary sense of these words, some people clearly can, while others cannot, will that m should be a law. Many soft-hearted people couldn't possibly will such a thing -- and not just because they would be terrified at the thought of m's becoming a law. But others, hostile and supremely self-confident or angry at a world they would be glad to leave, would have absolutely no trouble willing that everyone should energetically act on m. Thus, if Kant is to avoid the consequence that acting on m is permissible for some but impermissible for others, he must have some special sense of "can will" in mind, or some special conception of being able to will something.

I think it is fair to say that Kant does have a special conception of willing here. The first thing special about it is that, according to it, one cannot will anything impossible, whether one realizes it or not. As I pointed out earlier, Kant attempted to derive two classes of duties from his moral law, duties of justice and duties of virtue. As he made clear in his *Metaphysics of Morals*, he thought each of these classes is derivable from the moral law in a distinctive way, a way identifying a general reason why acting on a maxim and willing that it shall become a universal law cannot be willed. The first general reason is that the conjunction willed is impossible in some way. In arguing, in the *Groundwork*, that it is morally impermissible to act on the maxim "Whenever I believe myself short of money, I will borrow money and promise to pay it back, though I know I will never, in fact, repay it," Kant claims that if one considers "how things would stand" in the world if this maxim became a law of nature, one can see that "promising and the very purpose of promising ... [would be] impossible."[5] He concludes from this impossibility, which is (by the way) empirical rather than logical, that the relevant action *cum* law cannot be willed in the relevant sense. It would thus be useless for Joe Shmoe, who doesn't appreciate the physical impossibility in question, to insist "But I can certainly will such a thing."

Kant's general position is that duties of justice can be deduced from the impossibility of various maxims being universal laws and also being acted on. But if a maxim passes this test -- if, that is, it could be a

---

5. *Groundwork*, 422. The maxim Kant refers to here assumes the conditional form I described earlier when the purpose implicitly identified by the antecedent "when I believe myself short of money" is explicitly identified and when the consequent is shortened to "I will borrow money and *falsely* promise to pay it back."

law and also be acted on -- then if one could still not will that it be a law, a duty of virtue is thereby derivable. This, of course, still leaves us with some doubt about how we are to understand the relevant impossibility (or inability) of willing something that is itself possible. As is clear from Kant's treatment of his famous third and fourth examples in the *Groundwork*, the examples concerning the development of one's talents and helping others in need,[6] the relevant willing is impossible in the sense of being incompatible with the will of a rational being -- a being that is, at the very least, clearheaded, prudent, consistent in his or her thinking, and disposed to will the necessary means to willed ends.

Since the cost of developing all one's talents (assuming that it is physically possible to do so) may far outweigh the benefits of having every talent developed (drawing, playing tennis, singing, gardening, speaking eloquently, etc., etc.), I doubt that a truly rational being would undertake the arduous course Kant believes (or says) is obligatory. On the other hand, a rational being with a realistic view of him or herself and the world would naturally anticipate needing (as Kant says) the help of some other people at some time or other. Yet a person who is rational in these ways (or this sense) may yet feel hostility to others, be tired of living, and unafraid of dying. Surely, a clear-headed person with these attitudes *could* will that the maxim I have mentioned should become a law. And a sado-masochist -- who enjoyed being beaten as much as he enjoyed beating others -- could also will, without any kind of inconsistency or obvious bad judgment, that the following maxim should become a law:

m: I will inflict pain on another if it pleases me to do so.

It goes without saying, I hope, that Kant would never allow that it is morally permissible to act on this despicable maxim.

The problem that arises here is that, no matter how rational a group of people may be (in the sense of being clearheaded, wise, and logically consistent), it is possible for them to differ radically in their attitudes and values and, consequently, to be able to will that significantly different maxims should become universal laws. If Kant is to identify moral obligations and permissions by reference to what a person "can will," he must be able to characterize such willing in a way that disregards the contingencies and the variability of actual human attitudes and valuations. If he cannot do this, his categorical imperative (or "moral law") is not much of an improvement on the golden rule, which is perhaps a useful formula to inculcate in children who must be taught to treat others "with consideration," but which is virtually useless for theoretical purposes. (I

---

6. *Groundwork*, 423.

can just hear the convinced Nazi saying, "If I were a Jew, I would demand annihilation," and I can recall a friend saying to me, in an argument about capital punishment, "If I were a murderer, I would insist on being hanged for my crime.")

Kant's actual conception of what a purely rational being could will is more complicated and more obscure than I have thus far indicated. To show why the moral law, as he describes it, is binding on us as imperfectly rational beings who occasionally commit fallacies and who more frequently succumb to our inclinations and act unjustly, Kant draws a distinction between the world (of which we are a part) as it appears and the world as it is in itself. Arguing that we may justifiably believe or assume (though we cannot know) that, as things in themselves, we are metaphysically free or have "free will," Kant eventually concludes that we are justified in believing that we are, as things in themselves, rational self-legislators, who make the laws that govern our activities. So understood, we are rational beings in a fairly mysterious sense: we cannot claim any direct knowledge of, or insight into, our rational nature. We must infer our nature as rational beings mainly from the laws that govern it. Although as imperfectly rational beings we have a practically adequate sense of our moral requirements and, therefore, of the laws specifying them, these laws are (Kant says in the *Groundwork*) theoretically identifiable only by reference to the moral law, which we can identify, he adds, by its highly general, formal character.[7]

To make these points is to make the problem that led to them all the more acute, for if our underlying rational nature can be known only from self-legislated laws that are inferable from the moral law (or categorical imperative), our knowledge of that rational nature cannot be required for the interpretation or systematic use of the moral law. How, then, does Kant expect us to apply the moral law in identifying specific duties of justice and virtue? The bare bones of the answer is to be found in the discouragingly short and obscure part of the *Critique of Practical Reason* called "Of the Typic of Pure Practical Judgment."

In the four and a half pages that bear this title, Kant argues that "the morally good," being an object of pure practical reason, is "supersensuous" and cannot therefore be discovered in nature.[8] To discover whether an action possible for us in the sensuous world is or is not "a case" prohibited or required by the moral law, we must use our practical judgment, he says, and form an "estimate" of what pure reason requires. We form such an estimate by considering "how things would stand" if the maxim in question had the universality of a law of nature --

---

7. *Groundwork*, 423.
8. Kant, *Critique of Practical Reason*, trans. Lewis White Beck (Indianapolis, 1956), pp. 70-74 (pp. 68-72 of Prussian Academy edition of Kant's works, vol. 5).

if, that is, the partially rational beings of our world, namely human beings, invariably acted according to it. If the maxim could not have that kind of universality -- or if we could not will the result if it were possible -- then it would be impermissible to act on it. Presumably, it would be permissible to act on it if it passed both tests.

This strategy provides some basis for identifying purely rational practical laws of justice (the ones inferable from the impossibility of a maxim having a certain kind of universality), but it is not helpful for identifying duties of virtue, which turn on the possibility of willing an outcome that is in other respects possible.[9] The difficulty is precisely that different partially rational beings belonging to nature are evidently capable (empirically) of willing different things, and Kant does not enrich his discussion with further points about the requisite kind (or sense) of willing.

In my book on Kant's theory of morals I argued that Kant has another strategy for dealing with this issue,[10] but before discussing it I want to point out corresponding difficulties in applying Kant's other versions of the categorical imperative. Consider this End-in-Itself formulation:

> So act in relation to every rational being (both to your-
> self and to others) that he may at the same time count in
> your maxim as an end in himself.

When Kant outlines his theory of natural ends in the second part of *The Critique of Judgment*, he makes it clear that an end in itself is an intelligent being that has ends in the sense of purposes. In the *Groundwork* Kant says that we treat a person as a thing in itself when we do two things; first, we act in ways that do not interfere with the realization of his or her ends; and second, we endeavor, so far as possible, to make those ends ours -- by which he means that we do what we can to help realize them.[11]

An obvious problem that arises here is this: The actual purposes of many human beings are immoral, and if anything pertaining to morals is clear, it is that not only should we not share those ends but we should do what we can to prevent their realization. Obviously, Kant's doctrine is plausible only if we draw a distinction between (roughly) good and bad ends: We should not interfere with others' attempts to realize their good ends; in fact, we should do what we can to realize them ourselves. Yet how are we to distinguish good from bad ends? We must draw the dis-

---

9. *Groundwork*, 424.
10. Bruce Aune, *Kant's Theory of Morals* (Princeton, 1979, pp. 51-60, 121f.
11. *Groundwork*, 430.

tinction if we can apply the categorical imperative, but the imperative is supposed to be the fundamental principle of morals and the basis, therefore, of all moral distinctions. What is to be done?

Kant's solution, I believe, is built on his two ways of regarding a human being. As a rational thing-in-itself, a person has only good ends, for good ends are nothing but ultimately rational ones. Kant can therefore say that we behave rightly toward a rational being just when we do not thwart but actually share in his or her ends. Unfortunately, the denizens of our imperfect world of appearance are not perfectly rational, and to deal rightly with them we must distinguish their good from their bad (or their rational from their irrational) ends. To do this, we need some kind of "typic" for the pure End-in-Itself principle. Kant does not, to my knowledge, discuss this point explicitly, but he makes remarks here and there that disclose the strategy he probably has in mind. In both the *Groundwork* and *The Metaphysics of Morals* Kant argues that certain purpose-ends are objectionable because they are *unnatural*, out of line with nature's purposes.[12] It is by reference to the doctrine of natural purposes that he attempts to prove that suicide, carnal self-defilement (or masturbation), contraception, and self-mutilation are not morally permissible.

There are two striking difficulties with this strategy. The first is that, from a purely secular point of view, the notion of a natural purpose is no longer credible. Those who believe in a supernatural creator may seek a scriptural basis for a doctrine of natural law by which natural occurrences can be judged as deviant or lawful, but the evolutionary bias of secular science renders the very notion of a natural purpose painfully anachronistic. The other difficulty is that, even if a unique system of natural purposes could be identified and defended on secular grounds, it is very implausible to suppose that every end or purpose that we find morally objectionable would count as unnatural.

In his *Groundwork* Kant argues that if every rational being treated every rational being always as an end and not as a mere means, a "Kingdom of Ends" would result.[13] Such a kingdom would be a "harmonious" system of ends in which each being pursues its ends without interference by others and in fact helps others achieve their ends (being similarly helped in turn). Kant therefore proposes another formulation of the moral law known as the Kingdom of Ends formulation. A pure version of the formula is this:

---

12. *Groundwork*, 422; *Metaphysics of Morals*, 425.
13. *Groundwork*, 433f.

> Act on the maxim of a member who makes universal law
> for a merely possible kingdom of ends.

As in the case of the other pure formulas, the key problem lies in its application. The difficulty is that different actual ends can always, in principle, be brought into harmony in different ways. The slaves of even highly oppressed societies can be brought up to regard the position they occupy as right for them. Thus, many different possible kingdoms of nature -- some to our eyes morally barbaric -- can instantiate the abstract notion of a kingdom of ends. The problem is to restrict the abstract notion so that only morally acceptable systems of nature can instantiate it. As I see it, Kant has not succeeded in effecting this restriction.

One of the questions about Kant's system of morals that I mentioned near the beginning of this talk concerned Kant's reasons for supposing his various formulations of the moral law to be, in fact, equivalent. I want to say something about this now.

As I see it, Kant's system involves four pure versions of the moral law and four corresponding typics or rules of judgment. The first pure version and its corresponding typic occur early in chapter 2 of the *Groundwork*. Paton refers to these formulas as "the Formula of Universal Law" and "the Formula of the Law of Nature."[14] They are as follows:

> C1. Act only on that maxim through which you can at
> the same time will that it should become a universal
> law.

> C1a. Act as if the maxim of your action were to become
> through your will a universal law of nature.

The next two formulas, both of which actually occur in the *Groundwork*,[15] concern ends in themselves. They are:

> C2. Act in such a way that you always treat rational
> nature, whether in your own person or that of
> another, never simply as a means but always at the
> same time as an end.

> C2a. Same as C2 except that "humanity" replaces
> "rational nature. "

The third set of formulas concern rational kingdoms:

---

14. Paton, pp. 88f.
15. *Groundwork*, 429, 433.

C3. So act as if you were through your maxims a law-
    making member of a possible kingdom of ends.

C3a. Same as C3 except for the addition of the clause
     "understood as a kingdom of nature."

Both of these formulas, or variations thereupon, occur in the
Groundwork.[16] The final pair of formulas involve the notion of autonomy:

C4. So act that your will can regard itself as making
    universal law through its maxims.

C4a. Same as C4 except that "universal laws of nature"
     replaces the more abstract "universal laws."

The key relations between these sets of formulas are as follows.
To begin with, although Kant often speaks of the "universal law" version,
C1, as fundamental, identifiable (not very rigorously) by reference to the
"bare conformity to law" that must be the aim of ultimately disinterested
rational choice,[17] he introduces the Formula of Autonomy mainly for
emphasis. In explaining why he thinks the moral law is binding on us as
imperfectly rational beings, he claims that we are justifiably regarded as
rational beings "in ourselves" who are not subject to "alien causes." As
ultimately free beings whose will is autonomous, we act according to laws
we have made for ourselves. We are rationally bound by these laws
because, in freely accepting or creating them, we commit ourselves to
them. Since to will that a maxim should become a law is to legislate or
make a law, it is clear that the formulas C4 and C4a are fundamentally
the same in content as the formulas C1 and C1a; they differ only in
emphasis.

Kant introduces the formula C2 by considerations pertaining to
rational motivation.[18] If, as he claims at the beginning of the *Groundwork*,
the only thing "in or out of the world" that is good without qualification is
a good will -- this being a will that (among other things) acts for the sake
of duty and, as a thing in itself, freely adopts the laws that govern its
behavior and define standards of right and wrong, good and bad -- then a
rational being's motive in adopting its own laws cannot be to bring about
some "effect" in the world, or create some new object. The motive must,
rather, concern some object that already exists. Kant claims that the
motive is one of respect and that it is directed to rational nature itself. As

---

16. *Groundwork*, 434, 436.
17. *Groundwork*, 402.
18. *Groundwork*, 428f.

I have explained, Kant thought that this attitude of respect has a positive and a negative aspect -- the negative being not to act against (or interfere with) other rational beings, and the positive being to assist (to the extent that one can) other such beings to realize their ends.

For reasons that I have discussed at length in my book on Kant's ethics, Kant thought that the negative aspect coincided exactly with result secured by the first test implicit in the formula C1, that is, the test of not acting on maxims that could not become universal laws. Thus, for Kant, the theory of natural justice (the duties of justice) were deducible from either C1 or C2 (or their typics). Similarly, the positive aspect of treating rational nature as an end coincided exactly, Kant thought, with the result secured by the second test implicit in the formula -- that of not acting on maxims that, though possible universal laws, could not rationally be willed to be such. The theory of virtue (the duties of virtue) are then inferable from either C1 or C2 (or from their typics).

As for the formulas C3 and C3a, Kant introduced them by reference to C2 and C2a, and their content is clarified in relation to the result that would be achieved if all rational beings acted according to C2, or all human beings acted according to C2a. Formulas that, if acted on, are bound to have the same result are plausibly regarded as equivalent in a strong sense -- and this explains Kant's confidence that they are merely different "formulations" of the same law or principle. The tacit qualification to this is that the pure laws should be understood as distinct from the corresponding typics.

I have now answered the questions I initially posed about Kant's theory of morals. I have explained how many different formulations of the moral law are at least implicit in his system if not explicitly offered by him. I have also explained why Kant thought that such seemingly different principles are so strongly equivalent that he should regard them as different "formulations" of the same basic law. I have even explained why he thought this fundamental law is binding on us as imperfectly rational beings. I now want to round off this talk by some critical observations about his moral system.

Although I have a great deal of admiration for the intricacy, the inventiveness, and the amazing scope of Kant's thinking on morals -- and although I also admire, in a different way, the earnestness, the decency, and (contrary to a common opinion) the lack of moral fanaticism that is apparent in his writings on morality -- I have to say that his philosophical theory of morality is not, in my judgment, a success, or even close to it. I have already called attention to a number of difficulties in applying the categorical imperative; these difficulties disclose the inadequacy of that imperative as a "first principle" from which our liberties and obligations are derivable. I have also, in passing, expressed my serious doubts about the plausibility of Kant's idea that the moral law and the obligations sup-

posedly derivable from it are binding on us because, as things in themselves and in ways unknown to ourselves, we have freely committed
ourselves to them. To conclude my remarks, I shall briefly explain why I
think that Kant's attempt to show that moral principles can be identified
by reference to rationality itself is unsatisfactory as well.

As I explained earlier, Kant thought that, if a maxim could not
possibly become a universal law or a law of nature, it is morally
impermissible to act on it. This condition was the basis, I said, of his
system of natural justice, or juridical duties. Reflection shows, however,
that Kant's thinking on this point is untenable. Consider a maxim that I
discussed in my book on Kant's theory of morals:

> m. If I decide to become a parent, I shall marry some
>   eligible woman who also decides to be a parent and,
>   with her consent, etc., have a child by her.

The problem here is that, although almost anyone not opposed to the
institution of marriage would allow that a man (= a male human being) is
morally entitled to act on this innocent maxim, Kant's theory has the consequence that any action on it is morally impermissible. The reason is
obvious: the generalization of the maxim m could not be a law of nature
because no woman could (consistently with nature's purposes) act on it:
to do so, a woman would have to impregnate another woman, which is
impossible.

Defenders of Kant are apt to object to this criticism, saying that
there is a related maxim on which Kant would allow anyone to act -- a
maxim that differs from the one considered in speaking not of marrying a
woman but of marrying a person of the opposite sex. The objection misses
the point, however. The difficulty is not that we cannot find a maxim
passing Kant's test; it is that Kant's test renders immoral a patently
innocent human action. In doing this, his test (or the larger criterion in
which it is embedded) is defective. Once we see this, we can appreciate
the reason for the defect, which is that Kant's criterion exaggerates the
moral significance of every feature of a maxim (even a purely logical feature) that renders its generalization impossible. A well-meaning but
ignorant backyard inventor might demonstrate his ineptitude by acting on
a maxim prescribing a means of creating a perpetual-motion machine; yet
the impossibility of his success (let alone the impossibility of his maxim's
becoming a universal law) has no implications for morality.

If the purely rational tests implicit in Kant's categorical imperative are excessively stringent in disallowing numerous (actually, countless) innocent actions, that imperative is clearly defective as a basic moral
principle. This defectiveness is compounded, if I am right, by the
problems of application that I mentioned earlier. If, in addition, one

considers the general implausibility of Kant's view that ordinary human beings can reasonably be regarded as rational lawmakers who are bound by practical laws because they freely commit themselves to them, I think one will have to agree that Kant's philosophical system of morality is an extremely shaky structure. I, in fact, can go a bit further than this. Although I believe that my understanding of moral philosophy has been greatly enriched by the time I have devoted to Kant's writings on the subject, I find it difficult to point to an important, distinctively Kantian theoretical-ethical contention that, when carefully considered and dispassionately assessed, turns out to be acceptable or true. This is a severe verdict, but it is one that honesty compels me to make.

Classical Utilitarianism

Fred R. Berger
University of California, Davis

Much recent philosophizing within moral theory has taken as its starting point criticisms made of what is denoted "classical utilitarianism." The phrase has been used to pick out the moral theory of Jeremy Bentham, and James Mill and John Stuart Mill are sometimes also included as well. Some critics have been reluctant to include the younger Mill, as it is recognized that in places he clearly endorsed views that are straightforwardly inconsistent with the views labeled "classical utilitarianism." Until recently, the standard way of treating this anomaly was to hold that John Stuart Mill was simply given to embracing inconsistencies. The standard account held that he inherited doctrines from his father, and from Bentham, onto which he grafted other views not compatible with those of his mentors. Raised on a pablum laced with doctrinaire utilitarianism, it has been thought, his better instincts led him to a wider view of human nature and a more humane set of moral principles that could not be fully digested in combination with a strict utilitarian diet. Thus, unable to shake off his infantile security blanket, he could be charged with inconsistency and equivocation. On the old account of Mill, he came off as a good, kind, benevolent man whose basic morality and humaneness outstripped his moral theories, and, thus, as a morally admirable fathead.

I have endeavored to correct this picture of Mill in a book-length work devoted to examining his moral and political theories.[1] I have come to believe that Jeremy Bentham and James Mill depart *also* from the set of views labeled "classical utilitarianism" in a number of important ways also. Thus, in this paper, I want to examine the standard critique against

---

1. Fred R. Berger, *Happiness, Justice and Freedom: The Moral and Political Philosophy of John Stuart Mill* (Berkeley and Los Angeles: University of California Press, 1984). (Hereafter referred to as, HJF.)

the writings of these three figures. I believe that the conceptions of utilitarianism that emerge do not as readily succumb to the standard criticisms, and thus have significance for the contemporary defense of consequentialism. I do not claim that these views are immune from revised forms of those criticisms, but it is something of a scandal that accounts of these philosophers, and the criticisms of "classical utilitarianism" should for so long have been based on such gross misrepresentations.

I shall start by outlining the standard depiction of the classical theories, and the criticisms that have been thought to follow.

I. The Standard Critique

The standard account begins by attributing a value theory to these figures that maintains that it is certain mental states that have value, viz., pleasures, while pains have disvalue.[2] It is sometimes also held that the classical theory treats pleasures and pains as simple sensations that are produced by, and hence both conceptually and psychologically separable from the actions of which they are the consequences.[3] The value of an act, then, is just a matter of summing up all the pleasures or pains that are produced as a consequence. Actions, then, have no value in themselves; their value is derivative from the pleasures or pains contingently produced. Similarly, since the value of an act is a direct function of the sum of pleasures and pains produced, no distributional considerations enter in. So long as an act will produce more pleasure than any alternatives, that act has greater value than the others, regardless of how the pleasures and pains that result are *distributed*. A further consequence of this feature of the theory is that the evaluation of an act must be what has been called "person" or "agent-neutral," i.e., it is immaterial to *whom* the pleasures or pains accrue. Indeed, some writers go so far as to claim that persons, together with their ties to others, are lost entirely in utilitarian calculation.[4]

---

2. The standard view is concisely summarized by R. G. Frey in his introduction to *Utility and Rights*, ed. R. G. Frey (Minneapolis: University of Minnesota Press, 1984), pp. 3-19. Many of the articles in this book reflect typical, widely repeated depictions and criticisms of classical utilitarianism.
3. See, Joseph Raz, "Right-Based Moralities," in *Utility and Rights*, pp. 48-49.
4. Amartya Sen and Bernard Williams, "Introduction," *Utilitarianism and Beyond* (Cambridge: Cambridge University Press, 1982), pp. 4-5.

Now, some critics of the classical view sometimes also attribute *another* sort of value theory to the classical writers, viz., the theory that accords value to an act according to its fulfillment of desires or preferences on the part of people.[5] This sort of preference-maximizing theory is widely employed by social choice theorists in contemporary versions of utilitarianism. Not only is such a theory sometimes attributed to the classical thinkers, the two theories are sometimes conflated.[6] These *are* different theories, however. What is desired may not provide pleasure when achieved. And, what turns out to provide pleasure may not have been desired or preferred. Life *is* sometimes serendipitous. While there are some interesting aspects of some of the classical utilitarians' views that bear this latter interpretation (especially in J. S. Mill's work), I shall not pursue them. As I shall maintain, I do not believe John Stuart Mill is correctly understood under *either* banner, which I have argued at length in the work mentioned earlier. I believe the "pleasure" account does come closer to the views of Bentham and James Mill, but I believe their theories are misrepresented by the account as given. Let me turn to the criticisms of utilitarianism that have been made on the basis of attributing this sort of value theory to it. The importance of the correctives I shall indicate will be highlighted by seeing what is at stake.

The most central and important criticism of classical utilitarianism begins from the alleged fact that it holds what is sometimes referred to as an "aggregative" conception of the good. This means that it is concerned *solely* with aggregating goods, i.e., with maximizing the total *amount* of pleasure. Since there are not distributional constraints in the base of the theory, this would permit, it is alleged, overriding basic rights of persons whenever that will produce greater pleasure than would respecting the right. Rights have no inherent value in a utilitarian theory, hence, respecting a right has value only to the extent that it produces pleasure. Now, many contemporary critics recognize that as a matter of fact there *are* utilities that result from respecting rights, but, they maintain that

---

5. Frey is careful to distinguish these. The "preference" version he labels the "modern" view (see, "Introduction," *Utility and Rights*). Sen and Williams also mark the distinction, but virtually all of their criticisms deal with the preference account solely. Some writers, however, seem to take this account of value as exhaustive. David Gauthier, for example, refers to it as part of "the conceptual framework within which utilitarian ethical theory was developed." (See, David Gauthier, "On the Refutation of Utilitarianism," in *The Limits of Utilitarianism*, ed. Harlan B. Miller and William H. Williams (Minneapolis: University of Minnesota Press, 1982), pp. 144-163.

6. While John Rawls clearly marks the distinction that is being discussed, he takes "classical" utilitarianism (apparently, that of Bentham, Sidgewick, and Edgeworth) to accept the preference theory of value, which he describes as seeking to maximize the satisfaction of desire. But, he often slips into talking about maximizing people's "satisfactions," which begins to suggest the pleasure/happiness account. See, John Rawls, *A Theory of Justice* (Cambridge, Mass.: Harvard University Press, 1971), especially, pp. 25-27.

it is *in principle* possible that the score will come out in favor of rights-violation.[7] So-called "rights-based" theories have developed that are designed to provide guarantees for basic values or rights.[8] As I do not believe the theories that have thus far been presented are entirely adequate either as general moral theories *or* as theories that *do* provide just the right safeguards, I believe it of utmost importance to see just how plausible this criticism is when utilitarianism is put in its best and most defensible forms.[9]

A second criticism that has been made of the classical theory is that it must give full value to *all* sources of satisfaction, including those of malevolence. It has been pointed out that Bentham explicitly mentioned the pleasures of malevolence in his writings. *As* a pleasure, however, it cannot be distinguished from any other, and clearly, giving weight to it at all is questionable, while, in given contexts, it could have weight that outweighs the pleasures produced by respecting someone's rights. Similarly, if every pleasure has to be taken at face value, then we could not distinguish "urgent objective needs" from "strong subjective preferences."[10]

It is further alleged of the classical view that it cannot give full value to certain important moral and value considerations. Acts of friendship, for example, have value to us *as such*, not merely for the pleasures that are produced. Indeed, many activities, valuable *in themselves* can only be accorded derivative value, so it is alleged. Since the pleasurable sensations of acts of friendship, experiencing works of art, listening to fine music, and so on, are "capable of being caused in some other way and therefore only contingently connected with" the activities that produce them, these activities or acts can have no intrinsic value.[11] Just as respect for rights cannot be accorded value on the utilitarian view, so it is thought to be incapable of accounting for the value of acts of friendship or love or

---

7. Rolf Sartorious, "Persons and Property," in *Utility and Rights*, pp. 196-197.
8. See, Ronald Dworkin, *Taking Rights Seriously* (Cambridge, Mass.: Harvard University Press, 1977); J. L. Mackie, "Rights, Utility, and Universalization," in *Utility and Rights*, pp. 86-105; and Sartorious, "Persons and Property," in *Utility and Rights*, pp. 196-214.
9. Robert Nozick, Rawls, and Dworkin all permit extreme circumstances to override the rights they support; this suggests the need for a "deep" theory to explain and justify such a position. Some sort of consequentialist position, of course, could, logically speaking, yield their respective theories. For Nozick's theory, see, *Anarchy, State, and Utopia* (New York: Basic Books, Inc., 1974).
10. See, Sartorious, "Persons and Property," p. 197. Sartorious attributes the point to Thomas Scanlon. A similar view is expressed by Sen and Williams.
11. Raz, "Right-Based Moralities," pp. 48-49. Charles Taylor makes a related point in an article I shall discuss below.

gratitude.[12] This has been thought an especially grievous failing as much modern moral theory, curiously, stemming from emphases in John Stuart Mill's writings, has emphasized the importance of being an autonomous, self-determining person. Rights-theorists tend to give strong emphasis to this notion.[13] But, it has been thought, according intrinsic value to living autonomously is not consistent with the utilitarian outlook, hence, any such view, it has been said, must go "beyond utilitarianism."[14]

Finally, it has been held that since utilitarianism is commmitted to a "person-neutral" value theory, pleasures and pains can be transferred from one person to another so long as the magnitude is preserved with "no morally significant difference." And this means that it ignores the "separateness of persons." Persons are mere receptacles of pleasure and pain; they have no intrinsic value as such.[15] As Sen and Williams express the point, "persons as persons have dropped fully out of the assessment of states of affairs," since utility information alone is needed to assess those states of affairs.[16]

I think it is fairly clear that these criticisms rest on two of the chief features of the account of value that it is alleged the classical utilitarians held. First is the claim that at the base of their theories no distributional considerations enter in. Secondly, it is claimed that they were committed to separating acts from the sensations of pleasure produced by them, hence, as unable to attribute value to acts themselves. I want to show that these interpretations are either flat out false of the classical philosophers, or that there is virtually no ground for these attributions.

---

12. This point is made about consequentialism in general by Michael Stocker in, "The Schizophrenia of Modern Ethical Theories," *The Journal of Philosophy* 78 (1981), pp. 453-466. It is urged against act-utilitarianism in particular by Michael Slote in, *Goods and Virtues* (Oxford: Clarendon Press, 1983), p. 81. I have made a partial defense of utilitarianism on this score in, "Love, Friendship and Utility: On Practical Reason and Reductionism," in *Human Nature and Natural Knowledge*, ed. A. Donagan, N. Perovich, and M. V. Wedin (Dordrecht: D. Reidel Publishing Company, 1986), pp. 3-21.
13. See, for example, Mackie, "Rights, Utility, and Universalization;" and Sartorious, "Persons and Property."
14. Sen and Williams, "Introduction," in *Utilitarianism and Beyond*.
15. The criticism seems to have originated in John Rawls' *A Theory of Justice*, but has been picked up by others, e.g., Mackie.
16. Sen and Williams, "Introduction," *Utilitarianism and Beyond*, pp. 4-5.

II. A Revisionary Account -- Mostly Bentham

I should like to begin by noting that there is an important and illuminating tension between two of the criticisms I have cited of the classical value theory. A central claim holds that the account is insensitive to distributions of pleasure and pain, whereas a further criticism holds that the utilitarian must give weight to the pleasures of malevolence. Indeed, it is true that Bentham listed such pleasures (and pains as well) in his catalogue.[17] A bit of reflection on malevolence, however, reveals that it produces what might be called "second-order" pleasures, i.e., pleasures that concern the pleasures or pains of *others*. If, for example, I dislike a certain person, then if *that* person experiences a hardship, especially one that I sought to produce, I may experience pleasure -- a pleasure of malevolence. But one important thing to notice is that it matters *who* experiences that pleasure. If, in a malevolent fit, I strike out at my enemy but inflict the intended pain on my lover, I do *not* get the pleasure that would have accompanied my enemy's experiencing that pain. Indeed, by virtue of its being my *lover* who suffers the pain, I shall probably feel pained, rather than being pleasured. Clearly, it matters in *both* cases who experiences the pain. *Some* pleasures and pains, then, have a distributional aspect *built into them*. (I should add that it also seems to matter sometimes who *produces* the pleasure. There are *certain* pleasures which, when my lover experiences them, I am pleased at if they are produced by me, whereas I might experience the opposite reaction if I discover they were produced by someone else. I shall ignore *this* distributional aspect in the subsequent discussion.)

Now an important implication of this point is that if we are talking about the sum of pleasures or pains produced by an act, we may very well be masking the fact that in real life that sum is likely to be a function of distributions of prior pleasures and pains. The importance of this point can be seen by taking a closer look at Bentham's views on malevolence. After listing the various main categories of pleasures and pains in his most noted work, *An Introduction to the Principles of Morals and Legislation*, Bentham made the point that they fall into two classes -- the self-regarding, and extra-regarding. The pleasures and pains of the extra-regarding class are those of benevolence and malevolence. In *both* cases, Bentham made clear, the pleasures and pains are ones arising from other people experiencing pleasure or pain.[18] It hardly needs to be added that insofar as we act from sympathy or benevolence, it is the pleasure of

---

17. Jeremy Bentham, *An Introduction to the Principles of Morals and Legislation*, eds. J. H. Burns and H. L. A. Hart (London: Athlone Press, 1970), p. 49.
18. *Ibid.*

someone *else* we are seeking, not our own. But a point that is crucial to the entire utilitarian project must now be stressed. The pleasures and pains of malevolence and benevolence are *not* coordinate in an important respect. Bentham held that we are naturally inclined to be benevolent; we have *no* natural inclination toward malevolence. "Happily," he wrote, "there is no primeval and constant source of antipathy in human nature, as there is of sympathy."[19] And, in the *Deontology*, he remarked: "Scarcely can that human being ever have existed to whom, unless when afflicted by the contemplation of some unfortunate state of circumstances or agitated by some tumultuous passion, the sight of a fellow creature though a stranger to him in a state of apparent comfort was more gratifying than the sight of a fellow creature equally a stranger to him in a state of apparent sufferance."[20]

It should be clear from these points that at various stages in utilitarian calculation, the distinction among persons is crucial to the calculations, as well as the ties and interconnections they may have. This fact is hidden by the final score that an act gets *in* the calculation, but that score is a *function* of the ways in which the particular utilities are distributed and of the special relationships we have with others. These points, then, help to refute the Sen and Williams claim that persons and their ties do not matter, and they also go some way toward dispelling the claim that utilitarianism ignores "the separateness of persons."[21]

Bentham also held that our gratification at the well-being of others increases with the *numbers* of those so affected.[22] Since we have no *natural* inclination to be pleased at the ill-fare of others, producing ill-fare more extensively will not be likely to increase pleasure even *when* a pleasure of malevolence has been experienced. Indeed, Bentham made the point that malevolence or antipathy generally has bad effects, and must be controlled by considerations of overall utility. It is generally "productive of the very worst effects," he wrote.[23] We are so constituted by nature, then, that acts that distribute pleasure widely and diminish pain

19. *Ibid.*
20. Jeremy Bentham, *Deontology Together with a Table of the Springs of Action and the Article on Utilitarianism*, ed. Amnon Goldworth (Oxford: Clarendon Press, 1983), p. 129.
21. A much different defense of utilitarianism on these points is made in Leslie A. Mulholland, "Rights, Utilitarianism, and the Conflation of Persons," *The Journal of Philosophy* 83 (June, 1986), pp. 323-340. Mulholland goes on to criticize act-utilitarianism, however, for its alleged inability to account for rights within a legal system. I believe the arguments, however, confuse utilitarianism as a criterion of right and wrong action with the theory regarded as providing the sole rule for determining how one is to act. The latter was explicitly rejected by Mill, and is not a necessary part of the baggage of an act-utilitarian. I have argued these points at some length in, HJF, ch. 3.
22. Bentham, *Deontology*, p. 129.
23. Bentham, *Principles of Morals and Legislation*, p. 32.

are naturally pleasing to us. Furthermore, having cited the bad effects of malevolence, Bentham stressed good effects of benevolence -- it tends to produce further such acts, and builds up a "Saving Bank" of "good will" that tend to the benefit of both actor and society.[24] We should note that these are *very* compelling reasons for thinking that any actual case in which an act has produced the greatest sum of pleasure will also be one that reflects certain rather than other distributions.

With respect to the question of distributions of pleasure and pain, there is a curious passage in his essay entitled "Article on Utilitarianism," in which he maintained that we are so constituted that the quantity of unhappiness we can experience greatly outweighs the amount of happiness we are capable of. For this reason, he held, it was not necessary to speak of the greatest happiness *for the greatest number*. The latter phrase can be dropped since the distributive aspect is automatically looked to by virtue of the facts of our natures.[25] I suspect that the view here is a version of the not implausible principle of diminishing marginal utility -- once we have achieved a certain level of well-being, further increments of such are not as valuable or pleasurable as at the lower levels. James Mill explicitly argued from this principle to the conclusion that the distributive phrase is unnecessary in the Principle of Utility.[26]

I argued in my book that Bentham's famous "hedonic calculus" is best viewed as a device for planning future acts, and that it represents a strategy for maximizing good consequences. From the point of view of adopting strategies likely to produce the greatest good, the considerations already given provide strong ground for inculcating general dispositions to act benevolently -- a position Bentham in fact stressed[27] -- and, though Bentham did *not* make this point, it could provide a ground for downgrading or even discounting entirely prospective pleasures of malevolence. Thus, in practical decision making we would have strong ground for giving great weight to distributive issues by virtue of the *substantive* account of what gives pleasure to human beings as such.

I want to add that this account of Bentham's views is perfectly consistent with, may even imply the view that not all pleasures are separable from the circumstances or activities in which they arise. If we are constituted so as to take pleasure in benevolent acts, then they are pleasing to us *in themselves*. *Those* pleasures could not be produced, say, by eating an ice cream cone. Though Bentham sometimes described pleasures as "sensations" this was usually in connection with physical plea-

---

24. Bentham, *Deontology*, p. 184.
25. Bentham, *Article on Utilitarianism: Long Version*, p. 310.
26. James Mill, "'The Greatest Happiness Principle'," in *Utilitarian Logic and Politics: James Mill's 'Essay on Government,' and Macauley's Critique and the Ensuing Debate*, eds. Jack Lively and John Rees (Oxford: Oxford University Press, 1979), p. 149.
27. Bentham, *Deontology*, p. 183, 186.

sures. Most of the pleasures he described were not physical, and most often he wrote of the sensations that "accompany" an activity, suggesting thereby that he did not think of them as separable from the activity. James Mill did write that "acts are performed, not for their own sake, but for the sake of their consequences," but this was in a context where it is clear he was referring to an act as a "muscular contraction," whereas it was his view, as it was that of Bentham and John Stuart Mill, that a full-fledged act is a movement together with an intention. And, in another place, he did agree that there are acts in the full sense that we like and seek for their own sakes.[28] It is surely open to a utilitarian to adopt such a view, and I believe it evident that John Stuart Mill explicitly held such a view and gave an elaborate account of how it is possible.[29]

These points would invalidate the claim of Charles Taylor that utilitarianism must value acts solely "as a function of the consequences they have." On Taylor's view, this leads to the conclusion, among others, that we could not value integrity for itself. We may, he says, value it for its effects, but this cannot be the whole story: "It will certainly matter to us intrinsically as well as consequentially."[30] But this is to mistake the theory of value one holds with the theory of right action. To be sure, the *rightness* of an act, according to the utilitarian, is a function of its consequences -- the values that are produced or maintained by the act. But the *value* of the act need not rest on its consequences, and, we have seen how it is possible to regard acts as having value in themselves.

It would be well to direct our attention to the views of John Stuart Mill, as there is an aspect of the standard critique of classical utilitarianism that I do not believe Bentham's version fully addresses. Contemporary critics have been concerned not merely with the possibility that by virtue of a lack of concern with distributions, the theory could result in the utter *sacrifice* of some for the greater good -- a point made by John Rawls.[31] The account of Bentham just given surely makes that possibility close to being only logical at most. But there has been no reason to think that just the *right* distributions will result, and, in particular, ones that are sensitive to basic rights that people have. Bentham's well known opposition to rights independent of an institutional setting makes such an account unlikely to be forthcoming. Mill, on the other hand, had a well considered view about rights and their role in practical reasoning that I think is capable of accounting for most of the rights

---

28. James Mill, *A Fragment on Mackintosh* (London: Longmans, Green, Reader, and Dyer, 1870), p. 310. The point that acts *In the Full Sense* can be objects of liking and dislike for their own sakes is made at p. 85.
29. I have discussed this in HJF, especially, p. 146.
30. Charles Taylor, "The Diversity of Goods," in *Utilitarianism and Beyond*, p. 144.
31. Rawls, *A Theory of Justice*, pp. 22-27. Also, Nozick, *Anarchy, State, and Utopia*, pp. 30-33.

the critics want to press. Where it cannot do so, I rather suspect the critics are the ones who are wrong. Let us turn, then, to consider the Millian contribution.

III. The Contribution of J. S. Mill

Early in *Utilitarianism*, Mill wrote: "By happiness is intended pleasure, and the absence of pain; by unhappiness, pain, and the privation of pleasure."[32] This has almost universally been accepted as Mill's endorsement of Bentham's theory of value. And, it has been held that this theory is inconsistent with Mill's later endorsement of a distinction between "higher" and "lower" pleasures. But immediately after the sentence quoted, Mill wrote that "much more requires to be said; in particular, what things it includes in the ideas of pain and pleasure."[33] The discussion that ensues reveals that what he took to have ultimate value is happiness, composed of pleasure, perhaps, but requiring certain kinds rather than others. The underlying notion, I have argued, is that happiness consists in whatever is requisite for the exercise and fulfillment of our special capacities as human beings, as well as the provision of those things we require as the unique individuals that we all are. Creatures with the faculties of human beings cannot be well off without the pleasures of their specifically human faculties of intelligence and sociality. The point of the "higher pleasure/lower pleasure" distinction is that happiness arises in the development and exercise of what is peculiar to our natures and that these include the sense of freedom and whatever is requisite for human dignity.[34] On this conception, living an autonomous, self-determining life just *is* living well, hence, freedom is intrinsically good, and autonomy, *described* by Mill as requisite for dignity, is desirable for its own sake, *as well as* for whatever good consequences it produces by way of enabling us to better achieve our individual ends.

We should note that this conception of well-being does not leave all pleasures on a par. Not only will we be able to distinguish silly or momentary or trivial pleasures from deep needs, we shall have grounds for wanting to guarantee or protect those aspects of well-being that are essential. This notion -- that there are some things that are crucial to well-being that must be provided special protection -- can provide the foothold

---

32. John Stuart Mill, *Utilitarianism*, in *Collected Works* (Toronto: University of Toronto Press, 1967), X, p. 210.
33. *Ibid.*
34. *Ibid.* p. 212.

for a serious theory of rights. Indeed, it will not only provide a foothold, but a basis for distinguishing *what* rights should be recognized and how they are to be weighed against one another in cases of conflict. There is reason to believe that any rights-based theory that does not consist in the bare assertion that certain rights exist will depend on just such an account of human good.[35] Let us turn, then, to Mill's account of rights.

Crucial to Mill's views on rights is his emphasis on the role of rules in practical decision-making. There has been considerable controversy in recent years over whether Mill's moral *theory* was act- or rule-utilitarian. As these terms are commonly defined, I think it is fairly clear that his theory was not, strictly speaking, either. Each theory implies that every act is morally right or wrong, whereas Mill appears to have held that self-regarding acts do not raise issues of moral duty. I have examined the evidence for various accounts of his moral theory and have concluded that no account is likely to find definitive support. What I think *can* be said with some assurance is that his view concerning *practical* decision-making was that generally useful rules would be relied on, except for exceptional cases where a great deal is at stake and calculation of consequences can be relied on.[36] I have argued that such a position is open even to an act-utilitarian to adopt, and many of the critics of classical utilitarianism are willing to concede that it is open to act-utilitarians, at least at the level of social policy, to adopt even strictly applied rules.[37]

The arguments for utilitarians to rely on rules are well-known -- the difficulties of case-by-case calculation, the difficulties of assessing the effects on general rule-observance, the importance of developing general habits and states of character, and so on. But, there is a further reason to stress the importance of one class of rules in Mill's case, viz., the rules of justice. These are rules that define *rights* that people have. Mill's idea was that there are *certain* interests that people have that are so crucial to well-being that they should be protected as a matter of general rule. Rules forbidding people from harming one another, taking others' property, and so on, guarantee security. Moreover, he indicated that among the most important rules of justice are the rules that protect freedom. Furthermore, I have argued that his various writings on social and economic justice are best understood as attempts to argue in terms of those rights that are crucial for preserving one's status as an autonomous person.[38]

I believe that such an account can go a long way toward meeting many of the common objections to utilitarian accounts of justice. Of course, the value theory it presupposes is markedly different from that

35. See L. W. Sumner, "Rights Denaturalized," in *Utility and Rights*, pp. 20-41.
36. The various positions are canvassed and assessed in HJF, ch. 3.
37. See, e.g., Sartorious, "Persons and Property."
38. See, HJF, ch. 4.

which the critics typically foist on the classical view. But to some, it will still appear unsatisfactory because it gives rights a "derivative" status, a status dependent on facts about human nature. As I suspect that the most defensible rights-based theories ultimately depend on such facts also, I am not much moved by this objection. However, it is sometimes also stressed that what is wrong with the utilitarian account is that it can give no intrinsic value to rights. Their value is assessed solely by their contribution to the general well-being. Now I believe it is possible to develop the Millian account in ways (which Mill did not) that permit the utilitarian to go some distance in meeting this further objection.

Recognized rights of the strong kind the critics favor tend to appear in modern complex societies where conflicts of interests tend more to be highlighted. In any such society that incorporates even a rudimentary system of rights, those rights are strongly connected with one's sense of one's worth as a person. One's status is defined and protected by those rights and one asserts and maintains dignity by "standing on rights." The violation of a right is an affront to dignity *as such*. An act of respecting or of violating a right expresses the agent's regard for the rightholder; it has value or disvalue in itself. I have already argued that the consequentialist can consistently ascribe *value* to whatever he or she thinks *has* value, including actions, and surely ones that express regard, concern, respect, are desired for their own sakes, regardless of whatever further consequences they produce. Insofar as such acts have features that are inseparable from *those* particular acts, and we value those features, the acts themselves are valued.[39] Of course, being committed to a consequentialist theory of *right*, the theorist must always regard it as a meaningful question whether the right in a particular case *should* be respected. But in making that decision, he or she can surely consider the value of the act in and of itself, and if that value is one of the most important kinds that go to comprise human well-being -- the value of dignity -- then considerable weight would be given to that value alone, apart from such further considerations as system-related effects, and so on.

I do not know if such a moral theory can ultimately survive various objections that could be fashioned to its special features. I believe this brief survey of some of the classical thinkers reveals that the standard criticisms seriously misrepresent the features of their theories. As Mill himself remarked: "There is no difficulty in proving any ethical standard whatever to work ill if we suppose universal idiocy to be conjoined with

---

39. As Nicholas White has made clear to me, this may mislead some readers to suppose that the acts have a value apart from anyone's valuations, needs, wants or desires. But, whatever values inhere in the acts acquire their value, on the theory, in the same way as all other values, i.e., as being ultimately connected with human wants, needs or desires.

it." I would urge that there are more lessons to be learned from the classical utilitarians if we would only give them credit for having a bit more sense than it is customary to suppose them to have had.

Fairness to Indirect Utilitarianism

Richard Brandt
University of Michigan

Anyone who wonders how much to give for the starving in Africa, or whether to have an abortion, must want to have some guidance, different from reliance on isolated personal intuitions or analogical inference from these, of some justified general normative theory. No one denies that utilitarianism at least purports to be such a theory. But critics find it an unconvincing theory. All species seem to come in for vigorous criticism. In what follows I wish to concentrate attention on one variety of what I take to be the oldest species of the theory, one explained and defended by Berkeley, and also present in the work of Hutcheson. The particular variety of this species of theory on which I wish to concentrate I think finds fullest expression in Mill's *Utilitarianism*. All varieties of this species have recently come in for criticism. For instance, quite recently T. M. Scanlon wrote that the species in general, which we may call "indirect" or "rule" utilitarianism, "strikes most people as an unstable compromise," an evaluation which Professor Foot seems to underwrite.[1] I wish to address some recent objections raised against this sort of theory, with my own Mill-type variety in mind, and see what there is to them.

---

1. P. Foot, "Utilitarianism and the Virtues," *Mind* 94 (1985), p. 196.

I. What Is Indirect (Rule) Utilitarianism?

All utilitarianisms are normative theories, although some utilitarians have thought their normative thesis is entailed by a correct analysis of the meanings of ethical terms, for instance, Moore. All the forms of utilitarianism are agreed that whether an action is right or wrong is some function of desirable consequences, although perhaps a complex function. But how is a "desirable" consequence, or "utility," to be defined? Traditionally it was taken for granted that happiness, possibly in a broad sense, is the only thing desirable for itself, and hence to be viewed as synonymous with "utility." In recent years this view has been attacked, and most contemporary writers urge defining "utility" or "intrinsically desirable" in terms of *preferences,* actual or restricted in some way.[2] There are difficulties in this theory, and it has even been argued that it cannot be given a coherent formulation, but writers like Griffin[3] and Scanlon[4] have suggested lines along which such a theory might perhaps be worked out plausibly. However that may be, this issue seems to be one common to all types of utilitarianism, and hence I propose to ignore it here, and, for better or worse, consider utility to be definable in terms of happiness, as traditional writers did. More specifically, I shall take *total* utility to be the sum-total of life-time happiness of all sentient creatures who do or will exist. Some writers would take exception to this, following Sidgwick, but I propose to ignore the pros and cons on this point.

Utilitarians do or can agree among themselves that an act is the *best* act if it maximizes total happiness more than any other open to the agent -- or, in case happiness can be maximized only by some cooperative strategy of several persons, then the execution of this strategy by each will be the best act. And, they do or can agree that the *rational* act is the one which, on the evidence available to the agent, will maximize expectable happiness. But how about the concepts of the moral, or of the *morally right* act? The older (theological) utilitarians introduced this notion by reference to the will of God: what God requires on pain of punishment is one's *moral duty,* and what God requires is related in some way to human happiness because God is benevolent and wishes to maximize total happiness. What they thought God requires is conformity to a rule, the conformity to which by everyone would do the most good in the long run -- a view marking them as rule-utilitarians of a sort. This theological conception of God's law was replaced by more modern writers like Mill

---

2. R. Brandt, "Two Concepts of Utility," in H. B. Miller and W. H. Williams (eds.), *The Limits of Utilitarianism,* 1982, University of Minnesota Press, Minneapolis.
3. J. Griffin, "On Life's Being Valuable," *Dialectics and Humanism* 8 (1981), No. 2
4. T. M. Scanlon, "Preference and Urgency," *Journal of Philosophy* 72 (1975).

by a secular notion: by the idea of the requirements of a *social moral code*. Thus Mill wrote: "We do not call anything wrong unless we mean to imply that a person ought to be punished in some way or other for doing it -- if not by law, by the opinion of his fellow creatures; if not by opinion, by the reproaches of his own conscience. This seems the real turning point of the distinction between morality and simple expediency."[5] On this view, an action is wrong not because God forbids it and will punish infractions, but because it will be punished by disapproval of others and guilt feelings, in other words, by the prevalent social moral code. On Mill's view, the *optimal* social moral code is the one the prevalence of which would be utility-maximizing. That fact makes him a rule-utilitarian of a sort. Other rule-utilitarians, e.g., John Harsanyi, say that a morally right act is one which conforms to correct "rules," which are those, the *following of which by everybody* would yield the highest possible social utility, it being assumed that everyone can figure out what these rules will be.[6]

II. What Is a Personal Moral Code?

It will be helpful to digress briefly and explain the conception of a "moral code" which Mill seems to have had in mind -- forgetting the part about law (since it may be desirable that the law punish over-parking, but this fact hardly makes over-parking a matter of morality.) I think Mill would say, and I think it is reasonable today (although not uncontroversial) to affirm that subscribing to a moral system is primarily to have a certain *set* of *motivational* dispositions regarding certain *types of action*. For instance, if a person thinks breach of promise *prima facie* wrong, it will be true of him (1) that he will have some *aversion* to any breach of promise by him, for no self-interested reason (and, as being basic, not derivative from any other moral aversion); (2) that he will tend to feel guilty or remorseful if he fails to keep a promise (and what Ross called "compunction" even if the totality of his moral aversions moves him not to keep the promise in a concrete situation); that (3) he will *disapprove* and, in more serious cases, be *indignant* toward a person who fails to keep a promise; and finally (4) that he will believe these dispositions justified in some appropriate way.[7] From now on I shall refer

---

5. J. S. Mill, *Utilitarianism*, ch. 5.
6. J. Harsanyi, "Rule Utilitarianism and Decision Theory," *Erkenntnis* II (1977) p. 32.
7. This view is similar to that of K. Baier, "Moral Obligation," *American Philosophical Quarterly* 3 (1966), 210-26.

to this complex as a person's "moral code." We might call (1) the strictly "motivational" part of a person's moral code, and (2) and (3) the "reactive" part. In most societies the reactive parts will not be aroused toward the agent of an act if it was "excused," that is, occurred in circumstances such as to block the normal inference from act to the level of the agent's moral aversions. Some "strict liability" moralities do not have this feature, e.g., the Greece which sympathized with Ulysses' slaying of all his wife's suitors.[8] Of course, a person's moral code may be much more finely honed, say, for example, than just to contain an aversion to breach of promise. A person may be motivated differently depending (as Ross suggested)[9] on whether the promise was recently made, was solemnly made, made in response to a deliberate and fraudulent misrepresentation, etc.

Motivations pro or contra certain act-types can direct behavior contrary to the non-moral wishes of the agent -- unless the non-moral motivation is stronger, in which case the agent will not conform. Sometimes, of course, moral motivations will pull an agent in different directions. In such a case, if an agent, on reflection, eventually finds himself leaning in one direction, he will be apt to say to himself, "That is my duty," and when he does this he will activate a strong secondary aversion (etc.) to failing to perform that act. He may do this even when there was no conflict. So, at any rate, in the conscientious person, the desire to do one's duty is obviously not the only moral motivation in his code. Of course, much verbal reflection may go on in a concrete situation, with the effect of highlighting relevant features of the situation, so that the moral aversions to them are activated. In conflict situations, a person may feel it necessary to identify the features of a situation which make him inclined as he is, and possibly to formulate corresponding principles; and he may be led to question why he should be motivated as he is.

We can say that a person's moral code *requires* a certain act if the total moral motivation would, if not conflicting with non-moral motivation, bring the act about, and if failure to bring it about would normally arouse guilt or disapproval.

We might want to include as part of a person's "morality" that he admires good acts not morally required, but which manifest to a high degree some moral motivation required only to a lower degree; but I shall not expand on this.

Moral aversions are rather similar to other motivations which may lead to the same actions. For instance, I have a friend who is ill in a hospital. I go to visit him, not because I think I shall have a good time, but because, caring for him, I want him to be cheered up by my visit. Of

---

8. A. W. H. Adkins, *Merit and Responsibility* (Oxford: Clarendon Press, 1960), pps. 53-57.
9. W. D. Ross, *Foundations of Ethics* (Oxford: Clarendon Press, 1939), 100-1.

course, I could have seen this act as a significant service to another at small cost to me, thereby engaging moral motivation -- not that I need *say* to myself, "This is my duty," a judgment that activates a further motive. A morally sensitive person, then, may do the very same thing a caring friend would do; the difference is that moral motivation concerns *act-types* not general affection for friends, and that we morally condemn its absence. Here morality is a "back-up" system. If I were not impelled by caring for my friend, I would have done the same thing from moral motivation. The act is surely better done out of moral motivation than not done at all.[10]

The *moral code* of a *society* can be defined as a kind of statistical artifact: a profile of the typical moral codes of its members. Its moral *system* includes this but is wider: it includes the methods of sustaining its moral code over time -- teaching children, etc. In estimating the *cost* of a moral system we must include all this -- as well as the cost to agents of their moral commitments spilling over into areas it is better they not be, neurotic guilt-feelings, and so on. My kind of rule-utilitarian affirms that an action is morally right if it is permitted by the social moral *system* which would maximize (expectable) utility.

III. The Contrast Between
Act and Rule Utilitarianisms.

Act utilitarianism and my kind of rule utilitarian can agree, I think, that a *morally right* act is one permitted by the moral system which maximizes (expectable?) utility. In this they follow Mill. But why should they make this move from permission by a utility-maximizing moral system to moral rightness at all? At this point, I think, one thing the utilitarian may do is dilate on the fact that people who have moral motivations think them *justified*. But what is it to be "justified?" Here I think the utilitarian may go in for some metaethics, specifically for deciding what, all facts about man and moral codes taken into account, is the best reconstruction of the term "justified." He will want to consider whether a "justified" moral attitude is one that would be chosen from a Rawlsian original position, or by a fully rational person, or by an Ideal Observer, or by a person requiring moral prescriptions to be universalizable in Hare's sense. Or he may follow Mill's route, or some other one. Whichever route he chooses, he will then go on to affirm that a

---

10. See the discussion by Marcia Baron, "The Alleged Moral Repugnance of Acting from Duty," *Journal of Philosophy* 81 (1984), 197-220.

moral system that maximizes expectable utility has the property of being "justified," as he has reconstructed that term.

But why should one say that the "morally right" act is one permitted by the *justified* moral system, or the "morally obligatory" act one required by the justified moral system? Why go along with Mill in contrasting "morally obligatory" with "expedient?" The right answer seems to be that specifically moral language is used *within* a moral system, just as the term "illegal" is a term used within the law to apply to acts forbidden by it. We do need terms to mark the fact that in a given moral system some act is required on pain of justified guilt and disapproval, as distinct from just saying it is expedient. Moreover, we need this distinction because it can be that an act which is by itself expedient is not an act which would be required by a utility-maximizing moral system, when we make a total cost-benefit analysis of moral systems, taking into account the cost of teaching, undesirable psychological effects, and so on.

If we agreed on this, we may then locate the real point of disagreement between act and rule utilitarians. The act utilitarian thinks that the utility-maximizing social moral system (which identifies right acts) consists in just one moral motivation; to do what in the circumstances will maximize expectable utility. The rule-utilitarian (my kind) holds that the utility-maximizing social moral system (which identifies right acts) is a plural set of motivations -- the ones the moral system including which will maximize (expectable?) utility when applied in practice. Will these alternative proposals lead in practice to different forms of behavior? There has been controversy about this. But it seems the right answer is affirmative; for instance the rule-utilitarian will think it wrong to break a promise in order to realize a marginal benefit (to one's self), whereas the act utilitarian will deny this. I am assuming, of course, that we can know it would be a bad rule to permit breach of promise in cases of this sort.

It has sometimes been argued that prevalence of the one-principle act-utilitarian moral system obviously would have worse consequences than some kind of rule-utilitarianism. But I think this comparison is not as simple as at first it may seem. For act-utilitarians will point to inductively supported rules of thumb about which types of action tend to produce the most good. The agent, according to him, should bear these rules in mind, although there is no agreement about when an agent should follow one of these rules, and then follow his own judgment based on his total evidence. Heavy reliance on these inductive rules may bring the act-utilitarian closer to the rule-utilitarian conclusions. Still there is a difference. The act-utilitarian is using inductive inference to find which act will not maximize utility, whereas the rule-utilitarian is asking which act is required by that moral system, prevalence in the agent's society will be optimal in the long run. Evidently the inductive evidence might be that more good is done if a promise is broken in this situation -- an event which will presumably have little effect on future practice and expectations. Whereas it might be clear that a moral system permitting -- and being known to permit -- breach of promise in this type of situation might not be utility maximizing.

A good deal has been written about benefits of life in a society of committed rule-utilitarians, as compared with a society of committed act-utilitarians. It has been argued that persons of rule-utilitarian persuasion will behave more predictably, and hence we shall be able to plan accordingly. And it is true that we may count on committed rule-utilitatians having high concern for promise keeping. But, while it is true that we can identify many moral principles which intelligent agents of rule-utilitarian persuasion will try to live by, it is also true that there are areas in which such prediction will not be easy. It is one thing to have the concept of an optimal moral system, but quite another thing to identify its exact content. Will all convinced rule-utilitarians come out at the same place -- even on such a matter as when it is justified to break a promise? Moreover, the convinced rule-utilitarian will want to keep up to date his views about what a utility-maximizing moral system will be like. Will it be easy to predict what he will think should be the utility-maximizing moral system in view of advanced types of amniocentesis? (I incline to think that these arguments about predictability have some force, but we shall see that some writers come to exactly the opposite conclusion.)

It will be evident from the foregoing remarks that I consider it is part of being fair to indirect utilitarianism, that we do not think the supporting arguments better than they are.

It may be worthwhile to explain why I think it better to define rule-utilitarianism in terms of a utility-maximizing *moral system* as I do, than in terms of the optimality of *universal behavior* in conformity with certain rules, as the theological utilitarians seemed to hold and as has been proposed b y John Harsanyi, and in his case with the farther assumption that everyone would know what this optimal system is and that at least morally committed people would follow it. First, my proposal permits and encourages counting the cost of teaching a certain moral system, both in terms of the difficulty of conditioning and the psychological impact on the individual. Second, it leads to the idea that different moral motivations may be set at different levels of strength; and we don't want motivations set so high as to guarantee that certain behavior will occur in all cases. It is not only *behavior* which can be desirable. Third, differences of strength enable us to make a sense of moral intuitions in case of a conflict of rules -- the strongest one being the one we take to be our duty. Fourth, although here the difference may be slight, we might want to talk of a moral code which is optimal even if nobody in fact follows it or knows its content.

IV. Objections to Rule-Utilitarianism

I begin a review of influential objections to rule-utilitarianism by considering some which strike me as less weighty.

First, Professor Williams' critique in his 1973 volume (with Smart)[11] deserves review, although he never explicitly defines what he thinks the rule-utilitarian theory ought to be. Indeed, he seems doubtful whether the implications for action of this theory differ from those of act-utilitarianism. In the end, however, he seems to accept roughly the contrast drawn above.

His main objection, however, is that[12] indirect utilitarianism, in retiring to a more indirect level, and urging only that moral motivations be adopted which are optimific, leaves it "entirely open whether they are themselves of a distinctively utilitarian kind." In that case, he says, "I hold that utilitarianism has disappeared, and that the residual position is not worth calling utilitarian." He cites Rawls as taking the same line.[13] But, as I see it, Williams is here leaving out of account the fact that the correct rules, for the rule utilitarian, are those which are identified as those which maximize expectable utility, so that the thesis is far from deserting the centrality of the concept of utility-maximization. Williams seems to be moved by the fact that utility *may* not be *mentioned* by *most* of the rules of an optimific code.

I turn now to objections more widely mentioned, and perhaps more weighty.

(1) The Alleged Irrationality of 'Rule Worship.'

Various writers follow J. J. C. Smart in thinking that "to refuse to break a generally beneficial rule in those cases in which it is not most beneficial to obey it seems irrational and to be case a of rule-worship."[14] Professor Foot says, "Surely it will be irrational, we feel, to obey even the most useful rule if in a particular instance we clearly see that such obedience will not *have the best results*."[15] (Both seem to be objecting to

---

11. Bernard Williams in J. J. C. Smart and B. Williams, *Utilitarianism: For and Against* (London: Cambridge University Press, 1973), pp. 118-35.
12. *ibid.*, p. 134 f.
13. *Theory of Justice* (Cambridge: Harvard University Press, 1971), 182-5.
14. J. J. C. Smart and B. Williams, *op. cit.* p. 10
15. P. Foot, *loc. cit.*, p. 198.

requiring a person to keep a promise when it would be marginally beneficial because of benefit to the promisor.)

Anyone who thinks a rule-utilitarian morality would require
actions knowably productive of seriously bad consequences may be over-
looking what an optimal set of moral principles would be like. Surely
everyone can know that an optimal morality would direct doing what is
necessary to avoid, say, a nuclear disaster. The Supreme Court has
regularly construed the force of the (absolute?) rights listed in the
Constitution in such a way as to permit preventing social disaster.[16] We
should also remember that among the optimal moral principles will be
"Everything being equal, do not harm other persons," and "Give aid to
those in distress when this can be done without excessive cost to yourself."

Still, the rule-utilitarian should admit that sometimes a rule-
utilitarian morality will require producing less good than would application of the act-utilitarian standard. Is this irrational? The answer is that
the rule-utilitarian is advocating his type of morality because he thinks it
is the best long-range strategy for maximizing utility, and that insistence
on conforming to it will in the long run produce more good than permitting exceptions whenever the agent thinks it would be beneficial to depart
from it. Do the critics not want a program with long-term benefits?

David Lyons has argued[17] that there is at least an embarrassment
here for the rule-utilitarian, for, as a utilitarian, he thinks actions should
maximize the good; yet he affirms that an agent may be morally required
to perform actions he knows will fail to do this. But, if a utilitarian has
decided that acceptance of a certain set of principles, by himself and
others, is optimal *in the long run,* it would be strange for him to turn
around and advocate departing from it in an individual case. It is true he
could *teach* a rule-utilitarianism morality for the sake of long-range utility,
but depart from it in action so as to maximize direct benefits in individual
cases and recommend to his friends to do likewise. But such a strategy,
despite Sidgwick's recommendation, would be counterproductive, as
Professor Gibbard has pointed out.[18] For such a strategy would prevent
the benefits of sincere discussion of moral and political matters, and
undermine one's firm commitment to the basic principles.

Professor Hare thinks it necessary to employ direct appeal to
utilities not only in identifying an optimal morality for one's society (to
which the rule-utilitarian would agree), but also when optimific rules for
society conflict, or when for some reason the requirements of this moral-

16. C. L. Black, Jr., "Mr. Justice Black, the Supreme Court, and the Bill of Rights,"
    Harper's Magazine 222 (1961), 64-68.
17. David Lyons, "Utilitarianism and Rights," *Nomos* 24 (1982), 107-38.
18. A. Gibbard, "Utilitarianism and Human Rights," *Social Philosophy and Policy* 1 (1984),
    101 f.

ity seem profoundly repugnant. The rule-utilitarian need not deny that there are reasons for re-examining what the optimal moral code for his society really is. But what he will insist on is that the difficulty must be resolved by refining his conception of the relevant socially-optimific principles. It is possible that Hare is right in suggesting that he might not be clear just what a rectified general principle would be, beyond seeing that somehow it must deal with a certain case in a certain way.[19]

(2) Difficulties of Identifying
a Utility-Maximizing Moral Code.

It is sometimes said that the difficulty act-utilitarianism has, about identifying which course of action will maximize utility, is exacerbated for the rule-utilitarian theory.[20] Will it not be difficult to decide which *moral system* -- something which affects many people over a long period of time -- would be most beneficial? This charge, however, seems mistaken. Granted a difficulty of knowing whether a given lie in specific circumstances will maximize benefit, it may be easier to show that a moral system will best incorporate a general prima facie obligation to speak the truth, in view of the importance of being able to rely generally on information from others. Imagine the perils of travel in a strange country, if the locals when invited to give directions felt no obligation to tell the truth, but only an obligation to maximize benefit as they saw it, and thought it desirable to discourage visits by outsiders.[21] One may agree that decisions about which priority rules to teach, e.g., about the types of circumstance in which truth-telling must give way to avoiding a certain level of injury, will be hard to document by appeal to the impact on utility. In any case they can hardly be taught except by examples: In this sort of case, keep your promise! But it seems unduly cautious to think we cannot reach reliable results by careful thought. It would be interesting to see, moreover, what alternative moral theories have to offer. The question about which moral rules one would accept in the original position seems no help; to answer the question, one needs to know how it would be to live in a society with a certain set of rules -- essentially the problem here at issue. Act-utilitarians will doubtless advocate relying on rules of thumb,

19. R. M. Hare, *Moral Thinking* (Oxford: Clarendon Press, 1981), p. 51.
20. R. G. Frey, "Act-Utilitarianism, Consequentialism, and Moral Rights," in R. G. Frey (ed.), *Utility and Rights* (Minneapolis: University of Minnesota Press, 1984), 73-80.
21. J. D. Mabbott, "Moral Rules," *Proceedings of the British Academy* 39 (1953), 97-117, especially 116 f.

inductively supported by past correlations between truth-telling and public benefit; but if such rules of thumb can be so supported, then the estimates on which the rule-utilitarian relies can hardly be seriously defective.

(3) The Argument from Integrity.

Professors Williams and Scheffler have objected to utilitarianism on the ground that it "violates" the *integrity* of the individual. And, although they say (in footnotes) that their criticism is not directed against rule-utilitarianism, they do not sympathize with it, do not regard it as giving a reasonable solution to their problem, and prefer to rest a normative theory on different foundations. It is therefore useful for us to take account of their "problem" and reasoning about it.

First, what do they mean by the "integrity" which utilitarianism is supposed to violate? Obviously they do not have in mind the most frequent, moral sense, "having integrity" being a rough synonym of "being honest and conscientious." Williams seems rather to have in mind some kind of wholeness, unimpairedness of the person. In what sense? He seems to think the core of a person is the "attitudes and projects" which a person "takes seriously at the deepest level, as what his life is about." "It is absurd," he says, [for morality?] "to demand of such a man ... that he should just step aside from his own project." (This could include his moral commitments.) He gives a clue to what "project" means by offering a list: "One can be committed to such things as a person, a cause, an institution, one's own genius or the pursuit of danger." These, he says, may be more "permeated with character than the desire for the necessities of life."[22] It is the wholeness of these that morality may not violate.

There are several critical observations to be made about this. (1) Suppose he is thinking of a person's *moral* commitments: say a person's belief that it is morally wrong to engage in war and hence that it is wrong for him to take a position in a munitions factory, or to kill an innocent person, no matter what. What should a person think a utility-maximizing morality will say to a person who concludes these moral stances are misguided? I believe it will obviously be part of a utility-maximizing morality that the sincere moral views of other persons be treated with respect, and that people not be condemned for them unless holding them shows some defect of character. But it will presumably also permit a critic to feel free

---

22. Bernard Williams in Smart and Williams, *op. cit.*, p. 116, 111.

to put forward, to them, his own view and the reasons for it: and free not to encourage executions of the other's moral commitments or even to prevent carrying them into action. (2) But it also seems absurd to say that a person's non-moral projects may not be expected to stand aside on moral grounds. Suppose J. O. Urmson was deeply committed to writing a book at the time his unit was ordered to cover the evacuation of British troops at Dunkerque. Williams seems to be saying he was morally free to slip away, if he could. Perhaps Williams has in mind only less obvious cases, such as that of an artist who leaves his family in order to paint in the South Pacific. If there is such a limitation, one would like to see it all spelled out. (3) The "deep commitments" of some people may be evil, like that of Hitler to exterminate the Jews. Was Hitler morally free to execute his design? Surely Williams needs to qualify his principle. (4) Rule-utilitarians (and Sidgwick) agree that a person is free on utilitarian grounds to pursue his own goals even if he thinks more good would be done if he cooperated with others in pursuing their goals. One way of putting this is to say that freedom to have one's own goals and make plans accordingly (when this is within the bounds of morality) is itself a good.[23] At any rate, the rule-utilitarian will insist that a utility-maximizing moral system will permit and encourage persons to develop and execute their own projects, as well as to feel special obligations to persons with whom they are especially related in one way or another.

Scheffler argues only to a somewhat more qualified conclusion: that agents are permitted morally "to devote energy and attention to their projects and commitments *out of proportion* to the weight from the impersonal standpoint of their doing so . . ." (italics mine).[24] He calls this the "liberation" thesis. (He makes an exception: this permission may be outweighed by the obligation to keep promises except when this would be contrary to the general welfare, since this exception does not "undermine one's integrity, since it would apply only to obligations incurred as a result of one's voluntary action."[25]) He gives no clue to the size of the dispro-portionate weight nor how one might decide a relevant case. He denies, however, that such issues should be decided by appeal to "efficacy of such activity as an instrument of overall benefit,"[26] as the rule-utilitarian would have it.

Scheffler admits that rule-utilitarianism might reach moral verdicts similar to his. But, he says, he is not aiming to evaluate that thesis

23. John Harsanyi, "Some Epistemological Advantages of a Rule Utilitarian Position in Ethics," in P. A. French, T. E. Uehling, Jr., and H. K. Wettstein (eds.) *Midwest Studies in Philosophy* 7 (1982), p. 392.
24. S. Scheffler, *The Rejection of Consequentialism* (Oxford: Clarendon Press, 1982), p. 211
25. *Ibid.,* 23, 86.
26. *Ibid.,* p. 17.

in his book, and wants to show only that there is "independent ground" or "rationale" for his conclusions.[27]

He mentions a "maximization thesis," alternative to the "liberation" thesis stated above, to the effect that a person "should act in a way that will serve to maximize the number of people who are successfully pursuing their projects and plans."[28] This view, he says, is close to his "liberation" thesis, because it requires paying attention to the *number* of persons successfully pursuing their life plans, instead of adopting the straight utilitarian maximization thesis which, in Williams' terms, regards persons as a "sea of preferences."[29] Both theories recognize the fact that morality should "embody a set of demands it is reasonable to make of human agents."[30]

Scheffler says he is not attempting to "give a conclusive proof" of these theses, and indeed is not claiming even that "it is appropriate to seek an objectively correct moral theory."[31] But nevertheless he says that he, as contrasted with the intuitionism of Ross, has a *rationale* for his theses. What is this rationale? He says his proposal "conceives of [personal] independence as an especially important fact . . . and embodies an evidently rational method for taking account of the fact. . . ."[32] The liberation strategy "embodies a rational strategy for taking account of the nature of a person as a being with an independent point of view . . . a fact about human agency." The independence of the personal point of view "fundamentally affects the character of human fulfillment."[33] He sums up by saying that an adequate conception of right "must first of all embody a set of demands it is reasonable to make of human agents. And there may be features of human agents in virtue of which it is rational to require of them something other than the constant production of the best states of affairs or the best overall sets of happenings."[34]

To this, two comments seem in order. (1) It would be inconsistent to adopt this view and criticize rule-utilitarianism as being rule-worship: for this theory also authorizes acting in a way that is not welfare-maximizing. (2) Suppose we agree with him that personal independence is an especially important fact. But why need we think that his proposals are "an evidently rational method for taking account of the fact?" I do not think Scheffler makes clear what "his independent rationale" comes to.

---

27. *Ibid.,* 16, 53.
28. *Ibid.,* 60.
29. Bernard Williams, *Ethics and the Limits of Philosophy* (Cambridge, Mass: Harvard University Press, 1985), p.56.
30. Sheffler, *op. cit.,* 125.
31. *Ibid.,* 65, 67, 125, 126.
32. *Ibid.,* p. 63.
33. *Ibid.,* p. 64.
34. *Ibid.,* 135 f.

(4) The Argument from Justice and Equality.

A standard criticism of utilitarianisms including rule-utilitarianism has been that, when some policy which distributes goods among individuals is evaluated, they affirm that that choice should be made which maximizes benefit. This view has been regarded as wildly counterintuitive. The criticism has mostly been aimed at act-utilitarianism, but the objection, if valid, seems to be a point also against rule-utilitarianism, since at the level of government policy the two types of utilitarianism seem to be at least nearly identical, and some principles for ordinary interpersonal relations, (e.g., whether parents should treat their children equally) appear to involve the same issues. The basic difficulty with the view is often located in the alleged failure to recognize the separateness of persons ("person-merging"); it is thought that the utilitarian regards trading one person's welfare for another as like one person sacrificing one satisfaction (or time of life) for another, the latter not being open to moral criticism (it is thought), but not the former.[35] The issue is unquestionably important practically: for tax/welfare legislation, for the system of criminal law (the criminal sacrificed for the benefit of others, on the deterrence theory?), conscription into the army, decisions whether severely defective infants should be given life-saving treatment in the face of prospective enormous cost to others.

I am going to excuse myself from discussing this issue. It is not a novel criticism, and has been much discussed in the literature. Moreover, I have nothing to add to what I have said in other places.

(5) The Argument from the Problem of Partial Compliance.

A complicating problem is raised for the rule-utilitarian conception as proposed above, by the fact there may be, in a society, not merely imperfect but *very* partial compliance with the optimal (on the rule-utilitarian view) moral code. (It is also a problem for Rawls.)[36] Suppose a certain moral principle is in fact part of an expectable-utility-maximizing moral system for a given society: and suppose that therefore this principle identifies which actions are morally right or wrong, if the

---

35. H. L. A. Hart, "Between Utility and Rights," first published 1973; reprinted in H. L. A. Hart, *Essays in Jurisprudence and Philosophy* (Oxford: Clarendon Press, 1983), 199 ff.
36. J. Rawls *op. cit.*, 303 ff.

rule-utilitarian theory is correct, justified in the way a normative theory can be. But suppose now a great many people in this society have discrepant moral commitments, e.g., embrace racial discrimination or oppose inter-racial marriage, and think their view is justified somehow. Or perhaps at least a great many people will not conform in *behavior* to the system that would be optimal if there were strict compliance. Might it not cause great harm for the rule-utilitarian to follow the optimal moral code in this situation, and will he not, therefore, as a utilitarian, refrain from following his rule-utilitarian commitments? Does this show that the expectable-utility-maximizing system for the society, if there were complete agreement and compliance, cannot be seriously said to be a person's moral duty? A disposition to perform acts of certain types (or feel guilty, disapprove of others, etc.) which would otherwise be beneficial may not be at all desirable if the moral code of which it is part is not shared by others. That is a real problem.

I think the solution to it is to show that such suppositious cases are compelling only if we suppose an unduly simple conception of moral rules, and of their prevalence. What is needed for a solution of the problem is to show that a rule can be formulated such that *both* (1) it is optimific if prevalent in the society as a whole, and (2) it is also optimific if prevalent only among a minority, perhaps a minority of one.

It is judicious to bear in mind, however, that in fact partial compliance will reach relatively few issues. Contemporary individuals will agree morally to almost all the prohibitions of the criminal law in the states of the U. S. A. Nor will they fail to agree that there should be some uniform law about enforcement of contracts. But as Feinberg[37] and others have pointed out, following the optimal moral code in a society which is fiercely intolerant of some of the components of a code, optimal if prevalent, may lead to serious strife. So one question the rule-utilitarian must face is what the theory is to recommend for a situation of this sort. In discussing this issue I shall help myself to ideas in the work of Roy Harrod and Donald Regan.

We must ask how a moral code which would be optimal if there were strict compliance might also be optimal for a committed few if there were neither strict compliance nor agreement about some principle which would be optimal if there were strict compliance. Suppose one lives in South Africa. It seems clear that the long-range-utility-maximizing moral system will be one prohibiting race discrimination. But now? Let us consider the person (group) which already accepts the moral principle of non-discrimination. Let us then consider how much good and how much harm will be done, in the long run, for this group (or individual) to stand

---

37. J. Feinberg, "Review of the Forms and Limits of Utilitarianism," *Philosophical Review* 76 (1967), 383-8.

up and be counted as condemning race discrimination and refuse to practice it in their own affairs, as contrasted with submitting to the accepted code, or taking some compromise stance. An important reason for standing up is the reflection that if no one does, race discrimination may persist for a long time. Further, although a single person may not be able to do much to change the status quo, his example may inspire others to join the cause. For more substantial good to be done, however, it appears that an individual must identify, as far as possible, others with the same aspiration, and join forces with them in an integrated program of education, demonstrations, etc. What it is welfare-maximizing to do will depend on the size of the group. Perhaps the well-being maximizing strategy for a given group will be something of a compromise: say, avoiding the most offensive things such as interracial sexual contacts, but writing and speaking and demonstrating in favor of a completely nondiscriminatory system. Suppose it will be optimific if this group adopts some such strategy. (It could be that the cost to some individuals -- or their families -- would be so large that doing the optimific thing would be for them a supererogatory act, or excused even if not justified by necessity.) Then why not say that this strategy is the one they are morally bound to follow?

Is there any way in which we might say that such a stance can be part of the optimal morality for the *society as a whole*? The answer seems to be that the *optimal* morality for the society will include *disjunctive rules* (as part of the basic motivations of the optimal conscience), with the first part of the disjunct having prior force, such as: Treat everyone as deserving equal respect as a person; but in case such conduct would produce serious social harm, then do what it is utility-maximizing, for all of society (future as well as present), for you (your group) to do, as a means to social change. If we think such rules are optimific, then the optimific moral code for a society, in some situations or at some stage of development, will need to be more complex than we at first thought.

Is this conception really a capitulation to act-utilitarianism, since it is now said that a person (group) is to do what a benefit-maximizing strategy would call on them to do? I think not. The conception appears only as part of a complex rule, part of which applies only if most people are not complying with and oppose the first part of the rule. Moreover, the activity of the individual (group) can be viewed as essentially *teaching*, and the rule to be taught is "No racial discrimination except. . . ." They are aiming to get the optimal code accepted, and when it has been the escape clause can fall into desuetude, and the second clause will apply only when there is not compliance with the first part.

But can any such set of disjunctive rules be successfully taught to any large proportion of the population? If not, one of the criteria for identifying a benefit-maximizing *moral system* -- that it can be taught and taught without prohibitive cost -- seems to be infringed. Can *everyone* absorb a principle like "Do this if condition A obtains; but if B obtains, do that?" It is possible that we cannot teach such a kind of motivation to all. Perhaps we cannot teach it to children or maybe persons with an I. Q. below 100, but this fact should only serve to stimulate the rule-utilitarian to be a bit more precise (and less demanding) when he says the *right* act is one permitted by a moral code the *prevalence* of which in the agent's society would be optimific. There is a trade-off here. If the rule-utilitarian insists that an act is right only if permitted by a moral code the prevalence of which, in a sense requiring that it was or could be learned and interiorized by *absolutely everyone* in the society without prohibitive cost, would maximize expectable utility, he may find himself with a crude and minimal set of prohibitions. Alternatively, we can say that a moral code is prevalent (accepted), even if we know that not all of it can be interiorized by some procedure to everyone without prohibitive cost, if at all. Then when we say that an act is wrong if it would be prohibited by a code the acceptance of which would be optimific, we may get a code which is reasonably sensible. I suggest that the rational course for a rule-utilitarian to take is the latter. This would be consistent with the utilitarians's view that the social institution of morality be utility-maximizing.

But perhaps we go too far if we disparage the possibility of learning such a complex morality. It may be that such a principle is no more difficult to learn than when and how strongly a promise is binding, or in which situations a person is not subject to moral disapproval for not fulfilling one -- complications which seem to be learned very well by the time most people in our society become adults. In fact, it seems that, as things are, reflective educated and conscientious people have consciences -- moral motivations -- along the complex line I have suggested for race-discrimination. Civil rights leaders and civil disobedience groups appear to think exactly in this way. Most or all of the principles which moral people actually find persuasive in situations of conflicting views of this sort are ones it maximizes benefit to have in the moral code of the community.

Does all of the above imply that a person who does not object to race discrimination should be condemned as immoral by those who do? As hinted earlier, only in certain circumstances -- it *could* be that their view is not a consequence of any defect of character (but being so obtuse to the suffering of others may itself be one). But it might be utility-maximizing for the anti-discrimination persons to express condemnation of them, as the only way of making their point effectively, even though they do not feel disapproval because they think the view of these people is excused. Or, if condemnation is a bit dishonest (albeit a dishonesty which would have the blessing of Sidgwick), they can at least honestly say that these persons are failing in their moral duty. (To say that it is one's duty not to do A is the same as to say it is reprehensible to do *A without an excuse.*)

The normative (moral) implications of this and the preceding responses to alleged difficulties for rule-utilitarianism appear to have implications which correspond at least roughly with the convictions of thoughtful people, in reflective equilibrium -- for whatever force that fact may have.

A Contemporary Natural-Law Ethics

Germain Grisez
Mount Saint Mary's College
Emmitsburg, Maryland

1. Introduction

In 1959, I began working on ethical theory by studying St. Thomas on natural law. Over the years, I made the modifications required by modern and contemporary problems, phenomenological descriptions of moral realities, linguistic clarifications of relevant expressions, and a constant effort at critical reflection and systematization. Other philosophers, especially Joseph M. Boyle, Jr., and John Finnis, have been helping with this work. The theory we are developing is *a* -- not *the* -- contemporary natural-law ethics.

This paper only summarizes the theory. For its further explanation and defense, those interested may look into works listed in the bibliography.

Like consequentialist, Kantian, and other natural-law theories of morality, ours is cognitivist but not intuitionist. We think there are true moral principles from which the most specific moral norms can be deduced and by which judgments of conscience can be criticized. The theory we propose is less familiar than its consequentialist and Kantian alternatives, and can be initially situated by reference to them.

Consequentialist theories are teleological; they try to ground moral judgments in human well-being. Kantian theories are deontological; they try to ground moral judgments in the rational nature of the moral subject, whose inherent dignity they emphasize. Teleology appeals to many because it does not absolutize morality but subordinates it to a wider human flourishing. But deontology also has its appeal, for it tries to defend the absolute dignity of human persons, especially against any attempt to justify using some as mere means to the goals of others.

Our theory tries to combine the strengths and avoid the weaknesses of teleology and deontology. Morality, we hold, is grounded in human goods -- the goods of real people living in the world of experience. Still, each person's dignity is protected by moral absolutes, and it never is right to treat anyone as a mere means.

2. The Idea of Basic Human Goods

In the widest sense in which the word "good" is applied to human actions and their principles it refers to anything a person can in any way desire. But people desire many things -- e.g., pleasure, wealth, and power -- whose very pursuit seems to empty a person and to divide persons from one another. However, there are other goods -- e.g., knowledge of the truth and living in friendship -- whose pursuit of itself seems to promote persons and bring them together. Goods like these are real parts of the integral fulfillment of persons. We call them "basic human goods" -- *basic* not to survival but to fulfillment.

Some goods are definite objectives, desired states of affairs -- e.g., losing twenty pounds, getting an enemy to surrender, or successfully completing a research project. But in themselves the basic human goods -- e.g., health, peace, or knowledge of the truth -- are not definite objectives. Pursuit of these goods never ends, for they cannot be attained finally and completely. Interest in them goes beyond particular objectives sought for their sake, for they transcend states of affairs which instantiate them. It follows that persons acting alone and in various forms of community can contribute to the realization of such goods and share in them, but can never become wholly identified with them.

But if the basic human goods are not definite objectives, how do they guide action? By providing the reasons to consider some possibilities choiceworthy opportunities. An enemy's surrender becomes an objective to be pursued because of the belief that it will contribute to peace; the loss of twenty pounds is sought, perhaps, for the sake of health; particular projects of theoretical research are carried out in the hope that their results will advance knowledge. These reasons for choosing and acting provided by basic human goods do not require any prior reasons. The prospects of human fulfillment held out by peace, health, knowledge, and so on, naturally generate corresponding interests in human persons as potential agents.

Thus, human practical reflection begins from the basic human goods. They are expanding fields of possibility which underlie all the reasons one has for choosing and carrying out one's choices. This fact gives human life both its constant and universal features, and its diversity and open-endedness. The basic human goods explain the creativity characteristic, in our experience, only of human beings. They provide the framework of ideals necessary for the unfolding in history of human cultures.

3. Which Are the Basic Human Goods?

Some goods, though important, are not basic, for they are not intrinsic to personal fulfillment. No external good -- nothing a person makes or has, considered as distinct from the person -- can be basic. Individuals and communities always seek such goods for ulterior reasons, which culminate within persons.

Even goods of a more personal and interpersonal character are not yet basic if they can be desired only for their instrumental value. Liberty, for example, is a great good, but not basic; by itself it does not fulfill persons, but only enables them to pursue various forms of fulfillment. Thus, people want liberty to pursue the truth, to worship as they believe right, to live in friendship, and so on.

"Enjoyment" refers to a variety of states of consciousness, which have in common only that they are preferred to their alternatives. A preferred state of consciousness is at best part of a person's sharing in some good; in other words, it is part of the instantiation of a good. Thus enjoyment is not basic. But since "enjoy" refers to conscious participation in one or more of the basic goods, one needs no ulterior reason to enjoy oneself.

Both reflections on one's own deliberation and observation of the diverse ways in which people organize their lives make it clear that there are several basic human goods. For example, truth and friendship plainly mark out distinct fields of concern. Neither is reducible to the other nor to any more fundamental concern. This diversity of basic human goods is no mere contingent fact. Rather, since such goods are aspects of the integral fulfillment of persons, they correspond to the inherent complexity of human nature, both in individuals and in various forms of association.

As *bodily beings,* human persons are living animals. Life itself -- its maintenance and transmission -- health, and safety are one category of basic human good. As *rational,* human beings can know reality and appreciate beauty and whatever intensely engages their capacities to know and feel. Knowledge and esthetic experience are another category of basic

good. As simultaneously *rational* and *animal,* human persons can trans-
form the material world by using realities, beginning with their own bodily
selves, to express meanings and/or serve purposes within human cultures.
The fullness of such meaning-giving and value-creation is still another category of basic good: excellence in work and play.

Everyone shares to some extent in the preceding goods prior to
any deliberate pursuit of them. Life, knowledge, and various skills are first
received as gifts of nature and as parts of a cultural heritage. But children
quickly come to see these goods as fields in which they can care for,
expand, and improve upon what they have received. Life, knowledge, and
excellence in performance are basic human goods insofar as they can be
cherished, enhanced, and handed on to others.

There is another dimension of human persons. As *agents through
deliberation and choice,* they can strive to avoid or overcome various
forms of conflict and alienation, and can seek after harmony, integration,
and fellowship. Choices themselves are essential parts of this relational
dimension of persons. The already given aspects of personal unity and
interpersonal relationship provide grounds for this dimension, yet it goes
beyond what is given.

Most obvious among the basic human goods of this relational
dimension are various forms of harmony between and among persons and
groups of persons: friendship, peace, fraternity, and so on. Within individuals, similar goods can be realized; inner peace, self-integration, authenticity. And beyond human relationships, there can be harmony between
humans and the wider reaches of reality and its principles. Concern for
this last good underlies such diverse activities as believers' worship and
environmentalists' work to save endangered species.

The relational goods are instantiated by a synthesis of elements --
feelings, experiences, beliefs, choices, performances, persons, and wider
realities. Ideally, harmony enhances its diverse elements, but, in fact, conflict is seldom overcome without loss to the elements synthesized.
Defective forms of harmony often are built upon a significant level of conflict. For example, established, working relationships between exploiters
and exploited are a sort of peace, yet radically defective. Such defective
harmonies, as harmonies, are intelligible goods; they can serve as principles of practical reasoning and action. Yet they are mutilated forms of the
basic human goods.

4. The First Moral Principle

To understand right and wrong, one must bear two things in mind. First, the possibilities of human fulfillment are indefinite and always unfolding, for there are several basic human goods, and endless ways of serving and sharing in them. Second, human beings, even when they work together, can only do so much. No one can undertake every project and serve in every possible way. Nor can any community. Choices must be made.

Compulsive behavior, ineptitude, and the unwelcome results of mistakes and bad luck are not moral wrongs. Only in choosing can people go wrong morally. On any ethical theory, moral norms tell people how to choose.

On the account of human goods outlined above, it might seem hard to see how anyone can choose badly. Without reasons for choosing grounded in basic human goods, there would be no options; yet the choice of an option is never rationally necessary -- otherwise, there would not be two or more real options. Thus, on the preceding account, every choice is grounded in some intelligible good, and to that extent is rational, yet no choice has a monopoly on rationality. Moreover, virtually every choice has some negative impact on some good or other. Thus, no choice can be made without setting aside some reason for not making it.

Partly in response to this real complexity, consequentialists try to distinguish good from bad choices by their effectiveness in maximizing good and minimizing evil. But consequentialism is unworkable, for although one may be able to commensurate the measurable value and disvalue promised by different instantiations of goods, one cannot commensurate the goods and bads which make diverse possibilities choiceworthy opportunities, for these goods and bads go beyond what is definite at any moment of choice.

But if consequentialism is unworkable, how can basic human goods mark the moral distinction between choosing well and choosing badly?

There are two ways of choosing. First, one can accept the inevitable limitations of choosing and regard any particular good one chooses as a mere participation in the wider good; choosing thus, one sees the good one chooses as part of a larger and ever-expanding whole, and chooses it in a way which allows for its harmonious integration with other elements of that whole. Second, one can choose in a way which unnecessarily forecloses some further possibilities of fulfillment; one treats the particular good one is realizing here and now as if it were by itself more complete than one knows it to be.

Choices made in the first way are well made, for they are entirely in accord with reality; choices made in the second way are badly made, for they are partly at odds with reality. This distinction between choosing well and choosing badly is the first moral principle. It can be formulated: *in voluntary acting for human goods and avoiding what is opposed to them, one ought to choose and otherwise will those and only those possibilities whose willing is compatible with integral human fulfillment.*

This formulation can be misunderstood. "Integral human fulfillment" does not refer to individualistic self-fulfillment. Rather, it refers to the good of all persons and communities. All the goods in which any person can share also can fulfill others, and individuals can share in goods such as friendship only with others.

Nor is integral human fulfillment some gigantic synthesis of the instantiations of goods in a vast state of affairs which might be projected as the goal of a U.N.O. billion-year plan. Ethics cannot be an architectonic art in that way; there can be no plan to bring about integral human fulfillment. It is a guiding ideal rather than a realizable idea, for the goods are open-ended.

Moreover, integral human fulfillment is not a supreme good, beyond basic goods such as truth and friendship. It does not provide reasons for acting as the basic goods do. Integral human fulfillment only moderates the interplay of such reasons so that deliberation will be thoroughly reasonable.

5. Specifications of the First Moral Principle

One might like the ideal of integral human fulfillment but still ask: How can the formula proposed above be a serviceable first moral principle? How can any specific moral norm be derived from it?

None can be derived directly, but the first principle does imply intermediate principles from which norms can be deduced. Among these intermediate principles is the Golden Rule (or universalizability principle), for a will marked by egoism or partiality cannot be open to integral human fulfillment. And this intermediate principle leads to some specific moral judgments -- e.g., Jane who wants her husband Jack to be faithful plainly violates it by sleeping with Sam.

Thus, there is a route from the first moral principle to specific moral norms. This route can be clarified by reflection on a case such as the intuitively obvious relationship between the first principle and the Golden Rule, and between the Golden Rule and specific norms of fairness.

Human choices are limited in diverse ways. Some limits are inevitable, others not. Among inevitable limits are those on people's insight into the basic goods, ideas of how to serve them, and available resources. Insofar as such limits are outside people's control, morality cannot require that they be transcended.

But some limits on choices are avoidable; one can voluntarily narrow the range of people and goods one cares about. Sometimes this voluntary narrowing has an intelligible basis, as when a person of many gifts chooses a profession and allows other talents to lie fallow. But sometimes avoidable limitations are voluntarily set or accepted without such a reason.

Sources of limitations of this last kind thus meet two conditions: (1) they are effective only by one's own choices; and (2) they are nonrational motives, not intelligible requirements of the basic human goods. Normally, the acting person either can allow these nonrational limiting factors to operate or can transcend them. For they are one's own feelings or emotions, insofar as these are not integrated with the rational appeal of the basic goods and communal fulfillment in them. Such nonintegrated feelings offer motives for behavior yet are not in themselves reasons for choosing.

The first principle of morality rationally prescribes that nonintegrated feelings be transcended. The Golden Rule forbids one to narrow interests and concerns by a certain set of such feelings -- one's preference for oneself and those who are near and dear. It does not forbid differential treatment when required by inevitable limits or by intelligible requirements of shared goods.

Nonrational preferences among persons are not the only feelings which incline people to prefer limited to integral human fulfillment. Hostile feelings such as anger and hatred toward oneself or others lead intelligent, sane, adult persons to choices which are often called "stupid," "irrational," and "childish." Self-destructive and spiteful actions destroy, damage, or block some instantiations of basic human goods; willing such actions obviously is not in line with a will to integral human fulfillment.

Behavior motivated by hostility need not violate the Golden Rule. People sometimes act self-destructively without being unfair to others. Moreover, revenge can be fair: An eye for an eye. But fairness does not eliminate the unreasonableness of acting on hostile feelings in ways that intelligibly benefit no one. Thus, the Golden Rule is not the only intermediate principle which specifies the first principle of morality. It follows that an ethics of a Kantian type is mistaken if it claims that universalizability is the only principle of morality. Respect for persons -- treating them always as ends and never as mere means -- must mean more that treating others fairly.

Not only hostile feelings, but positive ones can motivate people to do evil -- i.e., to destroy, damage, or impede an instantiation of some basic human good. One can choose to bring about evil as a means. One does evil to avoid some other evil or to attain some ulterior good. In such cases, the choice can seem entirely rational, and consequentialists might commend it. But, as I explained above, the appearance of complete rationality is based on a false assumption: that human goods do not matter except insofar as they are instantiated and can be commensurated.

Thus, it is unreasonable to choose to destroy, damage, or impede some instance of a basic good for the sake of an ulterior end. If one makes such a choice, one does not have the reason of maximizing good or minimizing evil -- there is no such reason, for the goods are noncommensurable. Rather, one is motivated by different feelings toward different instances of good. In this sort of case, one plays favorites among instantiations of goods, just as in violating the Golden Rule one plays favorites among persons.

And so, in addition to the Golden Rule and the principle which excludes acting on hostile feelings, there is another intermediate principle: Do not do evil that good may come.

Because this principle generates moral absolutes, it often is considered a threat to people's vital concrete interests. But while this principle may be a threat to interests, the moral absolutes it generates also protect real human goods which are parts of the fulfillment of actual persons; and it is reasonable to sacrifice important concrete interests to the integral fulfillment of persons.

The Golden Rule and the other principles just enunciated shape the rational prescription of the first principle of morality into definite responsibilites. Hence, we call such intermediate principles "modes of responsibility." In all, we distinguish eight of them.

6. Human Action

Specific moral norms are deduced from the modes of responsibility. But one cannot explain this process without first saying something about human action.

Many people, including philosophers, unreflectively assume a rather simple model of human action, involving three elements: (1) a possible state of affairs which a potential agent wants to realize; (2) a plan to realize it by causal factors in the agent's power; and (3) the carrying out of a more or less complex set of bodily performances to bring about the desired state of affairs.

This model of action is inadequate, yet it does refer to something: to what Aristotle called *making* as distinct from *doing*. Kant saw the inadequacy of this model; he knew there is more to moral life than the pursuit of one goal after another. But because he separated the noumenal realm from the world of experience, Kant did not challenge at its own level the oversimplified account of human action. Yet reflection upon our experience as persons living our own lives will verify a more complex model.

As explained above, the basic human goods are broad fields of human possibility. Interest in these goods underlies the desire to realize any particular goal. For persons, whether acting as individuals or in groups, projects first appear as interesting possibilities, worthy of deliberation and perhaps of choice, because they seem to offer ways of uniting persons as open to fulfillment with goods which are intrinsic aspects of that fulfillment. For instance, beyond the specific objectives of any course, dedicated teachers want their students to become mature and cultured persons; beyond all his strategic objectives, a statesmanlike military commander hopes to contribute to a more peaceful and just world.

Thus, from a moral point of view, actions primarily are voluntary syntheses of acting persons or communites with basic human goods. There are at least three ways to make such a synthesis. These constitute three senses of "doing" which, from the moral point of view, are irreducibly diverse.

First, one acts when one chooses something by which one directly participates in a good. For example, when one gives a gift as an act of friendship, one chooses to realize a certain state of affairs -- giving the gift -- as a way of serving the good of friendship, the very fulfillment of self and other in this form of harmony, which is instantiated by giving and receiving the gift.

Second, one acts in a different way when one chooses something not for itself but as a means to an ulterior end. What is chosen is not willed as an instantiation of a basic good, but as something through which one expects to bring about an instantiation of a good. For example, many people work only to get their pay. The chosen means need not be such that it would never be chosen for its inherent value; for business purposes one sometimes makes a trip one might also take as a vacation.

Third, one acts in a still different way when one voluntarily accepts side effects incidental to acting in either of the two prior ways. Here one is aware that executing one's choice will affect, for good or ill, instances of goods other than those on which one's interest directly bears. Although one does not choose this impact on other goods, one foresees it and accepts it -- sometimes reluctantly (e.g., when one accepts the loss of a diseased organ to save one's life), sometimes gladly (e.g., when one accepts the bonus of making new friends when one agrees to participate in a philosophy workshop).

Because the three sorts of willing distinguished here relate acting persons to goods in different ways, they ground three distinct meanings of "doing." The significance of the distinction emerges most clearly in negative cases. One may reveal shameful truths about another out of spite, or to arouse shame and provide an occasion for repentance, or as a side-effect of preventing harm to some other, innocent person. In all three cases, one can be said "to destroy a reputation." But the three types of action destroy reputation in different senses.

7. The Derivation of Specific Moral Norms

Specific moral norms can be derived from modes of responsibility. That is plain from the work of many philosophers with the principle of universalizability and from the examples given above pertaining to other modes. I shall now try to clarify the process of derivation.

Its heart is a deduction which can be formulated in a categorical syllogism. In the simplest case, the normative premise is a mode of responsibility, which excludes a certain way of willing toward relevant goods. The factual premise is a description of a kind of action; it indicates what willing which bears on basic human goods would be involved in doing an action of that kind. The conclusion is that doing an act of that kind is morally wrong. Actions not excluded by any mode are morally permissible; those whose omission would violate some mode are morally required.

Many ways of describing actions, especially with a focus on results, do not reveal what is necessary to derive a moral norm. For example, if killing is defined as any behavior of one person which causes the death of another, the description is insufficient for moral evaluation. Descriptions of actions adequate for moral evaluation must say or imply how the agent's will bears on relevant goods. Such descriptions indicate which of the three sorts of doing, distinguished above, will be involved in an action.

Not all the modes of responsibility apply to all three sorts of doing.

Universalizability does. Parents who show affection for a favorite child but are cold toward another violate the Golden Rule in a doing which immediately instantiates the good of familial fellowship. Superiors who assign harder jobs to subordinates they dislike and easier jobs to subordinates they like violate universalizability in choosing means. Dormitory residents who party through the night while others try to sleep but complain when others make noise during daytime hours are unfair in accepting side effects.

Thus accepting side effects of one's choices can be wrong if one does it unfairly. Similarly, even without unfairness to anyone, someone excessively attached to some good can go wrong in accepting grave side effects -- for example, the aging, champion boxer who ruins his health in trying to retain his title.

However, one cannot act at all without accepting some bad side effects. In any choice, one at least devotes a certain part of one's limited time and other resources to the pursuit of a limited good and leaves unserved other goods for which one might have acted. Hence, it is impossible to have a general moral principle entirely excluding the willing of every negative impact on a basic human good. One sometimes can accept bad side effects as inevitable concomitants of a fully rational response to the intelligible requirements of goods.

Thus, the principle that evil may not be done that good may come applies only to the choice of a means to an ulterior end, not to the acceptance of side effects. Sometimes the results of doing an evil and of accepting a bad side effect can be quite similar, yet the acceptance of the side effect, if not excluded by some other mode of responsibility, will be permissible. For example, a choice to kill a suffering person, whether by a positive performance or by a purposeful omission, is morally excluded, as a case of doing evil that good may come. But a choice to limit or terminate burdensome and costly treatment, with death accepted as a side effect, need not be wrong. The treatment of free choice in the next section will help explain why differences in willing have much great moral significance, even when the results are quite similar.

Actions can be described more or less fully. If a limited description of an action makes it clear that it involves a choice to destroy, damage, or impede some instance of a basic human good, then the wrongness of any action which meets that description is settled. Additional factors may affect the degree of wrongness, but further description of the act cannot reverse its basic moral quality. For this reason, moral norms derived from this mode of responsibility can be called "moral absolutes." For example, an absolute norm forbids killing one innocent person to prevent that person and several others from being killed by a mob.

Different modes work differently, so not all specific norms are absolute. Universalizability can exclude as unfair an action proposed under a limited description, yet allow as fair an action which includes all the elements of that description together with some other morally relevant features. For example, fairness demands promise keeping, whenever the only motive for breaking a promise is of the sort whose operation promises are meant to exclude. But someone who has another reason to break a promise -- for example, that keeping it would have such grave consequences that even those to whom it was made would agree it should be broken -- may break the promise without violating the Golden Rule.

In general, specific norms based on universalizability are nonabsolute. That may not appear to be so, since ordinary language sometimes builds the moral specification into the act description -- e.g., by limiting "stealing" to the wrongful taking of another's property. However, instances of justifiable taking can include all the elements which are present in unjustifiable taking; the addition, not the subtraction, of relevant features makes the taking justifiable.

8. Free Choice, Personal Identity, and Character

Classical moral philosophers sought the wisdom to live good lives. By their standard, the ethical theory summarized thus far is inadequate. For being a good person is more than conforming each of one's acts to an appropriate moral norm.

One makes a choice when one faces practical alternatives, believes one can and must settle which to take, and deliberately takes one. The choice is free when choosing itself determines which alternative one takes. True, factors beyond one's control provided options and limited them. But, if free, only one's choice determined which option one would adopt.

The particular goal realized by a successful action is sensibly good and experienced as such, but the appealing goodness with respect to which one determines oneself in choosing to do that action is intelligible and transcends that experience. For example, recovery from a particular illness is sensibly good; health, to which one determines oneself in choosing to do what is necessary to get well, is intelligibly good. In many successful human actions, the goods concretely realized can also be realized by natural processes or spontaneous human acts without choice; by contrast, the sharing in and service to goods to which one determines oneself by choice can only occur in one's self-determining choice.

As self-creative, free choices transcend the material world. They are not events or processes or things in the world; they must be distinguished from the performances which execute them. The performances of particular acts come and go, but a choice, once made, determines the self unless and until one makes another, incompatible choice. Self-determination through choice means that the self is actualized and limited; one's orientation toward further possibilities is more or less settled. By choices, one not only brings about instantiations of goods, but participates in definite ways in the basic human goods.

There are large choices, which put one in the position of having to carry them out by many small choices. Examples of large choices are to become a philosopher, to get married, and to take up photography as a hobby. Some large choices can be called "commitments." To make a commitment is more than to adopt a long-range goal. Commitments bear directly upon goods such as religion, justice, friendship, authenticity, and so on. Since these are interrelated, any commitment will somehow bear on all of them. And since they include interpersonal harmony, every commitment joins one to a particular person or group.

The first moral principle requires willing in line with integral human fulfillment. Such willing must meet the conditions for effective and consistent participation in basic human goods. Without an integrated set of upright commitments, one cannot participate in goods effectively and consistently. Therefore, each of us must discern which commitments are personally appropriate, make and integrate them, and faithfully carry them out.

Some aspects of personal identity are given: One has a certain genetic make up, is brought up in a certain culture, and so forth. But the matrix of moral self-identity is one's free choices; mature people define themselves by their commitments. Still, a morally mature, good person is more than a set of upright commitments. For to faithfully carry out upright commitments, the whole personality must be developed and limited in line with them; they must shape feelings, beliefs, experiences, modes of behavior, skills, and so on. Thus, a good person is one whose whole self is formed by a comprehensive set of upright commitments.

Such a person has good character, whose facets are called "virtues." Since there are many ways of distinguishing facets of character, there are many classifications of virtues. But however classified, virtues are moral fruits, not moral principles. For virtues are only parts of a personality shaped by the carrying out of morally upright commitments, and such commitments are upright because they arise from and are shaped by propositional principles of practical reasoning and of morality.

9. The Way of the Lord Jesus

Describing the good person is easy; living a good life often seems impossible. The good we achieve and enjoy is mutilated and threatened by ineptitude, failure, breakdown, ignorance, error, misunderstanding, pain, sickness, and death. We sometimes freely choose to violate known moral truths; we never perfectly fulfill our commitments. Perhaps we could live better private lives if we had the support of a good society, and we also need a good society because the human is naturally social. But there are many wicked people in the world, and powerful people seem especially likely to be wicked. Thus, every political society constitutionally compromises with systematic injustice and other sorts of immorality. All humankind lives in slavery, though some are always only slaves, while others sometimes also play the role of master.

Philosophical reflection seems unable to explain this situation and to show the way to freedom. Immorality, precisely insofar as it is rooted in truly free choices, is inexplicable and unpreventable. Apart from immorality, most repugnant aspects of the human condition are epitomized by death, which seems natural and inevitable. Wrestling with the mystery of the human situation, ancient and non-Western philosophers ignore free choice, and modern and contemporary Western philosophers deny it. Almost all try to evade the reality of death by making some sort of rationally indefensible distinction between the morally significant human person and the human organism doomed to die.

The Christian gospel, I believe, offers a more adequate account of the situation. According to this account, God is a communion of three persons, who created human persons so that they might share in divine communion and live in human fellowship. In creating, God promised to forestall death, naturally inevitable for the human organism as such, if men and women cooperated with the divine plan. But from humankind's beginning wrongful free choices blocked the formation and development of an inclusive human community, constitutionally uncompromised by evil. And so God permitted nature to take its course and humans to taste death, at least partly so that they might experience the wretchedness of their fallen condition, and be eager to escape it.

Human liberation, according to the gospel's proposal, can be gained in two stages, by any who truly desire it. One of the divine persons became the man Jesus, who lived a morally unblemished human life. In doing so, he not only provided a unique example of how to live uprightly in the broken human situation, but also made himself available as the head of the human community God had planned from the beginning. All are invited to make faith in Jesus and his cause the central commitment of their lives. In making such a commitment, the gospel teaches, Jesus' disciples enter not only into fellowship with one another but into the communion of the divine family.

The gospel teaches Christians that if they live their lives to implement their faith in Jesus, they will live the best human lives possible in this broken world. Following the way of the Lord Jesus, individual Christians can become good people, and on the basis of their common bond with Jesus they can work together to build up decent community in the Church and in their Christian families.

Yet this first stage of liberation is incomplete, since the upright must suffer at the hands of the wicked and all must suffer the human misery which culminates in death. The second, and final, stage of liberation requires a divine act of re-creation. This re-creation, according to the gospel, began with Jesus' resurrection from the dead, and will be completed by the raising up of all who die in faith, and their reunion in an unending divine-human fellowship, protected forever from the wicked.

If the Christian gospel is true, the normative ethical theory outlined in the previous sections remains adequate. The basic human goods remain, though they unfold in unexpected ways. The modes of responsibility remain, though they generate many specifically Christian norms, to govern actions people without faith either could not think of at all or would not think of as choiceworthy.

Most important, the Christian need not accept an Augustinian or Thomistic version of neo-Platonism, with its supposition that the human heart is naturally insatiable by human fulfillment, and naturally drawn to fulfillment in the Beatific Vision of God. For faith does not substitute a supreme instantiation of a supernatural good for integral human fulfillment.

Rather, it holds out the hope of an unending marriage feast. In this communion of divine and human persons, all the basic human goods will be instantiated without the defects imposed by death. And the more-than-human fulfillment which is naturally proper to God alone also will be enjoyed by his adopted sons and daughters.

Selected Bibliography

Germain Grisez, *Contraception and the Natural Law* (Milwaukee: Bruce, 1964), xiii + 245. Chapter three is an early version of the theory; for understanding its mature form, only the critique of "conventional" natural-law approaches remains helpful. The critique of consequentialism ("situationism") here, and up to "Choice and Consequentialism," mistakenly focuses on the noncommensurability *of the different categories* of basic human goods.

_____, "The First Principle of Practical Reason: A Commentary on the *Summa Theologiae*, 1-2, Question 94, Article 2," *The Natural Law Forum,* 10 (1965), 168-201; abridged version: *Modern Studies in Philosophy: Aquinas: A Collection of Critical Essays,* ed. Anthony

Kenny (Garden City, N. Y.: Doubleday and Co., 1969), 340-82. (Kenny did some significant, unauthorized editing, so it is best to use the original.) Of works listed in this bibliography, this article and the next are Grisez's only attempts at Thomistic exegesis. Elsewhere, he tries to do philosophy or theology, not history, and freely parts company with St. Thomas, often without saying so.

_____, "Man, Natural End of," *The New Catholic Encyclopedia*, 9:132-38. By examining the efforts of various groups of Thomists to make sense of St. Thomas's teaching on the natural end of human persons, and by pointing out many inconsistencies in what he says about the ultimate end, this article deliberately comes within a step of rejecting his position (and with it, the positions of both Aristotle and St. Augustine) on the ultimate end of human persons.

_____, *Abortion: The Myths, the Realities, and the Arguments* (New York and Cleveland: Corpus Books, 1970), ix + 559. Chapter six is a restatement of the theory, with its application to abortion and other killing, including capital punishment and war. Some find this presentation of the theory especially attractive, perhaps partly because it is easier to follow than later, more adequate versions. Certain critics, including Richard A. McCormick, S. J., still deal with this statement of the theory, and make objections whose answers they could find in later works.

_____ and Russell Shaw, *Beyond the New Morality: The Responsibilities of Freedom*, 3rd ed. (Notre Dame: University of Notre Dame Press, 1988), xi + 256. Intended for use with beginning students as part of an introduction to ethics, this version of the theory is accessible, but somewhat simplified. Many important aspects of the theory and arguments for it are deliberately omitted, even from the third edition.

Joseph M. Boyle, Jr., "Aquinas and Prescriptive Ethics," *Proceedings of the American Catholic Philosophical Association*, 49 (1975), 82-95. A clear account and critique of Hare's prescriptivism.

Germain Grisez, *Beyond the New Theism: A Philosophy of Religion* (Notre Dame and London: University of Notre Dame Press, 1975), xiii + 418. The metaphysical foundations of the ethical theory are explained and defended in this book, which had the benefit of many years of work with Boyle and Tollefsen, especially on the book listed next. Chapters six through thirteen are an exposition and criticism of the modern and contemporary alternatives; chapter twenty-three deals with the irreducible complexity of the human person and community of persons.

Joseph M. Boyle, Jr., Germain Grisez, and Olaf Tollefsen, *Free Choice: A Self-Referential Argument* (Notre Dame and London: University of Notre Dame Press, 1976), xi + 207. The most complete account of free choice and related elements of action theory, and a criticism of alternative views of these matters, which are so essential to ethical theory.

The Teachings of Christ: A Catholic Catechism for Adults, ed. Ronald Lawler, O.F.M. Cap., Donald W. Wuerl, and Thomas Comerford Lawler (Huntington, Ind.: Our Sunday Visitor, 1976), 640. Finnis and Grisez (Finnis more than Grisez) did the first draft of chapters eighteen through twenty-one, but their draft was revised considerably by the editors. Work on this project was the most important starting point of the subsequent development of the ethical theory in the context of moral theology.

Germain Grisez, "Choice and Consequentialism," *Proceedings of the American Catholic Philosophical Association,* 51 (1977), 144-52. The first presentation of the mature version (which corrects earlier ones) of the argument against consequentialism based on the noncommensurability of those goods and bads which are the intelligible grounds for the options between or among which a *free* choice must be made.

_____, "Against Consequentialism," *The American Journal of Jurisprudence and Legal Philosophy,* 3 (1978), 21-72. The most thorough critique of consequentialism.

Joseph M. Boyle, Jr., "*Praeter intentionem* in Aquinas," *The Thomist,* 42 (1978), 649-65. A clarification of the notion of *side effect.*

Germain Grisez and Joseph M. Boyle, Jr., *Life and Death with Liberty and Justice: A Contribution to the Euthanasia Debate* (Notre Dame and London: University of Notre Dame Press, 1979), xiii + 521. Chapters eleven and twelve benefit from Boyle's work in action theory; everything necessary to deal with life and death issues reaches nearly mature form here. The political philosophy in this book needs development and, perhaps, certain corrections. The authors now think it is usually wrong to withhold food and water from comatose patients.

John Finnis, *Natural Law and Natural Rights* (Oxford: Clarendon Press, 1980), xv + 425. Chapters three through five deploy the ethical theory with originality, as a basis for Finnis's altogether independent philosophy of law. He gives special attention to epistemological issues raised by the empiricist tradition. There are some differences in ethical theory between Finnis, on the one hand, and Grisez and Boyle, on the other. But most differences are in formulation rather than in substance, and the more important substantive differences concern applications rather than the theory itself.

Joseph M. Boyle, Jr., "Toward Understanding the Principle of Double Effect," *Ethics,* 90 (1980), 527-38. A defense of the principle of double effect, with a clarification of the theory of agency it presupposes.

John Finnis and Germain Grisez, "The Basic Principles of Natural Law: A Reply to Ralph McInerny," *The American Journal of Jurisprudence and Legal Philosophy,* 26 (1981), 21-31. A defense against a Thomist of stricter observance.

John Finnis, *Fundamentals of Ethics* (Oxford: Oxford University Press; Washington, D. C.: Georgetown University Press, 1983), x + 163. Finnis restates much of the theory, and engages in a rich dialectic both with the history of philosophy and with contemporary English-language work in ethical theory.

Germain Grisez, *The Way of the Lord Jesus,* vol. one, *Christian Moral Principles,* with the help of Joseph M. Boyle, Jr., Basil Cole, O. P., John M. Finnis, John A. Geinzer, Jeannette Grisez, Robert G. Kennedy, Patrick Lee, William E. May, and Russell Shaw (Chicago: Franciscan Herald Press, 1983), xxxiv + 971. Chapters two through twelve are the most mature and complete statement of the theory thus far. Boyle contributed a total of more than six months of intense, *full-time* work to this volume. The rethinking in a theological context of the whole theory without reference to any particular issue (such as abortion or euthanasia) led to many important developments, and a considerable increase in the tightness of the system. Chapters nineteen and thirty-four provide a theological account of the ultimate end of human persons; chapters twenty-five and twenty-six explain the specificity of Christian ethics.

John Finnis, "Practical Reasoning, Human Goods, and the End of Man," *Proceedings of the American Catholic Philosophical Associattion,* 58 (1984), 23-36. A conciliatory comparison of the ideal of integral human fulfillment with the ultimate end as St. Thomas understands it. Finnis, whose view is closer than Grisez's to that of St. Thomas, here emphasizes points of agreement.

Joseph M. Boyle, Jr., "Aquinas, Kant, and Donagan on Moral Principles," *The New Scholasticism,* 58 (1984), 391-408. A criticism of Donagan's nonconsequentialist (Kantian) ethics.

John Finnis, Joseph M. Boyle, Jr., and Germain Grisez, *Nuclear Deterrence, Morality and Realism* (Oxford and New York: Oxford University Press, 1987), xv + 429. A fresh, philosophical presentation of the theory, with a careful application to the morality of nuclear deterrence. The present paper is in part a considerable revised version of a first draft of chapter ten of this book.

Germain Grisez, Joseph Boyle, and John Finnis, "Practical Principles, Moral Truth, and Ultimate Ends," *The American Journal of Jurisprudence*, 32 (1987), 99-151. A restatement, clarification, and updating of many elements of the theory often criticized (and generally misunderstood) by philosophers in the (broadly speaking, Thomistic) natural-law tradition from which the theory was developed.

Imperfect Duty Situations, Moral Freedom, and Universalizability

Marcus G. Singer
University of Wisconsin, Madison

"What is right (or wrong) for one person must be right (or wrong) for any similar person in similar circumstances." That is a minimal paradigmatic statement of what I have called the generalization principle and what Sidgwick called the Principle of Justice, and what is now usually called, in some of its versions at least, the Principle of Universalizability. Does this principle imply that if I ought to do act A in situation S, then every relevantly similar person ought to do A in S, or that if I judge that I ought to do A in S then I must also judge that every relevantly similar person ought to do A in S? It is tempting to think so, many proponents of universalizability do, and for a long time I did. But I now see that it does not, and this is an important restriction on universalizability and fact about it. There are limitations if not exceptions to the Generalization Principle, which need to be specified and understood. These limitations will be seen to strengthen not to weaken it.

I earlier discussed this principle in a paper published in 1955, and then in a book published in 1961,[1] and over the past thirty years or more it has been much discussed by a number of philosophers, though usually under the name of universalizability. Now I have no wish to be especially stubborn about it, but I still prefer the name "generalization principle," because the term "universalizability" has been overgeneralized so as to cover processes and principles that are fundamentally different from each other.[2] For instance, in Kant's ethics (though Kant did not himself use the

---

1. "Generalization in Ethics," *Mind* LXIV, July 1955, pp. 361-75; *Generalization in Ethics* (New York: Alfred A. Knopf, 1961; Atheneum, 1971).
2. This point is argued in "Universalizability and the Generalization Principle," in *Morality and Universality*, ed. by N. Potter and M. Timmons (Dordrecht: D. Reidel Publishing Company, 1985), at pp. 48-58.

term) universalizability is the test for the maxims of action: a universalizable maxim is one that can be willed to be a universal law, and it is only on such maxims that one is justified in acting. In Hare's ethics, universalizability is used to cover a number of different things. Thus universalizability is said to be common to "all judgments which carry descriptive meaning,"[3] so that it is characteristic of statements of fact and value judgments alike, from which it follows, in Hare's words, that "any singular descriptive judgment is universalizable" (FR, 12). One of his own examples is that "This is red" is universalizable because it entails "Everything like this in the relevant respects is red" (FR, 11). But Hare also maintains that all ought-judgments, where the word "ought" is properly used, are universalizable. He says: "in by far the majority of judgments containing the word 'ought,' it has the sense that requires them to be universalizable; there *may* be some peripheral cases where it does not have this sense; but at any rate in its *moral* uses . . . it always does . . . the logic of the word 'ought' in its typical uses . . . requires universalizability . . . ." (FR, 35, 37). For Hare universalizability is a merely logical thesis; "offenses against . . . universalizability are logical, not moral;" they consist in "abusing the word 'ought';" so on Hare's view "no moral judgment or principle of substance follows from the thesis [of universalizability] alone" (FR, 32). Therefore, whereas on Kant's view not all maxims are universalizable, on Hare's view, since they all have descriptive meaning, they all are. And what is on Kant's view a moral test is on Hare's view only a logical thesis, albeit one that is capable of employment in moral argument (FR, 35).

I am not here presenting any argument about or against Hare's moral philosophy. I meant to show only that universalizability has been overgeneralized, is thus ambiguous. Hence although the universalizability principle is often the same as the generalization principle it is not so always, and the generalization principle is not the same as Kant's test of universalizability, or the Categorical Imperative. But henceforth in this discourse I shall use the expressions synonymously. By "universalizability," or the Principle of Universalizability, I shall here mean the Generalization Principle, and nothing else.

Now in the book of 1961 I claimed about the generalization principle that it is the fundamental principle of morality, that it is not vague or useless or inapplicable, that it is at the heart of moral reasoning, is involved in or presupposed by every genuine moral judgment, and is an essential part of moral reasoning (GIE, 34). This large claim has since been subjected to a number of probing criticisms. On the present occasion I want to examine one line of such criticism.

---

3. R. M. Hare, *Freedom and Reason* (FR), 10. See References at end for other abbreviations.

The line of criticism in question is to the effect that there is a class of cases in which one makes a moral judgment that is not universalizable. This class is one in which one is pressed to decide between conflicting considerations of equal or nearly equal weight and judges that he ought to act in one way rather that the other -- if only because he *has* to decide one way or the other -- but yet does not think that anyone else similarly placed ought to decide or act in the same way. This results from the fact that one is called upon to make a decision or a judgment that is peculiarly personal, so that one does not regard it as generalizable to anyone else. In such a situation one can think, "Here is how I have decided I ought to act, I think this act would be right for me, but someone else in this situation might well decide it differently." Given this, it is claimed, the universalizability principle has no logical force; moral judgments are not generalizable beyond this particular case to a class of similar cases. One decided the individual case on the basis of the considerations applicable to it, and need not consider anything beyond it. So it is claimed.

I. Agent's Judgments -- Billy Budd and the Sartre Case

Let us consider then this class of agent's or first person prospective judgments. Do such judgments have this special character?

(a) Billy Budd

Consider, as does Peter Winch, the case of Billy Budd and Captain Vere as presented in Melville's short novel *Billy Budd*. In particular let us, in Winch's words,

> consider the moral dilemma of Captain "Starry" Vere, captain of *H. M. S. Indominable*, on active service against the French in the period following the Nore mutiny, when further mutinous outbreaks aboard H. M. ships were feared at any time: a situation "demanding," Melville writes, "two qualities not readily interfusible -- prudence and rigour." Billy Budd, a foretopman of angelic character, is impressed into service on the *Indomitable* from the merchantman *Rights of Man* on

the high seas. He is persecuted by the satanic master-at-arms of the *Indominable*, Claggart, in a campaign which culminates in Claggart's falsely accusing Billy, before Vere, of inciting the crew to mutiny. In the stress of this situation, Budd is afflicted with a speech-impediment which prevents him from answering the charge. Frustrated, he strikes Claggart, who falls, strikes his head and dies (Winch, p. 200).

In Melville's words:

> In the legal view, the apparent victim of the tragedy was he who had sought to victimize a man blameless; and the indisputable deed of the latter, navally regarded, constituted the most heinous of military crimes. Yet more. The essential right and wrong in the matter, the clearer that might be, so much the worse for the responsibility of a loyal sea commander, inasmuch as he was authorized to determine the matter on that primitive legal basis.

And Winch observes that

> Vere ... sees the military code as ... something to which he himself is morally committed. For him the conflict with which he is faced is an internal moral one ... (W, 201).

Vere feels obligated both to abide by the naval code, under which Budd's act is a capital offence, and therefore to prosecute Budd for murder, and also to urge that Budd, persecuted and oppressed by Claggart, be acquitted. As he says to the court-martial, "can we adjudge to summary and shameful death a fellow-creature, innocent before God, and whom we feel to be so?" (W, 202). Vere thus feels a conflict between two moral considerations, not just a "conflict between morality and military law" (W, 201). Vere's decision is to urge that Billy Budd be convicted. "Tell me whether or not, occupying the position we do, private conscience should not yield to that imperial one formulated in the code under which alone we officially proceed?" And this decision troubled him for the rest of his life. Mortally wounded in a later engagement, Vere's dying words were "Billy Budd, Billy Budd," but Melville tells us that "these were not the accents of remorse" (W, 211). Now Winch claims that, given the sort of person Vere was, it was not "morally possible" for him to have acted differently. Therefore, says Winch, Vere had concluded "This is what I ought to do." However, he maintains, Vere was not "logically committed to the corollary, 'And anyone else in the same situation ought to act likewise'."

Winch arrives at this conclusion by imagining himself in Vere's position and asking himself what he would have said and done in such circumstances:

> I try, as does Melville in depicting Vere's line of thought, to discount the possibilities of failure of nerve and softness in the face of a terrible duty; I try, that is, to confine myself to the genuinely moral features of the situation. Having done this, I believe that I could not have acted as did Vere; and by the 'could not,' I do not mean 'should not [read 'would not'] have had the nerve to,' but that I should have found it morally impossible to condemn a man 'innocent before God' under such circumstances . . . I do not think that I should [read 'would'] appeal to any considerations over and above those to which Vere himself appeals. It is just that I think I should find the considerations connected with Billy Budd's peculiar innocence too powerful to be overridden by the appeal to military duty (W, 207-8).

But, Winch says, this does not mean that he thinks Vere acted wrongly in doing the opposite. And, he adds, he does not hold the "Protagorean view," according to which whatever someone holds to be right is right for that person. "This Protagorean position," he says, is not his. His position is this:

> I am holding that if A says 'X is the right thing for me to do' and if B, in a situation not relevantly different, says 'X is the wrong thing for me to do,' it can be that both are correct. That is, it may be that neither what each says, nor anything entailed by what each says, contradicts anything said or implied by the other. But this certainly does not mean that, if A believes that X is the right thing for him to do, then X is made the right thing for A to do by the mere fact that he thinks it is. It was clearly important to Vere that he did the right thing, and he did not think that whatever he thought would be the right thing would in fact be so (W, 209).

What Winch goes on to argue is that Vere's judgment is not a universalizable one, that there is "a certain class of *first person* moral judgments in a special position as not subject to the universalizability principle" (W, 203). What he is claiming, then, is that there is a class of first person or agent's prospective moral judgments, expressing the outcome of deliberation between conflicting moral demands, that are not universalizable. That is to say, the first person judgment, expressed by either Vere or Winch, that I ought to do this, or it would be wrong for me to do this, does not imply that everyone similarly placed ought to do this, or that it would be wrong for any similar person in similar circumstances to do this. And this runs or seems to run counter to the generalization principle. "Deciding what one ought to do," says Winch, "is not a matter of finding out what anyone ought to do in such circumstances." It does involve "finding something out," but "what one finds out is something about oneself, rather than anything one can speak of as holding universally" (W, 212).

(b) The Sartre Case

Before going to the question whether this is a valid counterexample to universalizability, I want to consider another case somewhat and superficially like it. This is the example used by Sartre, which has come to be perhaps the most widely discussed example in recent moral philosophy, of one of his students, who, as Sartre described it, came to see him under the following circumstances:

> his father was on bad terms with his mother, and moreover, was inclined to be a collaborationist; his older brother had been killed in the German offensive of 1940, and the young man, with somewhat immature but generous feelings, wanted to avenge him. His mother lived alone with him, very much upset by the half-treason of her husband and the death of her older son; the boy was her only consolation.
>
> The boy was faced with the choice of leaving for England and joining the Free French Forces -- that is, leaving his mother behind -- or remaining with his mother and helping her to carry on. He was fully aware that the woman lived only for him and that his going-off -- and perhaps his death -- would plunge her into despair. He was also aware that every act that he did for

his mother's sake was a sure thing, in the sense that it was helping her to carry on, whereas every effort he made toward going off and fighting was an uncertain move which might run aground and prove completely useless; for example, on his way to England he might, while passing through Spain, be detained indefinitely in a Spanish camp; he might reach England or Algiers and be stuck in an office at a desk job. As a result, he was faced with two very different kinds of action: one, concrete, immediate, but concerning only one individual; the other concerned an incomparably vaster group, a national collectivity, but for that very reason was dubious, and might be interrupted enroute. And, at the same time, he was wavering between two kinds of ethics. On the one hand, an ethics of sympathy, of personal devotion; on the other, a broader ethics, but one whose efficacy was more dubious. He had to choose between the two.

Who could help him choose? Christian doctrine? Christian doctrine says, "Be charitable, love your neighbor, take the more rugged path, etc." But which is the more rugged path? Whom should he love as a brother? The fighting man or his mother? Which does the greater good, the vague act of fighting in a group, or the concrete one of helping a particular human being to go on living? Who can decide *a priori*? Nobody. No book of ethics can tell him. The Kantian ethics says, "Never treat any person as a means, but as an end." Very well, if I stay with my mother, I'll treat her as an end and not as a means; but by virtue of this very fact, I'm running the risk of treating the people around me who are fighting, as means; and, conversely, if I go to join those who are fighting, I'll be treating them as an end, and, by doing that, I run the risk of treating my mother as a means. If values are vague, and if they are always too broad for the concrete and specific case that we are considering, the only thing left for us is to trust our instincts. That's what this young man tried to do; and when I saw him, he said, "In the end, feeling is what counts. I ought to choose whichever pushes me in one direction. If I feel that I love my mother enough to sacrifice everything else for her -- my desire for vengeance, for action, for adventure -- then I'll stay with her. If, on the contrary, I feel that my love for my mother isn't enough, I'll leave. . . ."[4]

I have presented this account fairly fully, because I think that too abrupt summaries of it can lead to distortion of it. Sartre used the example to support the existentialist claim that there is no prior standard rule or principle to which the youth can appeal to decide this question, that he must simply choose, that the same thing is in general true in every genuine moral dilemma, and that in choosing one is in effect choosing oneself or the sort of person one is to be.

My analysis of this example, curiously enough, will lead to an odd confirmation of the existentialist thesis, or at least a portion of it. We can agree with Sartre that "there are no 'objective' criteria by which such a choice may be made" and that such a case cannot be decided by deduction from ready-made rules and copy-book formulas. If it could it would not constitute a problem. However, that does not show the Generalization Principle to be false. And the Sartre case has been made the basis of an argument, similar to Winch's, against the idea of Universalizability.

Thus Alasdaire MacIntyre has claimed that:

> Someone faced with such a decision might choose either to stay or to go without attempting to legislate for anyone else in a similar position. He might decide what to do [notice this terminology] without being willing to allow that anyone else who chose differently was blameworthy. He might legitimately announce his choice by saying, "I have decided that I ought to stay with my mother." If he did so, his use of "ought" would not express any appeal to a universalizable principle. . . . It would be a moral evaluation [but not universalizable].[5]

Now it may be agreed that "someone faced with such a decision might choose either to stay or to go without attempting to legislate for anyone else in a similar position." But that is true of everyone in a situation of moral decision. It is hard enough to decide one's own case without attempting to legislate for everyone else. This by itself does not preclude the use of the Generalization Principle in the context of moral judgment, which would provide a test of whether the decision made can pass moral scrutiny. (Similarly it may be agreed that one "might decide what to do without being willing to allow that anyone else who chose differently was blameworthy," but that also is true in general, and the shift to speaking of *blameworthy* is unfortunate and unnecessary, since it imports another

---

4. Jean-Paul Sartre, *Existentialism and Human Emotions* (New York: Philosophical Library, 1957), pp. 24-6.
5. Alasdair MacIntyre, "What Morality is Not," p. 326.

dimension of discussion. One can think that what someone did was wrong without thinking that that person is blameworthy.) It can also be agreed that one "might legitimately announce" one's choice by saying "I have decided that I ought to stay" without that expressing any appeal to either a universalizable or a universal principle -- though one can question the prudence of our protagonist in his special situation *announcing* any choice at all.

But consider. How does "I have decided that I ought to stay" differ from "I have decided to stay?" In the first locution there is perhaps a more definite suggestion that a moral conflict has been decided, but that interpretation is not precluded by the second locution, and the second may even be somewhat less misleading. For what is called for is some decision, not necessarily a moral judgment, and this is so even if one feels that one cannot arrive at a decision -- a decision as distinct from merely drifting into some course of action -- without resolving some moral problem. MacIntyre says that the use of "I ought" in such a case "is plainly to commit oneself, to allow that if I do not do what I say I ought to do, then I am blameworthy. It is a performatory use of 'I ought'," MacIntyre claims, "in that its use makes one responsible for performing a particular action where before" saying that one could not be held responsible. But to say "I ought to do so-and-so" is not to *do* so-and-so, nor is it to promise to do so-and-so. The overworked category of performatory or performative language is here out of place. MacIntyre thinks that "in this non-universalizable sense of 'ought' one could never say 'You oughtn't' but only 'I oughtn't'," but that is not so. In the context of giving advice, one can plainly say to another "I think you oughtn't . . .," and what is true of the first person use will be true of the second.

Simply to say "I ought" is not to *do* anything, any more than saying "I will" or "I shall," or "I think I ought." And one need not use "ought" either to announce or to express a decision. One can say or think, indifferently:

(a) I ought to stay

(b) I have decided that I ought to stay

(c) I think I ought to stay

(d) I have decided to stay.

(e) I am staying.

or

(f) I shall stay.

It is true that (c) "I think I ought to stay," expresses more hesitancy than (a) "I ought to stay" or (b) "I have decided that I ought to stay." But that is no great matter, nor is it to the point. And surely there is no difference between (a) "I ought to stay" and (d) "I have decided to stay." But there is no hint in (d) "I have decided to stay," or (e) "I am staying," of committing or obligating oneself or of a performatory use of a term.

One can quite appropriately say, in this setting, "I ought to stay." But, in this setting, this use of "I ought" is a purely personal one, and it is not surprising that it is not universalizable. I return to this matter in due course.

II. Imperfect Duty Situations

Before considering these two cases independently, I want to develop the notion of an Imperfect Duty Situation.

Kant (in the *Groundwork*) defines a perfect duty as one which allows no exception in favor of inclination.[6] An imperfect duty then is one that allows exceptions in favor of inclination. Kant's examples of imperfect duties are the duty to develop one's talents and the duty to help others in need of help. With respect to beneficence Kant maintains that the maxim of refusing to help others who are in need of help when one is not in need of help oneself cannot be willed to be a universal law, that is, breaches the Categorical Imperative. Suppose for the sake of argument that this is true. This would establish the duty to help others who are in need of help, and hence that beneficence as so understood is a duty. But it is an imperfect duty, because indefinite, not determinate. From the rule itself -- simply the duty to help others in need of help -- it cannot be determined who is to be helped, what sort of help is to be provided, under what circumstances, to what extent, in what way, and at what cost. It is up to the agent to decide this. And the agent *must* decide; there is no way of

---

6. Immanuel Kant, *Grundlegung zur Metaphysik der Sitten*, 53n = 422n.

determining the answers to these questions by deduction from prior rules or principles. The principles of morality determine the boundaries of these duties, and therefore what would be wrong in a situation of imperfect duty, but not what ought to be done in a situation of imperfect duty. Nothing does. One simply decides, has the right to decide, is in the realm of moral freedom. A person who, though perfectly capable of providing help to someone at some time or other, never helps anyone to any extent in any situation whatever, is in violation of this rule, and it is not morally open to anyone to decide to do this. Thus one who eliminates someone's need for help by eliminating that person from the land of the living is of course guilty of murder, but is also guilty of this breach of obligation, and has no more right to do the one than the other. Moral principles and perfect duties set limits or boundaries or parameters to the range of free decision, but otherwise determine nothing, and within these parameters one must simply decide. In making such decisions, one may call upon and use various decision procedures, and more power to anyone who finds them a help. But no decision procedure can relieve anyone of the need to decide. One, after all, has to decide to use a decision procedure.

Giving to charity is a special case coming under beneficence, as it is a special way of being beneficent. Everyone who has enough to live on has the duty to give to charity. But there is no duty to give to this charity rather than to that, nor can any general rule determine how much one should give or when. Here is where differences of character as well as of interest become manifest, and moral judgments can certainly still be made on people so situated. Some niggardly people give very little, and that grudgingly and under pressure. Some people are especially generous, even some who cannot afford to be. One who gives away more than she can afford is imprudent; one who gives away more than she has is irresponsible. Aristotle's doctrine of the mean is certainly relevant here, as it is in all cases of imperfect duties, and may even provide a sort of rough and ready guide for those who need one.

Contrast this with a perfect duty, such as the duty not to lie or not to make a lying promise, Kant's standard example. This is not indefinite in this way. Unless the occasion is one where one is justified in lying, one has no right to decide to whom one will not lie, to what extent, under what circumstances, and in what way. (There is still some indefiniteness, of course, since the duty not to lie is not the same as the duty to tell the truth; one is free to decide to remain silent.) Another example is the philosophically favored one of keeping one's promises. But one is normally free not to make a promise. Such difficulties aside, such perfect or determinate duties do not exhaust the field of duties; they only delimit it. It is within the limits -- parameters, as I call them -- determined by perfect duties, and ultimately by basic moral principles, that one has imperfect duties, and the area of imperfect duties is in the area of moral freedom. That is, within these limits, one is morally free to do as one pleases or as one thinks best.

Consider now the alleged duty of developing one's talents, and let us suppose, again, that this is established as a duty. What is thus established is the duty of developing one's talents, but that does not tell anyone which talents, to what extent, for what purposes, and at what cost to others, to one's inclinations, and to one's other talents. For no one can develop all of his or her talents. One who is a jack of all trades may be a master of none -- but that, in the light of the general duty, is also all right, if it reflects the decision of the jack in question to develop in that way. The duty to develop one's talents is not the duty to develop any one specific talent to its utmost at the cost of stultifying others. If one wants to do that one is, so far as the general duty goes, morally free to, though one may not be free to in the light of other claims on one's time and talents. Neither is the general duty a duty to develop all one's talents equally, stunting none but developing none to the utmost, though if one wants to do that one is morally free to. Each extreme has its merits and each has its costs, and it is part of the richness and the rewards of human diversity that not only do different people have different talents -- one for drawing, one for cooking, one for sewing, one for carpentry, one for medicine, one for government, and so on -- but also people are free to develop their talents, under any minimally reasonable form of society, in accordance with their own interests tastes and inclinations. Some choice, however, is necessary, and one of the prime functions of education is to enable people to make such choices wisely and intelligently, by helping them develop their capacities for so choosing.

Taking our cue from these examples, then, an Imperfect Duty Situation is a situation in which one has an imperfect duty. It is therefore one in which one has the latitude, discretion, freedom, responsibility, to decide what to do, and one is morally free to act in accordance with one's inclinations. Hence in an Imperfect Duty Situation one is free to do anything one wants or thinks best so long as it is in accordance with the general rules that define the situation and is also not in breach of other moral requirements and prohibitions. These other moral requirements and prohibitions are the moral parameters of the situation, and there is no imperfect duty situation without moral parameters. This is the area of moral freedom, and it is a very large one. When one is in a situation of moral freedom there is no point in continuing to ask "What *ought* I to do?" In such a situation one ought to do whatever one wants to do, as long as one doesn't want to do anything one ought not to do. I am not suggesting that this is easy to determine. It is, indeed, often very hard, which is one reason why some people turn to moral philosophy, mistakenly, to solve their problems for them, to tell them what they ought to do in every circumstance of life.

This, then, should explain Kant's description of imperfect duties as allowing exceptions in favor of inclination. They can even be described as permiting *modification* in favor of inclination, for in an Imperfect Duty Situation inclination not only plays a role but may even be allowed to prevail -- within the parameters. The catch -- and there is a catch -- is that so often it is unclear what our inclination is, and often our inclinations have to be reconciled with our interests, and what is in our interest is not always self-evident. Thus Mill, after alluding to "the common questions of right and wrong" spoke of "the far more difficult questions of wise and foolish" (*Utilitarianism*, ch. 2, par. 24, Everyman ed., p. 23).[7]

III. The Two Cases

Let us now turn back to the Sartre Case and the Billy Budd or Vere Case.

(a) We are not told why Sartre's pupil -- whose, name, I have since discovered, was Pierre -- is confronted only with the alternatives of leaving France to join De Gaulle or of staying to look after his mother. Why just these? These alternatives, though mutually exclusive, are not exhaustive. Pierre could, presumably, have joined the local Resistance, which would have enabled him to feel "that he was responsible as a patriot" without leaving France and hence without leaving his mother. This would have been one way through the dilemma. But perhaps there was no local Resistance in Pierre's area, so he could not have joined the Resistance without leaving his mother. Let us suppose that, and accept that this way through the problem was not available. The thing to notice, then, given only the alternatives of staying or going, is that there was no way of being sure that Pierre would succeed in *either* course. For suppose he had gone. Sartre mentions the possibility that he might have been detained in a Spanish camp, or stuck in a desk job. But he does not mention the possibility that Pierre could have been captured by the Nazis while en route. And if he had been, this might have led to reprisals against his home village. The idea that only "feeling is what counts" might then have presented itself in an especially heavy way. Sartre says "the only thing left for us is to trust our instincts." I am prepared to grant this, in

---

7. Mill also said, in another place: "Prudence, indeed, depends on a calculation of the consequences of individual actions; while, for the establishment of moral rules, it is only necessary to calculate the consequences of classes of actions -- a much easier matter" "Dr. Whewell on Moral Philosophy," in *Dissertations and Discussions* (Boston: William V. Spencer, 1868), vol. III, p. 156.

this sort of case, in the end. But not even feeling is a substitute for rational judgments of probability. "I ought to choose whichever pushes me in one direction." No. For that might push one in the direction of disaster, and that could be antecedently likely. If it were known that the Nazis, or their French collaborators, were mounting an unusually heavy vigil just at that time in order to catch people like Pierre heading off to join the Free French, no matter what feeling had said it would have been irrational for him to go. And the case would then have been decided, not by values, vague or not, but by a matter of fact, or by a judgment of what it is reasonable to believe (which can also be counted as a value, though it is no doubt not one of the values Sartre had in mind).

Alternatively, suppose Pierre had decided to stay (as he did in fact), and that shortly thereafter he had been rounded up in a Nazi drag-net designed to impress young Frenchmen Pierre's age into service on the Russian front. If he could have known in advance that that would happen, it would have been irrational for him to stay, for there would then have been no way he could stay at home and take care of his mother. Circum-stances, or the enemy, would not allow him. Or suppose that, having decided to stay -- or having decided even that he ought to stay --, Pierre had been rounded up as a hostage and then shot in reprisal for some raids the Free French or the Resistance were carrying on in the area. This again, if knowable in advance, would have been a fact or a probability tell-ing in favor of going. For, if his mother would have been upset by his going, she would have been a bit more than upset if he had been impressed into service in Russia or shot. Sartre says that going was an action that "concerned an incomparably vaster group, a national collectivity, but for that very reason was dubious." But that is false. In the circumstances, either course of action was dubious, and its dubiousness was not due to its concerning a collectivity or an individual. Suppose Pierre had decided to stay, simply because of his love for his mother, but she herself was then killed in a Nazi raid aimed simply at collecting Pierre for work in German factories? If feeling is all that matters, his feelings then would be rotten.

To be sure, information as to the outcome was not available and could not have been available in advance, and there was no way in which Pierre's decision could be based on this nonexistent information. None-theless, some reflection on the likely outcome and pitfalls must have crossed Pierre's mind, if he reasoned about the matter at all. For it was not simply a matter of what, given his feelings, he most wanted to do, but a matter of what, all things considered, including his feelings, he ought to do, which in this context incorporates the questions of what it would have been reasonable for him to do, given the uncertainties. The course of going was not inherently more dubious than the course of staying -- although more effort was involved in going, and if he had pondered the problem until the war ended he would in effect have decided to stay without ever *arriving at* that decision, or at any resolution of the problem. But it is important to realize how it could go wrong, no matter which alternative, staying or going, is chosen.

(Given a condition of ignorance of these future contingencies, or simply a stipulation of their equal unlikelihood, there appears to a disinterested observer nothing that can decide the matter one way or the other, with the exception of one rather far-fetched possibility, just alluded to. A decision to go is irrevocable; once Pierre is in England, or in Portugal, he could not decide to go back. But a decision to stay is not irrevocable; the problem could present itself over and over again. Though this would not be decisive for anyone whose mind stays made up once made up, it could cause some problems for someone with a more vacillating disposition. This is the only respect, so far as I can see, in which these alternatives are not evenly weighted, and whether it tells in favor of staying or going would also, it seems to me, be a matter for inclination or disposition.)

Given an equal likelihood of disaster or of success either way, then it is simply up to Pierre to decide which course to take. Neither course is antecedently wrong and neither course is antecedently right. If he decides "I ought to, all things considered . . . ," then, *whichever* he decided, that is right. For he is in an Imperfect Duty Situation, and no Kantian principle and no principle of any other ethical system can decide the matter. It is a misunderstanding both of Kantian ethics and of ethical theory to suppose otherwise. Pierre wants to know which course of action would be treating someone as a mere means to an end that person cannot share. The answer is, neither. Pierre, in trying to decide which course of action is right, is acting from a good will no matter which he decides on. It is of course not morally open to Pierre to kill his mother and then go off. This, indeed, is a monstrous idea that would have been perceived, if it had occurred at all, as monstrous. Such options, if such they be, are not within the terms of the problem, and do not present themselves as options, except to a moral monster. But a moral monster has no moral problems.

This last condition is one of the limits or parameters within which the problem arises and which determine the limits within which the problem can be dealt with. Within these parameters, whichever option Pierre were to choose would be right. And in being right for Pierre it would be right for anyone similarly situated. Only it is not right in the sense of mandatory. So it would not be wrong for anyone else so situated to choose the opposite.

Suppose Pierre had a twin brother, François. This would change the terms of the problem in only one respect -- Pierre could not then be his mother's "only consolation." If he were, then his brother François would not. If François felt similarly, the solution is easy -- François should go and Pierre should stay. If the mother had an equal regard for and need for both, then they could flip a coin -- use some decision procedure -- to determine who should stay and who should go. For there is nothing in the universalizability principle that implies that if one should stay they both should. On the contrary, the condition of one's going is that the other should stay, and conversely.

Suppose, not that Pierre had a brother François, but that he had a neighbor, Henri, on a nearby farm, who is in a similar situation. And let us suppose that Henri's mother has "her only consolation" in Henri. A rational solution is still in reach. For again, one could stay and the other could go, with the one who stays committed to helping out the other's parent. And again, there is nothing in universalizability or the Generalization Principle to imply otherwise. For, even apart from a cooperative solution, if one decided "I ought to stay" and the other "I ought to go," these judgments are not incompatible, either with each other or with the generalization principle. For here, in an Imperfect Duty Situation, one's deciding "I ought to do X" does not imply that, in some objective way, "it would be wrong for me not to do X" -- it only means "I have decided to do X" or "I have decided that I ought to do X," and this "duty" is an imperfect duty, and this "ought" a purely personal "ought," not universalizable. To suppose otherwise is to commit the fallacy of exclusive rightness, the fallacy of supposing that in every situation there is some act (or set of acts) that would be right, in the sense of mandatory, while every other act would be wrong. This is shown to be fallacious by the existence of Imperfect Duty Situations, in which there is quite plainly no such act.

There is, in short, no answer to the problem presented by the Sartre Case, if by an answer is meant a specification of just what Pierre *ought* to do. For the considerations are such that he both ought to go and he ought to stay and he cannot do both, and the situation is such that it is up to him to decide what to do. If, after suitable deliberation, he decides on one of these alternatives as what he ought to do, *that* is what he ought to do -- and that is all there is to it, though that is quite enough. But that is what he ought to do only in the sense that he is morally free to do either (though not to do just anything) and that is what he has decided to do, or decided that he ought to do. Within the parameters, neither course of action is in any sense something that he "objectively" ought to do. For either of the two mutually exclusive courses of action is morally permissible for him, and in that sense right.

(b) Let us turn now to the Billy Budd Case, superficially so like the Sartre Case. There are, it turns out, some important differences between the two.

In the Sartre Case the decision is a personal one. Pierre is not in a representative or executive position. Vere, on the contrary, is, and Vere's decision is not a merely personal one, if it is personal at all.

Sartre's Case is to be decided by just deciding, and that -- except for hindsight in the light of what happened afterwards -- is all there is to it. But in the Budd Case, that is not all there is to it. Vere is acting in an official capacity, as are the members of the Court-Martial, and their decision can serve as a precedent for future cases. In this sense, the Sartre Case is not a *case*. As just mentioned, if Pierre has a brother, François, they can decide that one should stay and the other should go and draw straws or toss a coin to determine who -- and there is no problem. (And if there is some emotional or physical reason why one should go rather than the other, that could decide it.) It is impossible to imagine anything similar in the Budd Case -- even if we imagine something just the same happening to Midshipman Jimmy Judd on the sister ship *H. M. S. Invincible* commanded by Captain Were. It is impossible to suppose -- as it is not in the Sartre situation -- that anyone can suppose that Captain Vere ought to recommend that Billy Budd be executed for killing Claggart and that Captain Were ought to recommend that Jimmy Judd not be executed for in the same "innocent" way killing master-at-arms Braggart. The reason is that Vere's decision is supposed to be based on reasons, reasons that would justify *any* one in the situation in acting in a given way, and they therefore do not apply uniquely or peculiarly to Vere, or Were, or Here, or any *one* else. As Atwell has pointed out, in this case "the original question 'What ought I ... to do?'" needs to be "re-formulated ... into its morally proper formula, 'What ought anyone to do'?"[8] -- or, to put it another way, "What ought to be done?" This question is not open to Pierre in the Sartre Case. His question is always and irretrievably, "What ought *I* to do?", not "What ought to be done in this situation?", and it arises because he cannot be in two places at the same time. If he could split himself in two he could resolve the conflict. But Vere cannot resolve his conflict by splitting himself in two.

Thus we see that these two cases are essentially different. Sartre's Case is an Imperfect Duty Situation, and it is up to the person involved to decide what to do. Vere's is not (except in an extended sense), and it is not up to Captain Vere just to decide what to do, though of course he has to decide what he is to do. It is no more up to Captain Vere just to decide what ought to be done than it is up to Captain Were just to decide what ought to be done. If Vere decides one way and Were the other, one of these actions is wrong -- though they can both be *justified* since the case is so hard. But if Pierre decides one way and François the other they can both be right, for they are both right -- neither course of action is morally wrong. But it is not the case that Captain Vere has the right to execute

---

8. John Atwell, "A Note on Decisions, Judgments, and Universalizability," p. 132.

Budd and Captain Were does not. There is a right answer in this case, though it may be impossible ever to know it for certain.

Of course, the cases are alike in being each very hard. And it is because they are so hard that one can readily be charitable, and ought to be towards anyone who decided or judged it differently. As one astute commentator has put it:

> When there are reasons to suspect that we do not know some centrally relevant facts about a person's concrete situation, we should refrain from judging. We should do likewise when the moral gains and losses appear equally balanced, whatever one decides to do. But this only shows that in cases like these *moral judgment is not in order* ; the description of decisions in such circumstances as right or correct is not appropriate, not called for. If, following Winch, we are inclined to say that an agent in such a conflict-ridden decision concludes 'it is right for me to do X,' or 'I ought to do X,' without implying that another person in the same situation also ought to do X, then no *judgment* is involved, although, no doubt, the agent does find out something about himself. Consequently, the content of that non-universalizable 'ought' in the expression 'I ought to do X,' which supposedly involves a deadlock between two conflicting moral obligations, is no more that 'I am inclined to do X,' or 'I am the kind of person who assigns greater importance to doing X rather than doing Y.'[9]

As mentioned before, Winch's argument for the conclusion that Vere's conclusion is not universalizable is that when he, Winch, asks himself what he would have done in the circumstances, he comes up with a different answer: "I believe that I could not have acted as did Vere. . . . I should have found it morally impossible to condemn a man 'innocent before God' under such circumstances. . . . I should find the considerations connected with Billy Budd's peculiar innocence too powerful to be overridden by the appeal to military duty" (W, 207-8). Yet Winch, as I earlier observed, does not think that Vere "acted wrongly" or "made the wrong decision;" what "Vere did was, for him [given his construction and personality], the right thing to do."

---

9. K. Kolenda, "Moral Conflicts and Universalizability," pp. 464-5.

This I find morally unintelligible. Vere's decision may have felt right to Vere, as Winch's hypothetical decision the other way feels right to Winch. And it may be that in a case as hard as this one this is as far as we can go. *May* be! But this does not entail that Vere's decision is right, for him or anyone else, or that Winch's would-be decision would be right. All that Winch has said -- and we can certainly believe him on this -- is that *he* would find it "morally impossible to condemn a man 'innocent before God' under such circumstances" (W, 208). But he does not find it morally impossible for Vere, or anyone else, to condemn someone "innocent before God" in such circumstances -- hence *he does not find it morally impossible for a person innocent before God to be condemned in such circumstances.* And this is odd, at least. (Notice that such a consideration could not apply in the Sartre Case.)

But it is not my purpose here to arrive at a sound conclusion of what ought to be done in a case like the Billy Budd Case. We can conclude about it either that it is so hard that every commander's decision in the field or at sea will have to be accepted as such, even if these decisions are diverse, or that the case is so hard that we don't know what the right course would be, even though we can be sure it is the same in every relevantly similar case. For present purposes it does not much matter. What matters is that there are cases in which the considerations are equally balanced, or in which what is decided by one person need not be decided by everyone similarly situated. The Sartre Case is one such, and there are others. And there are others like the Budd Case, where we might not know what the answer is -- we may be forever baffled by it -- but it does not follow that it is different for different people.[10]

---

10. There is an interesting complication worth mentioning though not emphasizing. Harold Beaver, in a note to his edition of *Billy Budd,* credits Hayford and Sealts, in their edition of the text, with the following observation: "according to British naval regulations in effect at this time, the trial was threefold illegal ... First, a captain was not authorized to punish a seaman beyond 'twelve lashes upon his bare back, with a cat-of-nine-tails;' any greater punishment required a court-martial; but to convene a court-martial a captain needed the permission of his squadron commander. Secondly, a regular naval court-martial could consist of commanders and captains only. Thirdly, a sentence of death, for crimes other than mutiny, could not be executed 'till after the report of the proceedings of the said court shall have been made to the lords commissioners of the admiralty, or to the commander of the fleet or squadron in which the sentence was passed, and their or his direction shall have been given therein'." (From Herman Melville, *Billy Budd, Sailor and Other Stories,* ed. by Harold Beaver (Harmondsworth: Penguin Books, 1967), p. 462, citing Harrison Hayford and Merton M. Sealts, Jr., in *Billy Budd, Sailor* (Chicago: University of Chicago Press, 1962), pp. 175-83, and John McArthur, *Principles and Practice of Naval and Military Courts Martial* (4th ed., London, 1813). Thus it can be argued that Vere acted precipitously. This indicates that Vere had more options available than Winch allowed for, and casts further doubt on the non-universalizability thesis.

There is still another way of looking at the matter, though it is not one that, given the time, we can look at for very long. This is to say that both decisions, though incompatible, are justified in the circumstances, and finesse all talk of right and wrong in these circumstances. There is no doubt that the decision to hang someone calls for justification, and in some circumstances, the circumstances of the Billy Budd case, the decision not to hang him would call for justification too. But not all decisions or actions or activities call for justification -- it is only the moralist's fallacy to suppose so. A decision or action taken in the area of moral freedom, or in an Imperfect Duty Situation, does not call for justification. What needs justification is the demand that everything be justified -- and it cannot get it.

IV. The Purely Personal "Ought"

A word or two now on what I earlier called the purely personal "ought." A genuinely moral use of "ought" is one that rests on reasons and is therefore universalizable. If a given use of "ought" is not universalizable that is because it is an expression of the agent's or speaker's personality. It is, in a perfectly good sense, subjective, which does not mean that there is anything wrong with it. An ought-judgment in an Imperfect Duty Situation -- whether it is the agent's or a spectator's makes no difference -- expresses the agent's (or the spectator's) preference or inclination, all things considered.

Pierre, in deciding to stay, say, is expressing a preference for staying, all things considered, and can express this, may even feel the need to express this, by saying "I ought to stay," or "I have decided that I ought to stay." But of course he cannot universalize this "ought." For this "ought" does not imply "It would be wrong for me to go." There are not sufficient reasons to warrant such a judgment. It implies at most "I feel that it would be wrong for me to go," and this in the context is equivalent to "It is my overall preference, my inclination, not to go." Similarly, François, in deciding to go, is expressing an all-things-considered preference for going. He might think and say "I ought to go." But this "ought" also cannot be universalized. "I am inclined, I prefer, I have decided, to go" does not imply "It would be wrong for me to stay," though for François also it could feel wrong for him to stay. If, on the other hand, François' decision to go were actually based on a genuine moral judgment that he ought to go, this in turn would be based on some reason relating to features of the situation or to features of François himself. If, for instance, François did not feel close to his mother, was inclined to be impatient with her, if he also took care to make arrangements for her care, if his staying would be likely to generate feelings of resentment and frustration and anger whereas if he went this would be likely to generate feelings of self-fulfillment -- he being a warrior type, say --, then he unquestionably ought to go, and this would be true of anyone in François' situation. If Pierre were like this, then he also ought to go. On the other hand, if Pierre was not the warrior type, if he was inclined to fear in the abstract the idea of battle, if he felt at home staying at home to take care of his mother, then he ought to stay, and so ought anyone so describable. Now these last are instances of genuine moral judgments, based on impersonal or objective reasons and governed by the generalization principle. But these genuine moral judgments are different from their pseudo-counterparts, which are either disguised statements of preferences or inclinations or else expressions of decisions to act, but not themselves moral judgments, even though they use the language of "ought."

So what here appear to be genuine moral judgments are not so, but for good and sufficient reason use the language and form of moral judgment. There are many other instances of statements that use the term "ought" that are not universalizable and not genuine moral judgments. We often say we "ought" to do something without meaning "ought" in any special moral sense. "We ought to see them more often" does not mean "We are under an obligation to see them more often" or "It would be wrong for us not to see them more often" but rather "It would be nice if we did" or "I should like it if we did;" and it is certainly not something universalizable -- as though it implied "Everyone relevantly similar to us ought to see them, or people relevantly similar to them, more often." I take the absurdity of this as self-evident. And I also take the example given as representative of a large class, which I shall not now further illustrate. All such statements, though they use the language of "ought," relate to and express preference, inclination, and personality. Such occurrences of "ought" or "should" are not universalizable, nor should they be supposed to be. In them the emphasis is on the "I" or the "you" or the "we," rather than on the "ought," and the "ought" is not impersonal but personal. (And we may note in passing that here we have the legitimate home for the emotive analysis of ought-sentences, which, it is to be noted, are not genuine moral judgments. They only appear to be.)

Now in an Imperfect Duty Situation, a situation of moral freedom, we can easily come to regard the decision one arrives at in a moral light and to feel that "*I ought*" to act in the way that I have decided to act or have come to feel I should act. After all, one felt oneself to be in a moral situation and to have a moral problem, so this is perfectly natural. And this is perfectly compatible with someone relevantly similar arriving at an opposite decision and having the same feeling about it. For in such a situation if I feel that I ought, then I ought, and if you feel that you ought not, then you ought not, and these "oughts" are not universalizable. They are in fact perfectly compatible with each other. As I have already said much more than once, they express inclination or preference, and not genuine moral judgments. The explanation is that they are expressed in an imperfect duty situation, the area of moral freedom.

Within the area of moral freedom, it can be said that the Generalization Principle, understood as an ought-principle, is not applicable. The inapplicability of the Generalization Principle, understood as a prescriptive principle, may actually be taken as defining the area of moral freedom. But there is still a perfectly good sense in which the Generalization Principle is applicable. It is not applicable to the inner-directed "ought," to an "ought" determined by one's feeling that one ought. But what is morally permissible for one person is morally permissible for every relevantly similar person, what is morally indifferent for one person is so for everyone relevantly similar, and what is an imperfect duty for one person is an imperfect duty for every relevantly similar person. These are other perfectly valid statements of the principle.[11] I conclude, not that universalizability or the generalization principle can weather any storm, but that it has weathered the tempest raised by these hard cases, and this is further confirmation of its validity, supposing any is needed.[12]

References

John E. Atwell, "A Note on Decisions, Judgments, and Universalizability," *Ethics,* vol. 77, no. 2, Jan. 1967, pp. 130-4.

Brenda Cohen, "An Ethical Paradox," *Mind,* vol. 76 (302), April 1967, pp. 250-9.

Norman C. Gillespie, "On Treating Like Cases Differently," *Philosophical Quarterly,* vol. 25, no. 99, April 1975, pp. 151-8.

R. M. Hare, *Freedom and Reason* (Oxford, 1963): FR

---

11. This point (along with a number of other important ones on this same subject) is made more briefly and more effectively by N. Gillespie in "On Treating Like Cases Differently," pp. 153, 156-7.
12. I am pleased to acknowledge my indebtedness, not just to the papers cited by Winch and MacIntyre, which provided the stimulus to this analysis, and to Sartre and Herman Melville for the examples, but to papers (listed in the References) by John Atwell, Konstantin Kolenda, Brenda Cohen, and Norman Gillespie, which provided many of the ideas contained in this analysis. Whatever mistakes may be found in what I have said can be attributed to one or all of these unconscious collaborators.

Konstantin Kolenda, "Moral Conflicts and Universalizability," *Philosophy,* vol. 50, October 1975, pp. 460-5

Carl R. Kordig, "Another Ethical Paradox," *Mind,* vol. 78 (312), October 1969, pp. 598-9.

Ronald E. Laymon and Peter K. Machamer, "Personal Decisions and Universalizability," *Mind,* vol. 79 (315), July 1970, pp. 425-6.

Alasdair MacIntyre, "What Morality is Not," *Philosophy,* vol. 32 (132), Oct. 1957, pp. 325-35.

M. G. Singer, *Generalization in Ethics* (Knopf, 1961): GIE

J. J. C. Smart, "Extreme Utilitarianism: A Reply to M. A. Kaplan," *Ethics,* vol. 71 (2), Jan. 1961, pp. 133-4.

Peter Winch, "The Universalizability of Moral Judgments," *The Monist,* vol. 49, no. 2, April 1965, pp. 196-214: W

Ethics and the Craft Analogy

James D. Wallace
University of Illinois

Contractarians, Kantians, natural-law theorists, and utilitarians -- practitioners of the dominant modes of moral philosophy -- from time to time discuss such virtues as benevolence, the sense of justice, and trustworthiness. No one doubts that the study of virtues and vices belongs to moral philosophy. A number of philosophers, however, have recommended the study of virtues as an alternative to the dominant modes of moral theorizing. It is the study of virtues conceived as a distinct mode of moral philosophy, different from and in competition with the other modes, I expect, that people have in mind when they use the term "virtue ethics."

Professor G. E. M. Anscombe described and to a degree recommended such a program in her 1958 paper, "Modern Moral Philosophy."[1] Several philosophers have explored this mode, including Philippa Foot, Stuart Hampshire, Alasdair MacIntyre, and the present writer.[2] There are, of course, important differences in the views of these individuals, but there are striking similarities, too. These philosophers find unsatisfactory certain epistemological assumptions that underlie much ethical theorizing of the last fifty years. They reject in its several forms non-cognitivism, the view that moral beliefs are not the sort of thing that can be either true or false. On the other hand, they do not subscribe to intuitionist cognitivist accounts that rely upon the alleged self-evident truth of fundamental moral beliefs. To explain what makes certain

---

1. *Philosophy* vol. 33, no. 124 (January, 1958), pp. 1-19.
2. See Philippa Foot, *Virtues and Vices* (Berkeley and Los Angeles: University of California Press, 1978); Stuart Hampshire, *Two Theories of Morality* (New York: Oxford University Press, 1977) and *Morality and Conflict* (Oxford: Basil Blackwell, 1983); Alasdair MacIntyre, *After Virtue* 2nd ed. (Notre Dame: University of Notre Dame Press, 1984); and James D. Wallace, *Virtues and Vices* (Ithaca: Cornell University Press, 1978).

moral beliefs true, they develop and adapt certain ideas they find in Aristotle, ideas in which virtues play a prominent role.

Despite the considerable differences in the accounts offered by these philosophers, a single model plays an important role in their thought. I will call this model the craft analogy. In what follows, I will describe in very general terms the role that the craft analogy plays in these views and discuss some problems that arise in connection with the analogy.

Moral epistemology provides one path to virtue ethics. The route is inviting to a philosophically sophisticated individual who holds the following views. Morality, properly understood, is an absolutely indispensable guide for reasonable and enlightened conduct. Without such a guide and a general recognition of its authority, it is impossible for individuals to live as they should, and it is impossible to sustain the conditions necessary for human social life. Non-cognitivist views, according to which moral beliefs are neither true nor false, despite the heroic efforts of their defenders, cannot in the end avoid the result that adopting one moral belief rather than a contrary one is arbitrary. This result is at odds with the conception of morality as a reliable authoritative guide indispensable for reasonable conduct. Intuitionist theories, on the other hand, according to which basic moral beliefs are known to be true because they proclaim their self-evidence directly to the understanding, are equally unsatisfactory. Such views cannot in the end distinguish between a belief's seeming true and its actually being true. The credentials of moral beliefs as guides for reasonable individuals are irremediably suspect on such a view.

The notion that moral beliefs have such ephemeral contents that either their truth can be grasped only directly by the intellect in an act of intuition or they are incapable of truth at all is incongruous with the idea that these beliefs are indispensable for living intelligently and successfully. That philosophers accept such a notion is symptomatic of serious disorders in their theories. In fact, living is an everyday occurrence that takes place in a complex and demanding world. Living intelligently, presumably, requires knowledge of how to cope with that world, a knowledge grounded in an understanding of the problems encountered in living and how these problems can be solved. The intellectual resources needed to pursue successfully the activity of living are no more ephemeral than the intellectual resources needed to pursue such activities as healing, carpentry, or playing a musical instrument. Here is the craft analogy.

What does one need to know to pursue a craft intelligently and successfully? The question can be answered by considering the point or purpose of the activity and the sorts of difficulties its practitioners encounter. The standards according to which the craft is practiced well or badly can be understood in these terms. That healers need to have certain traits and skills can be shown to be true by considering what healers do, what sorts of problems they face in doing it, and what is known about solving these problems. It is obviously true that there are better and worse ways of practicing crafts, and there is no need to invent extraordinary intellectual acts and faculties for apprehending these truths.

It is plausible to suggest that there are truths about how one should conduct one's life that are known in similar ways. We know that there are better and worse ways of conducting one's life, that certain qualities and capabilities are needed in order to live intelligently and successfully, and that certain ways of proceeding can be shown to be appropriate by reference to standards of acting well or badly -- standards that pertain to the conduct of life generally. We could provide an account of how these things are known to be true, if we could develop in a plausible way the idea that living is sufficiently like healing, carpentry, and playing a musical instrument. The craft analogy, of course, played an important role in Aristotle's ethics. He said, for example,

> Just as for a flute-player, a sculptor, or any artist, and, in general, for all things that have a function or activity, the good and the 'well' is thought to reside in the function, so it would seem to be for man if he has a function. Have the carpenter, then, and the tanner certain functions or activities and has man none? (NE 1097b 26-32)[3]

Aristotle maintained that the characteristic function or activity of human beings is activity involving the exercise of certain psychological capacities, specifically intellectual capacities. Such activity comprises the form of living that is peculiar to the human kind. One lives well when one continually performs such activities well, that is, in accordance with the standards appropriate to such activities, that is, in a manner that exhibits human excellences or virtues.

This view suggests two ways of proceeding to develop a more detailed account of better and worse living. One line of inquiry involves expanding the idea of a form of living that is characteristic of the human kind, studying the nature of such activity in an attempt to discover the standards of doing well appropriate to it. Alternatively, an investigator could study specific human excellences in an attempt to develop an account of what sort of activity exhibits those excellences. In either case,

---

3. The reference here is to the *Nicomachean Ethics*. The translation is that of W. D. Ross in volume IX of *The Works of Aristotle Translated into English* (Oxford: Oxford University Press, 1915).

the investigator would be developing an account of living successfully and intelligently.

In his ethics, Aristotle pursued both of these lines of inquiry. His positive account of living well and doing well for human beings -- in *Nicomachean Ethics,* Book X, for example -- is not very plausible to us. His account of the virtues is initially more promising; the Aristotelian world-view is less prominent in this discussion. For one who reads this account in search of some concrete data about the standards of living well, however, the result is disappointing. In Aristotle's ethics, moral virtue is defined by reference to the determinations a practically wise man, a *phronimos,* would make. When the account of practical wisdom, *phronesis,* as (roughly) wanting the things a man possessing the virtues would want and knowing how to get such things, is placed beside the account of moral virtue as (roughly) the disposition to choose in certain circumstances as a *phronimos* would think one should, it is apparent that the two accounts are circular. After traveling around the circle, one is no wiser about *how* the *phronimos* properly determines what choice should be made, what course of action should be undertaken. Aristotle was aware of this problem. In explaining the difficulty, he used the following analogy: "We should not know what sort of medicines to apply to our body if someone were to say 'all those which the medical art prescribed, and which agree with the practice of one who possesses the art'." (NE VI, 1138b 30-32) This was a serious difficulty for Aristotle, who thought that the point of studying ethics is to learn how to become good and how to help others become good.

For contemporary philosophers who see promise for an ethics based somehow upon the craft analogy, the program Aristotle sketches seems more important than the details of his execution of that program. Contemporary efforts to pursue Aristotle's program, however, encounter difficulty at the same points Aristotle's did. To show that a certain craft is better practiced in one way rather than another, it is essential to have a clear idea of what the point or purpose of the craft is. In order to pursue the craft analogy in developing a cognitivist account of ethics, we appear to need a clear idea of what the point or purpose of living is. A host of problems threaten to overwhelm us here. Yet, if we abandon the idea that there is something related to living that is analogous to the point or purpose of a craft, we seem to have to give up any hope that the craft analogy will shed light upon what makes beliefs about living well true or false.

There is another way to proceed that promises to circumvent the problem of establishing what the point of living is. We have notions of moral virtues, and our list corresponds, more or less roughly, to the classical virtues. We can undertake to explicate these notions. We know that virtues are exhibited in acting well and living well. Accounts of a representative selection of virtues, accounts that make clear what sorts of choices and actions exhibit those virtues, may reasonably be expected to yield an outline of the general nature of living well. Just as an understanding of the skills and traits possessed by a good physician would shed light on the point of medicine and the standards by which its practice is judged, so the study of human virtues can reasonably be expected to yield accounts of the point of living and the standards for living well or badly. This expresses succinctly the program of "virtue ethics."

In the course of developing accounts of the virtues, however, the circularity that infected Aristotle's views is a serious danger. We describe a certain virtue as a tendency and/or capacity to act in a certain way. What way? What actions exhibit the virtue? It seems impossible to avoid saying that it is acting *as one should* in certain circumstances, with respect to certain considerations or difficulties, that exhibits a certain virtue. So courage is exhibited not just by acting in the face of danger, but (roughly) by acting as one should in the face of danger. More specifically, courage is exhibited by choosing and acting in a dangerous situation in a way that shows that one has given the consideration of danger exactly the weight it *should* be given in the situation. What, though, determines how one should act in the face of danger or how much weight one should give the consideration of danger in a particular circumstance? If the aim of our inquiry is to make clear how such a determination is properly made, so that we see clearly what makes such a determination true or correct, then it will not suffice to say simply that there are standards of correctness here and that there are people especially well qualified to make judgments in accordance with these standards. We must undertake the project of explaining how one properly determines what weight to give a consideration in a particular decision. In other words, we need to produce an account of practical reasoning and of being good at practical reasoning -- practical wisdom.

Consider the following remarks by Philippa Foot.

> In the first place the wise man knows the means to certain good ends; and secondly he knows how much particular ends are worth. Wisdom in its first part is relatively easy to understand. It seems that there are some ends belonging to human life in general rather than to particular skills such as medicine or boat building, ends having to do with such matters as friendship, marriage, the bringing up of children, or the choice of ways of life . . . . The second part of wisdom . . . is much harder to describe, because here we meet ideas which are curiously elusive, such as the thought that some pursuits are more worthwhile than others, and some matters trivial and some important in human life . . . . But I have never

seen, or been able to think out, a true account of this
matter, and I believe that a complete account of wisdom,
and of certain other virtues and vices must wait until this
gap can be filled.[4]

It can be argued plausibly that certain virtues are perfections of
traits necessary for any form of life that would qualify as human. This
provides grounds for the judgment that we need such traits and that they
are good to have.[5] What makes such judgments true is clear. Alasdair
MacIntyre argues plausibly that certain of the goods we seek in a very
wide range of "practices" (including crafts) can be obtained only if we
possess virtues. This, he maintains, provides only a partial account of what
a virtue is.[6]

Such accounts of virtues as these are incomplete because they do
not address the problem of how to determine what weight a consideration
should be given in a particular decision. If virtue ethics is to provide an
account of morality as a guide for reasonable individuals that makes clear
the grounds for the truth of certain ethical beliefs, an account of practical
reasoning is necessary. It is not enough merely to say that a virtue involves
choosing in a way that shows that one has given considerations the weight
they should be given. We must indicate how one determines the weight
considerations should be given in a particular decision. Our difficulties in
carrying out this project are exacerbated by our tendency to accept certain
Aristotelian assumptions.

A number of things conspire to create this problem which
defeated Aristotle and plagues his modern followers. A contributor is the
notion that life is an activity with a point or function or *telos*, if you like --
as healing or carpentry has a point or function. This, of course, is a particular application of the craft analogy. Another conspirator is a particular
view of practical reasoning which I will call the fixed-goal conception of
practical reasoning. On this view, the paradigm of sound practical reasoning is choosing an effective means to a clearly defined goal. Assuming that
the goal is an appropriate one to pursue, the standard of correctness of
choice is, substantially, conduciveness of the action chosen to the realization of the goal. The appropriateness of the goal itself may be determined
by showing the conduciveness of its pursuit to still another appropriate
goal or by showing that the goal is good for its own sake. This scheme
may be complicated in various ways, but the central question with any
practical problem will be, which of the alternatives most contributes to
the attainment of the appropriate goal? With practical problems concern-

---

4. Foot, *Virtues and Vices*, pp. 5-6.
5. Wallace, *Virtues and Vices*, pp. 10-11 and *passim*.
6. MacIntyre, *After Virtue*, Chapter 14.

ing the general conduct of one's life, proper practical reasoning requires that there be an appropriate goal for one's life. The craft analogy -- the notion that thinking about how one should conduct one's life is similar in important respects to thinking about how one should heal or make things of wood -- suggests that living has a point or function as do healing and carpentry. This reinforces the requirement of the fixed-goal conception of practical reasoning that there be a goal in any reasoning concerning the conduct of life.

On the fixed-goal theory of practical reasoning, in order for us to be able to solve very many of our problems about the conduct of our lives, the conception of the appropriate goal -- the point or purpose of living, the effective pursuit of which will be the good life -- will have to be in certain respects concrete and detailed. The conception will have to make clear what the components of the good life are, and, if there is more than one component, what the priorities are among them. The relationship of these components to one another -- the life's structure -- must be clearly articulated. The more vague or unspecific the conception of the goal, the good life, the less useful it will be in solving actual practical problems -- that is, the fewer such problems there will be that admit of rational solution.

The fixed-goal view of practical reasoning, when it is applied to questions about the conduct of life in this way, places inordinate demands upon our idea of a good life. How, on this view of practical reasoning, are we to decide how the obvious candidates for important human goods are to be fitted together in the good human life? How are we to choose among the indefinitely many ways we can imagine things being put together? Actual human lives are led in concrete circumstances or contexts that differ from time to time and place to place. These contexts influence enormously how lives are lived; they restrict how lives can be led, what goods can be pursued, what goods can be fitted together. When we attempt to describe the ideal life, in what circumstances do we suppose the life is led? If we cannot supply *any* context at all, how are we to determine how the various desirable elements are to be fitted together? How are we to decide what the life's structure is? If, on the other hand, we describe the ideal life in a determinate context, how can this conception be used in *other* contexts? If proper practical reasoning is a matter exclusively of choosing what most conduces to this goal, what can possibly guide us in adapting the conception of a life led in one set of circumstances to our own quite different circumstances?

I do not mean to deny that it is sometimes useful to use another person's life as a guide for one's own. My point is that on the fixed-goal conception of practical reasoning, there is insufficient provision for the *intelligent* adaptation of a conception of an ideal life described in one set of circumstances to a different set of circumstances, insufficient indication of how the adaptation might proceed more or less reasonably. Thus, the choice to adapt a certain conception to my circumstances in one way rather than another will be to a degree arbitrary. Since the matter of how I adapt the conception will crucially affect what choices I then make to attain this goal, the arbitrariness will infect the subsequent choices as well.

In constructing an account of how choices about the conduct of life are properly made, the fixed-goal theorist is faced with the fact that there are many particular good lives that are importantly different from one another. There will be disagreements among serious people, moreover, about which of the candidates for the status of a good life are genuinely good. Puzzled by how to choose, the theorist may be tempted to look for what all such lives have in common. The description of the goal -- the ideal human life -- can perhaps mention what is common to all particular good lives, leaving out the differences. The result of this program, however, will be a very abstract and general description of the goal which we are supposed to seek in all reasonable decisions about the conduct of life. This, of course, is hardly the sort of determinate goal that will lead us to solutions of complex practical problems.

For a fixed-goal theorist, the problem of how to demonstrate the appropriateness of a putative life-goal is truly formidable. Either it must be shown that the pursuit of this goal conduces to the attainment of another appropriate goal, or the theorist must fall back upon the claim that the goal described is intrinsically good. It is difficult to see how this use of the fixed-goal theory can in the end escape some form of question-begging intuitionism about the certification of the appropriateness of "ultimate" goals.

This problem aside, however, the fixed-goal theorist faces a disheartening dilemma. The more specific the description of the goal for all decisions concerning the conduct of life, the more difficult it is to make plausible the claim that every correct choice about the conduct of life must advance *this* particular goal. Aristotle's description of the life of *theoria*, the contemplative life, might be offered as an example of a *relatively* specific goal. It is clearly less specific than a detailed biography of an ideally good person, but it is specific with respect to life's priorities -- there is but one. More plausible as a claim about what the best sort of human life is like is the thesis that an active life exhibiting a variety of excellences both of character and intellect is best. There is, of course, evidence in Aristotle's writings that, at least intermittently, he thought of "the good for man" as a complex of activities in accordance with several excellences. There is, however, no indication of how Aristotle thought such a conception of the good for man could be used to resolve conflicts among practical considerations -- when, for example, one must choose between loyalty to friends and loyalty to the *polis*. A goal, described simply as 'a life that combines (somehow) activity in accordance with many excellences' is too unspecific to determine what to do in situations involving conflict problems.

The reader of the *Nicomachean Ethics* is apt to receive the impression that Aristotle wavered between the notion that the ultimate fixed goal of practical reasoning is a life of *theoria*, and the view that the fixed goal is the less specific one of a life consisting of a pursuit of many goods, that exhibits a variety of moral and intellectual excellences. If indeed Aristotle did waver between these views, it may be that he was impaled upon the horns of the fixed-goal theorist's dilemma. A fixed-goal theory of practical reasoning cannot be worked out in a plausible way. This may explain why Aristotle did not have a developed account of practical reasoning.

The basic weakness of the fixed-goal theory of practical reasoning can be described succinctly in this way. For the idea of a certain life to play the role of the ultimate intrinsic good in a fixed-goal theory, it must be the idea of that which is, in effect, the goal promoted by the *correct* solution of every practical problem of moment -- past, present, and future -- concerning how human beings should lead their lives. How could anyone have sufficient grounds for the claim that a certain particular conception of the ideal life meets this condition?

The fixed-goal view of practical reasoning must be abandoned. What, though, is to replace it? A consideration of certain of the difficulties that beset the fixed-goal theory suggests that there are many different, more or less independent goals that human beings pursue, sometimes reasonably. Unfortunately, however, the human condition is such that often -- *very* often -- in pursuing one good, we must forgo another; circumstances force us to sacrifice one good to another. Many of our most difficult practical problems require us to chose one good rather than another. How do we *properly* make such choices? Presumably, we somehow determine which of the conflicting goods is in the circumstance more important or which has the stronger claim upon us. But how is this determined? Philippa Foot complains in the passage quoted above that she can find no satisfactory account of how one properly makes such determinations. If there is no rational way of making such choices, then a great many of the most important choices we make are arbitrary.

Alasdair MacIntyre's claim that we need a modern conception of the human *telos* is based, at least partly, upon his belief that the solution of this problem requires such a conception. He says,

> Unless there is a *telos* which transcends the limited
> goods of practices by constituting the good of a whole
> human life, the good of a human life conceived as a
> unity, it will *both* be the case that a certain subversive
> arbitrariness will invade the moral life *and* that we shall

be unable to specify the context of certain virtues adequately.[7]

In developing this point, however, MacIntyre seems to embrace a version of the fixed-goal theory of practical reasoning. If I understand him correctly, then he is offering an account that suffers from the difficulties of the fixed-goal view. "The good life for man," he says at one point, "is the life spent in seeking for the good life for man."[8] It is not clear, however, why a good human life *must* have as its central focus a quest for understanding of the good life, nor is it clear how aiming at *this* goal will enable one to "order" the other goods, how it will enable one to decide in a particular circumstance whether loyalty to a friend is more important than loyalty to the state, etc.

Giving up the fixed-goal theory of practical reasoning is easier said than done. It can be done, however -- and without introducing a "subversive arbitrariness" into our lives -- by taking very seriously the craft analogy. In Aristotle's ethics, the craft analogy suggests that living has a point or goal, and this fits neatly with the fixed-goal theory. I propose, however, that the craft analogy be applied in quite a different way. What has a point or purpose, analogous to the way that a craft has a point or purpose, is not living itself; rather it is practical considerations, requirements, and values that have points. How can such a thing as a moral consideration have a point in anything like the way that a craft does? Things that occur in practical reasoning as considerations have reference to learned ways of dealing with certain situations. There are sorts of practical knowledge that are needed only by some people -- people who, because of their circumstances, have special tasks to perform and special problems to solve. The division of labor in a community, for example, brings about such circumstances, and technical practical knowledge is needed. There is, on the other hand, practical knowledge that is needed by every individual in a community in the course of his or her life. Practical knowledge about the conduct of life generally is fundamentally a hodge-podge, a motley collection of learned ways of dealing with a variety of different problems that arise in our lives. These are ways developed by individuals in real-life situations and, often, modified by countless other individuals in order to adjust the ways to one another and to changing circumstances. Some of these ways were developed to deal with problems connected with the social character of human life -- problems we face in living with one another, cooperating with one another, resolving our conflicts with one another, etc. It is the more important of those ways that we tend to classify as "moral." The ways we have developed for dealing with

7. *After Virtue*, p. 203.
8. *After Virtue*, p. 219.

the myriad problems of living together were developed by the use of the same sort of intellectual resources that were employed in the development of agriculture, language, and medicine. It is particular moral considerations, such as the rule of law, respect for human life, and the commitments involved in friendship, that have points or functions analogous to the points or functions of crafts. These considerations refer to shared ways of considerable complexity for coping with certain problems that tend to arise in everyone's life. The ways have a history; they have been modified and adapted to enable them to function in altered circumstances, to solve novel variants of the original problems. In the course of their careers, the purposes and functions of these ways have changed, have evolved, too. Sometimes it is human practical intelligence that is the cause of such changes. What is going on in such cases, however, is not properly described as devising means of attaining a clearly defined goal. Rather, the aim is to resolve an unprecedented difficulty, using ways developed to deal with analogous but crucially different difficulties. In the course of resolving the difficulty, the ways themselves and the understanding of what constitutes a resolution may be significantly modified.[9]

One thing that recommends this contextualist and (in the philosophical sense) pragmatic view of morality and practical reasoning is the account it affords of how certain difficult problems are properly resolved. To determine the relevance of certain considerations and their proper weight in actual moral problems, it is necessary to understand the points of the considerations. The point or points of a consideration will lie in the function, the use of the way that the consideration embodies. The idea that an understanding of the points of moral considerations is indispensable for solving moral problems is plausible because we would not expect to be able intelligently to apply or to resolve conflicts between *any* rules or procedures whose uses and points we do not understand. The task with particular moral problems, on this view, is to determine the applicability of moral considerations and to resolve conflicts among considerations in ways that are intellectually defensible by showing that (1) the solution proposed retains, insofar as possible, the necessary functions of the old ways, (2) the solution addresses the needs of the present situation, and (3) the modifications of our ways implicit in the solution are ones we can live with. In order to develop such solutions, it is necessary to understand the points of the considerations involved, the uses of the ways.

---

9. Compare this with MacIntyre's description of the simultaneous evolution of "practices," the "goods internal to practices," and "standards of excellence" pertaining to practices. (*After Virtue*, pp. 187-191). See also John Dewey's account of the evolution of institutions in *Human Nature and Conduct* (New York: Henry Holt and Company, 1922), pp. 79-83.

David Hume's discussion of the "utility" of private property in Section III of *An Inquiry Concerning the Principles of Morals* is an example of an attempt to explain the points of certain considerations.

The account sketched above enables us to abandon the fixed-goal conception of practical reasoning, while retaining, in a modified form, the craft analogy. The notion that living itself is like a craft in that it has a certain point or purpose is replaced by the idea that the considerations we consult in practical reasoning have points analogous to the points of crafts. This modified version of the craft analogy retains its cognitivist implications for ethics. Beliefs about the correctness of certain solutions to problems about the conduct of life have an epistemological status similar to beliefs about the correctness of solutions to certain problems in medicine and other crafts.

What are the implications of such an account for the program of virtue ethics? What of the idea that by providing accounts of the classical virtues or some modern counterparts, we can develop an account of living well and the standards by which the conduct of life is properly assessed? The way in which the craft analogy is used in the Aristotelian account lends plausibility to this idea; just as the exercise of the skills and capacities of the good carpenter constitutes the activity of practicing the craft well, so the exercise of the virtues constitutes the activity of living well. The proposed modification in the use of the craft analogy replaces this tidy picture with one that is far more cluttered. It remains true that we need such virtues as courage, honesty, and justice in order to live as we should, but it is equally true that we need such virtues in order to practice crafts successfully -- in order to teach as we should, do research as we should, etc. No one, however, infers from the importance of these virtues for the practice of crafts that accounts of the virtues will provide adequate accounts of practicing the crafts well. No one supposes that by studying courage, justice, and honesty we will learn a great deal about the standards by which the practice of a craft is properly evaluated. The virtues, for all their importance, do not contain the particular dispositions -- the skills, knowledge, and commitments -- that are necessary for practicing a particular craft well. Similarly, accounts of such lists of "moral virtues" as have been offered recently cannot be expected to provide full accounts of the standards by which decisions about the conduct of life generally are properly evaluated. The store of knowledge, skills, and commitments that comprises our resources for dealing with particular moral problems is vast, complex, and specific. Philosophical accounts of the virtues lack the necessary specificity to enable us to draw out of them useful accounts of how difficult concrete practical problems are properly resolved.

I do not conclude from this that the program of virtue ethics should be abandoned. This program, I think, can be adapted to the proposed modification in the use of the craft analogy in ethics. A case can be made for thinking of the very considerations that occur in practical reasoning as having a locus in us in the form of learned disposition consisting of know-how, skills, concerns, values, and commitments. If moral considerations refer to shared learned ways of dealing with certain practical problems, we can think of the considerations themselves as character traits. So, such practical considerations as the rule of law or respect for human life are thought of as learned ways of acting, character traits. The number of character traits central to ethics will, on this view, far exceed the number of classical virtues. The traits, however, will have points or purposes deriving from the ways that exhibit them. These ways and their points will be far more specific in their application to concrete situations than the corresponding features of the classical virtues. On this conception, the relatively unproblematic phenomenon of adapting a practical skill to an unprecedented situation can provide a model for understanding how certain difficult moral problems might be resolved. This, however, is a topic for another paper.

Index